CW01218808

In the Ring
With
MARVIN HART

Adam J. Pollack

Win By KO Publications
Iowa City

In the Ring With Marvin Hart

Adam J. Pollack

(ISBN-13): 978-0-9799822-2-4

(hardcover: 55# acid-free alkaline paper)

Library of Congress Control Number: 2010932740

Includes footnotes, appendix and index.

© 2010 by Adam J. Pollack. All Rights Reserved.

No part of this book may be reproduced, or transmitted in any form or by any means, graphic, electronic or mechanical, including photocopying, recording, taping, or by any information storage retrieval system without the written permission of Adam J. Pollack.

Cover design by Gwyn Snider ©

Manufactured in the United States of America.

Win By KO Publications

Iowa City, Iowa

winbykopublications.com

Contents

1. Marvelous Marvin: The Louisville Knockout Artist ... 4
2. Stepping It Up: Becoming a Contender ... 19
3. The Carter War ... 41
4. The 6-Round Road Warrior and the Top Light-Heavyweights ... 46
5. Derailed By a Hand ... 73
6. Solidifying Contender Status ... 83
7. Three-Time Champion ... 88
8. Settling Matters ... 101
9. Hanging With the Heavyweights ... 112
10. Crossing the Color Line for Top Contender Status ... 133
11. Justifying The Shot ... 153
12. The Unfulfilled Match ... 179
13. Filling the Vacancy ... 186
14. Road to the Championship ... 191
15. To Be a Heavyweight Champion ... 203
16. A Title Fight ... 227
17. Next Up ... 233

Appendix: Marvin Hart's Record ... 239

Acknowledgments ... 242

Index ... 243

CHAPTER 1

Marvelous Marvin: The Louisville Knockout Artist

When James J. Jeffries retired as undefeated world heavyweight champion in May 1905, Marvin Hart and Jack Root fought for his vacated title on July 3, 1905. Following in the wake of a long-time champion who was considered unbeatable, without having won the linear title owing to Jeff's retirement, and without a lengthy reign, Hart has become the South's underappreciated and somewhat forgotten champion.

Although Hart may be one of the least-known heavyweight champions, his career deserves more discussion than the neglect that it is usually receives. Hart was known for his aggressiveness, hard punch, good conditioning, and ability to withstand punishment. He was a very exciting fighter who was almost always in entertaining fights. Not a fancy boxer, he was built for the fight to the finish. Think prime Arturo Gatti. Today, Hart would be a fan favorite, a fighter who you would like to see fight, win or lose. He was game and powerful to the core. Hart was Louisville, Kentucky's hero long before there was a Cassius Clay/Muhammad Ali.

Later known as "The Fightin' Kentuckian," during his career Hart was more often called "Marvelous Marvin," gaining that nickname well before Marvin Hagler did. He was listed as standing either 5'10 ¼" or 5'11 ½". At his heavyweight best, Hart fought at around 180-190 pounds, but he began his career in the neighborhood of 160 pounds, at times being called a heavyweight, and at others a light-heavyweight or even middleweight. At the time, the light-heavyweight division was just gaining recognition. When Marvin's career began, bantamweight was 116 pounds, featherweight 122, lightweight 133, welterweight 145, middleweight 158, and heavyweight was everything above middleweight. They were not as fixated on weight as we are today.[1]

Like many fighters, throughout his career, there would continually be some discrepancy about Hart's age. Primary source reports often listed Hart as being one to two years younger than what later sources and secondary sources have him. Like Bob Fitzsimmons, Hart fudged on his age just a bit.

In 1905, the *Police Gazette* confirmed that Hart was born on September 16, 1876, making him older than what many earlier accounts listed him.[2]

---

1 *Louisville Courier-Journal*, February 24, 1901.
2 *Police Gazette*, September 16, 1905. Hart's date of birth is also confirmed by his death certificate and military registration card. Special thanks to Tony Triem for providing me with these items.

Born in Fern Creek, Jefferson County, Kentucky, about 15 miles from Louisville, Marvin Abuary Hart was the 21st of 21 children – 13 boys and 8 girls. His father Samuel Hart had married three times, and Marvin's mother, whose maiden name was Carthage Swope, was his third wife. As a result of being the youngest child, Marvin said, "I have a niece a year older than I am." With the exception of two brothers, Marvin claimed to be the runt of the family. If so, "They must be a family of giants." Hart was of German ancestry.[3]

Hart said that when he was a young boy, he used to go out in the barn and punch a straw boy bare-fisted until he was tired. When his family moved to Louisville, he used the first money he earned to purchase boxing gloves. He enjoyed punching just for fun.

Marvin Hart began his pro boxing career in early 1900, at 23 years of age. The year before, James J. Jeffries had become the world heavyweight champion by knocking out Bob Fitzsimmons in the 11th round. Jeff had already successfully defended the title with a 25-round decision victory over Tom Sharkey. Jeffries was just one year and five months older than Hart.

Hart had not originally intended for boxing to become his occupation. Marvin initially earned his living for several years as a plumber. However, he eventually just drifted into the fighting business and his life became much different than anyone could have foreseen. Call it a twist of fate. Hence, some later called him the "plumber pugilist."

Marvin said the first time he fought for money was in Louisville. He was a plumber at the time. A fellow flunked out of a fight, and a friend of Marvin's said they should get him to substitute. Hart was matched against a husky guy from Marvin's end of town, but then that fighter also pulled out. Instead, Hart's supposed opponent sent his trainer as a substitute to fight Marvin. He was probably being set up to lose, but he did not. "I whipped the trainer in a hurry, and the next thing I knew my friends were telling around how great a fighter I was. They matched me against one man and then another…and I have been at it ever since." Hart quickly gained popularity as a result of his fighting ability.[4]

Quite an active fighter, the powerful Hart won at least 17 consecutive fights, possibly more, over a two-year span, knocking out every opponent (except for one disqualification victory). All of these bouts took place in Louisville, Kentucky, where he had a big local fan base. Marvelous Marvin was the popular powerful plumber.[5]

23-year-old Marvin Hart's professional debut took place in Louisville, Kentucky on January 15, 1900.[6] *The Louisville Evening Post* next-day report

---

3. *San Francisco Chronicle, San Francisco Evening Post*, March 24, 1905; *Louisville Courier-Journal*, July 4, 1905.
4. *National Police Gazette*, August 2, 1902.
5. *The Louisville Times*, July 4, 1905, reported that Hart's "pugilistic record dates from 1900."
6. Hart's pro debut was on January 15, 1900, despite later incorrect claims by semi-primary and secondary sources that the bout took place on the 17th.

said that a fighter named John Marbleheart had knocked out William Schiller with a right to the jaw in the 4th round.[7] This was Marvin Hart, not Marbleheart.

Many years later, Hart told the story of his first ring appearance, with Billy Schiller, which took place in 1900. Marvin said he weighed 150 pounds at the time.

> All I knew about fighting was to rush in and swing both hands. I had never seen Billy Schiller, who I was to fight, and when he climbed through the ropes I thought he looked as big as Jeffries. He outweighed me forty pounds, and when he looked over at me and scowled I'll admit that I was just a little bit scared.

Despite the size disparity, when Marvin met Schiller's first rush and easily tossed him away, the crowd cheered. Marvin thought they were cheering for Schiller. He was wondering how long it would take for the big fellow to get him. It was the longest three minutes of his life.

Hart did not get his confidence until the 3rd round, when he realized that he had taken Schiller's hardest punch on the jaw and found that Bill could not hurt him. At that point, Hart went right after him, and he managed to stop Schiller in the 4th round. "My seconds had to tell me I won. I was so excited I didn't know which one of us was out." Marvin had been a 10 to 3 betting odds underdog.[8]

Naturally, Hart's success in knocking out a much bigger foe that had been heavily favored to defeat him caused a local buzz, and so a rematch was in order. Less than a month later, on February 12, 1900 in Louisville, before a crowd of 500 people, Hart had a rematch with Schiller. This time, Marvin knocked him out cold in the 6th round. It took 25 minutes to restore Schiller to consciousness.[9]

Most sources list Charles Meisner as Hart's next opponent, but a June 1900 local reproduction of his record lists additional victories for Marvin before the Meisner bout. Heretofore, no official record has listed these bouts. It said that after the Schiller bouts, Hart scored a KO1 "Butch" Fletcher, KO2 "Stormy" Goss, and KO1 Paddy Minton, all local fighters.[10]

---

7 *Louisville Evening Post,* January 16, 1900. The interesting question is whether this article got Hart's name wrong, or if in fact it was his actual name, but he later changed it (less likely), or if Hart was using an alias.
8 *San Francisco Bulletin,* March 22, 1905.
9 *Louisville Times,* February 13, 1900. A local paper in June that year said that Hart had turned pro four months earlier, confirming the early 1900 pro debut of Hart. Another June report indicated that Hart and Schiller had fought twice, Hart having knocked him out in the 4th round in their first bout, and in the 6th in the rematch. *Louisville Times, Louisville Courier-Journal,* June 25, 1900. Some secondary sources incorrectly list this February bout as a KO4 for Hart (the result of their first bout), but the local primary sources and records indicated that Hart stopped Schiller in the 6th round.
10 *Louisville Courier-Journal,* June 10, 1900. Another June report said that Hart had in less than four months knocked out all the local fighters, making his pro debut sometime in early 1900. *Louisville Times, Louisville Courier-Journal,* June 25, 1900.

On April 2, 1900 at Louisville's Music Hall, the 5-0 Hart took on Charles Meisner, who had challenged him after the Schiller rematch. They were battling for the heavyweight championship of the city of Louisville or state of Kentucky, depending on the source. They only weighed about 165 or 170 pounds. Hart trained at the East End Athletic Club. Each man already had a large following in the "East End." Therefore, "A great deal of local interest has been manifested in the fight, and a good crowd will very probably be on hand." Both boxers were said to be "very scientific."

The bout was scheduled for 20 rounds, although it was not expected to last that long. Regardless, even from the start of his career, Marvin Hart was scheduled to fight in potentially lengthy bouts. Try to imagine a fighter today, with only five bouts of experience, being allowed to box in a 12-rounder, let alone a 20-round bout. Queensberry rules governed, although clean breaks were required.[11]

The "tall, lithe and graceful" Hart was three inches taller than Meisner. From the opening bell, Hart went right after him, and after the first feint, hit Charles on the jaw and he went down. The rest of the round was but a repetition of this sequence. Hart would rush, feint, and then throw a left or right, landing regularly. Meisner would drop regardless of whether or not he had been hit. Some felt that he suffered from stage fright. Possibly, he could not handle Marvin's punch. Meisner dropped to his knees half a dozen times in the round to avoid Hart's blows. Towards the end of the 1st round, Hart landed either a left swing or a right to the jaw (two local sources differed) that dropped Meisner to the ground in a groggy state, and the referee counted him out.

Hart was described as "well muscled, handles himself like a boxer, and has a knockout punch in either hand." He "is certainly a likely looking young man as far as boxing goes and there are many light heavyweights in this country whom he could give quite an argument." Hart had noticeable talent.[12]

Originally from London, England, the welterweight-sized Tommy Williams said that he would like to meet the winner of the Hart-Meisner bout, and he was granted his wish. They fought at "catchweights," meaning Hart went down in weight and Williams came up. The bout was scheduled for 20 rounds.

The fight result was very briefly mentioned in the *National Police Gazette*, showing it had more than just local significance. Williams, though smaller, "has had years of experience in the squared circle, and is an aggressive fighter and a hard puncher with either hand. His fight with Australian Jimmy Ryan in this city some time ago proved that he would take the 'gaff,' and that he was able to give as good as was sent." According to a secondary

---

11 *Louisville Times*, March 31, 1900; *Louisville Courier-Journal, Louisville Evening Post*, April 2, 1900.
12 *Louisville Courier-Journal, Louisville Evening Post*, April 3, 1900.

source, in September 1899, the very experienced Ryan had stopped Williams in the 4th round.[13]

A local newspaper called Hart "the ex-amateur," suggesting that he might have had some amateur bouts. The locals said that Hart, although inexperienced, was a hard puncher, "as game as they make them," and "one of the most promising middleweights ever turned out of Louisville." Still, Marvin was claiming the heavyweight championship of the South.[14]

Hart fought Tom Williams in Louisville on May 10, 1900. The splendidly proportioned Hart towered over his smaller opponent. What Williams lacked in size he made up for with skill and pluck. It was an exciting fight, for they mixed it up from the start, slugging away. Despite this, little damage was done in the 1st round, which was about even.

The 2nd round was another war, with Williams "jabbing Hart's head off. The latter was game and strong as a bull, and he was always coming. He ripped rights and lefts into Williams' ribs time and again, and got inside of Williams' swings." It did not last the round. "Toward the close of the second round Hart landed a right hook on Williams which put him down and out. It was a clean knockout."[15]

The following day, in New York, James J. Jeffries defended his world heavyweight championship with a KO23 over former champion James J. Corbett.

Continuing his monthly fighting pace, on June 12, 1900 in Louisville, Hart fought Lucas Siefker in a scheduled 20-round bout. Both were local Louisville prospects fighting for the heavyweight championship of the South. Siefker was said to have a better record, with 15 bouts under his belt, as opposed to only 7 for Hart (which included the local bouts previously overlooked by historians). Siefker's record included a 10-rounder with Jim Watts, a 4-round exhibition with Kid McCoy, a 4-round exhibition with Gus Ruhlin, and a 10-round draw with Watts. Although Hart was "practically a newcomer," he had "shown conclusively that there is good stuff in him. He is game to the core, and has a fair amount of science."[16]

Hart was expected to weigh about 160 pounds to Siefker's 150 pounds, although there was no official weigh-in, so no one knew for sure. Hart was properly listed as 23 years of age and standing 5'11" tall to Siefker's 27 years and 5'10 ½". This listing of Marvin's age is consistent with later accounts of his birth date, but as will be seen, Hart later claimed he was a bit younger.[17]

The boxers agreed to break clean, a modification of the Queensberry rules, which, unadulterated, allowed for punching on the break. Siefker had former Hart foe William Schiller as one of his seconds. English

---

13 *National Police Gazette*, June 2, 1900; *Louisville Courier-Journal*, May 9, 1900; Boxrec.com.
14 *Louisville Courier-Journal*, *Louisville Evening Post*, May 9, 1900.
15 *Louisville Courier-Journal*, May 11, 1900.
16 *Louisville Courier-Journal*, June 10, 1900; *Louisville Evening Post*, June 12, 1900.
17 *Louisville Courier-Journal*, June 12, 1900.

welterweight Tom Williams, whom Hart had knocked out the previous month, was Hart's trainer, and worked his corner.

The bout was a good, fast heavyweight fight with several mix-ups of hard punches in each round. Hart outpointed Siefker in every round, showing an unusual amount of cleverness. Although losing the rounds, Siefker put up a game, scientific battle and was not afraid to mix it with the aggressive Hart, who was taller and had a slight weight advantage. At the bell ending the 7th round, Lucas landed a left that staggered Hart.

In the 8th round, they went at it and exchanged left swings. Hart then stunned Siefker, the Kentucky barber, staggering him with an uppercut. Marvin followed with a vicious punch to the jaw, trying to finish. However, Siefker came back with a left that made Marvin's knees tremble. After a clinch and break, just before the bell rang, Hart landed a short half-arm hooking right jolt to the jaw that sent Siefker down, out cold. The bell actually saved him, but even after the one-minute rest, Lucas was unable to respond for the 9th round, forcing the stoppage. *The Louisville Courier-Journal* said Hart was no doubt the best pugilist that Louisville had ever produced. He was "tall, lithe as a panther, quick, eager and a hard puncher."[18]

Just two weeks later, on June 26, 1900 in Louisville, Hart, the South's heavyweight champion, took on Indiana's Harry Rogers in a scheduled 20-round bout. This was Hart's second fight against someone from outside of Louisville.

Scouting the bout, the local *Louisville Courier-Journal* said, "Rogers is generally accredited with being the cleverer boxer of the two, but Hart is probably the more rugged and a harder hitter." Quite frankly, this is what was said of Hart in relation to almost all of his opponents for the rest of his career. Rogers had put up good fights with "Jack Moffatt, Billy Stift and other high-class fighters." *The Louisville Times* called Rogers a "well-known pugilist" who had the advantage in experience.[19]

Both the local *Times* and *Courier-Journal* agreed that Hart would likely only weigh about 165 pounds to Rogers' 175 pounds, but nevertheless, regarded Hart as the harder hitter. Marvin said he would not weigh more than 165 pounds. However, after the fight, despite the pre-fight reports, it was said that Rogers weighed 163 pounds, while Hart claimed 160 pounds as his weight. No one knew for certain because the fighters were not required to weigh-in for heavyweight bouts. Hart was taller and had the longer reach. They agreed that if it went 20 rounds the bout would be declared a draw.

During the 2nd round of the fight, Hart broke his right hand. He concealed the break and often led with the right when he knew it would not land, just to set up the left. Another local paper said Hart showed gameness,

---
18 *Louisville Courier-Journal, Louisville Times, Louisville Evening Post*, June 13, 1900.
19 *Louisville Courier-Journal, Louisville Times*, June 25, 26, 1900. *The Times* said Hart had only been boxing as a professional for four months.

and although he broke his right hand early in the bout, it did not affect his use of it. After the fight, a doctor said a bone just above the wrist had been split, but that the injury was not necessarily serious or permanent.

Rogers put up a game fight, and his defensive work – blocking, ducking, and footwork, were complimented as effective and unique. *The Louisville Evening Post* said Rogers had the best of the battle and forced Hart about the ring. *The Post* contradicted itself a bit by saying that Rogers danced about and ducked, and also landed, but his blows lacked steam.

In the 5th round, Rogers staggered Hart with a right. In the 8th, Hart staggered Rogers with a left to the forehead. In the 11th, it looked like Rogers had it won, but Hart rallied and they hammered each other. The round was a slugging match. They continued fighting a fast pace up through the 14th round.

In the 14th round, Hart and Rogers engaged in a series of even mix-ups. According to the *Louisville Courier-Journal*, "Hart stuck a sizzling left-handed smash just below the solar plexus." Rogers dropped to the floor and the referee counted him out.

However, the *Louisville Times* reported that Hart stopped Rogers in a semi-controversial fashion. "The knockout blow was a left swing rather low in the stomach. Rogers was not completely knocked out, but was unable to continue. He claimed that he was struck in the groin by Hart's knee." *The Courier-Journal* agreed that the knockout blow was rather low in the stomach and also noted that Rogers claimed it was a knee in the groin that finished him. It speculated that his claim might have been true, because he was doing well and had no reason to lie down. Of course, a vicious punch might have been the reason. *The Louisville Evening Post* said, "Hart shot in a very low one, at the same time planting his knee in his adversary's groin. Down went Rogers, but he was not knocked out. He claimed he was hurt in the groin by the foul blow, and asked to be examined, but the referee gave the fight to Hart."[20]

It is possible that Hart might have gotten away with one. However, it is also possible that Rogers was just acting, and had been stopped with a body shot. Throughout his career, it certainly was not atypical for Hart to knock someone out with a single body or head shot. Seven years later, Hart and Rogers would meet again, and Hart would score a KO2 over Rogers.

That same night, in New York, Gus Ruhlin scored a KO15 over Tom Sharkey.

Hart's right hand could not have been broken that badly, and possibly was not broken at all, because he was back in the ring less than two months later, on August 13, 1900, again at Louisville's Music Hall, under the

---

20 *Louisville Courier-Journal*, *Louisville Evening Post*, *Louisville Times*, June 27, 1900. The local primary sources differed as to when the bout ended. *The Courier-Journal* and *Evening Post* both said it ended in the 14th round, which is what secondary sources report. However, the less detailed *Times* said it ended in the 12th round.

auspices of the Nonpareil Athletic Club. He met Lexington's Kid Hubert in a scheduled 20-round match. This was another big local bout.

Both Hart and Hubert were "young, eager, ambitious and promising." Hart was taller and a little heavier, "but Hubert is a big fellow himself, and is shifty and muscular." The husky Hubert also had a punch. The undefeated Hubert had "whipped all the fighters he has faced to date." Hubert was said to have a following of 200 fans that would attend the fight and be willing to wager on him. Former Hart opponent William Schiller trained Hubert at the Lion Garden.

Hart also had his own following. He expected to one day be the world heavyweight champion. He was the "pugilistic idol of the East End sports, and they think he is invincible." Marvin's fellow East End Athletic Club members were big fans of his, and they purchased half of the best reserved seats.

Marvin Hart

For this fight though, Marvin was training at his manager John Seitz's place at Shelby and Market streets. Training him was former opponent Tom Williams, as well as Charles Watts and Andy Schwartz. Marvin's friends said that he had improved since his last fight.[21]

On fight night, Hubert said he weighed 156 pounds, while Hart "admitted to 155 pounds." However, "Hart was taller than his opponent and looked considerably heavier." William Schiller was one of Hubert's seconds. The men agreed to break clean from clinches. This was to be the second Hart bout filled with some controversy.

1 - The round was warm. Hubert started as the aggressor, but it did not last long. Marvin missed a lot of hard rights, while the Kid was content to jab. They kept a fast pace. Honors were easy at the end.

2 - Hart was the aggressor, swinging right and left, landing a few, but Hubert ducked cleverly and landed a stiff right to the stomach. The crowd applauded the fast work. One of Hart's powerful rights was a bit wild, and in missing, he flung himself down.

3 - The round began with exchanges of jabs. Hubert avoided several vicious uppercuts. They exchanged lefts to the face. It was a fast pace, and both appeared tired at the bell.

---

21 *Louisville Times*, August 4, 13, 1900; *Louisville Courier-Journal*, August 12, 13, 1900.

4 - Hubert jabbed with his left to the head, while Hart countered on the head with his right. Hubert avoided several leads and they clinched. Hubert landed his left to the face and Hart his right to the body. At the bell, Hubert landed a left to the stomach.

5 - Hubert jabbed to the face. Hart came back with a hard right to the jaw that shook up Hubert. They went to work missing wild right and left swings. They clinched along the ropes. Hart landed a left that cut Hubert's eye. Hubert landed his right to the stomach. They exchanged lefts at the bell.

6 - The round was a corker, for they mixed it up continually. Hubert often ducked or rushed in with his head and struck Hart in the stomach with it. Referee Edmund Rucker warned Hubert to quit rushing with his head or shoulder into Hart's stomach, or be disqualified. "Hart acted like a wild man, rushing Hubert all over the ring, and every time he would swing hard at Hubert's head the latter would duck straight ahead and his head or one shoulder would land in the pit of Hart's stomach." Hart's seconds and hundreds of admirers began yelling, "Foul!" at the top of their voices when Hubert did this. The referee was on the verge of stopping it and disqualifying Hubert because "Hart was clearly weakened by the many collisions." He again warned Hubert.

7 - Despite the referee's warnings, the round was more of the same, and after Hubert ducked a Hart swing and landed his head into Marvin's stomach, Referee Rucker disqualified Hubert.

The Louisville Times said the referee disqualified Hubert in the 7th round for using his shoulder in the clinches. Both had fought fast, but Hubert "had a way of using his shoulder whenever they came to a clinch." Hubert had been warned several times, but was finally disqualified when he did not stop.

The Times said Hubert surprised many with his good footwork and ability to get away from vicious swings. Hubert "had all the best of it. In the seventh round Hart was groggy and would surely have been finished in the next round or so." That said, in years to come, it would not be atypical for a newspaper in one round to describe Hart as groggy or tired, and shortly thereafter describe him as looking fresh and strong as he administered a knockout blow. The ending was unsatisfactory and unpopular with the audience, because Hart was groggy at the time.

However, the *Louisville Courier-Journal*, which gave a more complete and balanced view of matters, said, "The crowd, after due deliberation, will agree that Referee Rucker was right." This was because Hart's grogginess was not owing to Hubert's punches, but his head and shoulder butts into Hart's stomach. This paper felt that although Hubert put up a game, fast bout, the decision was fair and honest, and the referee could not have decided any other way.

> The boxing rules provide expressly that a boxer shall use his hands only in fighting. When he uses anything else he shall be disqualified by the referee if he commits such acts intentionally or even if not intentionally, if such acts injure the chances of his opponent. In last night's contest, while Hubert's butting tactics may not have been intentional it certainly had a bearing on the result, and if Referee Rucker had allowed the contest to continue as it had been proceeding Hubert would have won.

Although it agreed that Hubert was on the verge of victory, the reason for his potential victory was because of his foul butting into Hart's stomach. Hubert was "very clever at ducking Hart's vicious leads," but would duck straight down and "come up under Hart's arm with his head in the pit of Hart's stomach, with the latter's face contorted apparently by pain. This did not happen once, but at least half a dozen times." Hubert would also do the same quite often with his shoulder, striking it into the pit of Hart's stomach.

Actually, Hubert "did not hit Hart more than a dozen good stiff punches," but the butts did the damage. "And yet Hart, as far as blows with the fists were concerned, had landed nearly twice as many as had Hubert." The referee repeatedly warned Hubert, but the Kid might have been unable to stop himself, for "both were very awkward at times." This clearly suggests that on legitimate points, Hart was winning. However, in terms of damage done, including his butts, Hubert appeared to be heading towards victory.

Hubert was complimented for having the superior science of the two. "He is certainly cleverer than Hart and showed last night considerable science in ducking and sidestepping Hart's vicious swings. He is a good, game boxer, for he took many a hard punch." The Kid appeared to have a stiff hook with either hand, but did not often "let himself out." Hart was more aggressive and busier, with Hubert playing defense more.[22]

Owing to the unsatisfactory ending, the fans wanted to see a rematch. Neither boxer was satisfied with the result, so they were eager to meet again. "It is dollars to cents that the hall will be packed, for the crowd which saw last Monday night's contest is about evenly divided as to the merits of the men."[23]

Although the Horton law expired in New York, rendering it illegal, boxing was alive and well in Louisville. There was great interest in a Hart-Hubert rematch. Hubert's friends noted that their man had the better of the first fight, and argued that if there was any fouling it was due to Hart's

---

22 *Louisville Courier-Journal, Louisville Times*, August 14, 1900.
23 *Louisville Courier-Journal*, August 16, 1900.

awkwardness in the clinches. Hart supporters claimed that in a fair contest, without Hubert's foul tactics, Marvin would easily defeat him.[24]

Hubert was the favorite going into the rematch, owing to his "wonderful cleverness and ability to stall off Hart's fierce rushes" in their first bout. "He was certainly cleverer than Hart, and, while he did not land many telling blows on the East-End champion with his fists, when the contest was stopped Hart was certainly weak." However, "Hart's weakness was caused by the many collisions between his stomach and Hubert's head."

The Louisville-Courier Journal said eight out of ten sporting men felt that Hubert would win before the conclusion of the 20th round. "But Hart must not be overlooked. He is big, tall and strong and willing, and carries a dangerous punch in either hand. If he ever lands his right on the point of Hubert's jaw the Lexington heavyweight will go down and out the same as all the other men Hart has faced." Hart's past performances had endeared him to the East-End sports, which were all prepared to back him, despite Hubert's good showing in their recent battle.[25]

On September 18, 1900, Marvin Hart and Kid Hubert fought a rematch at Louisville's Music Hall, again sponsored by the Nonpareil Club. The scheduled 20-round bout was for the heavyweight championship of the South. Both were called two of the best heavyweights the state had ever produced. They had been training faithfully for the past month, and both were in splendid condition.

The boxers agreed upon George Hassler, the well-known local amateur athlete, to referee the bout. Hart entered the ring first, accompanied by Tom Williams, Kid Husbands, John St. Clarie and Johnny Schwartz. Hubert entered a few minutes later, and walked over to Hart and shook hands heartily. One of Hubert's seconds included Pete Traynor, who would be Hart's next opponent. This gave Pete the ability to scout Marvin. The men appeared well matched in terms of weight, height, and reach, and both appeared to be in first-class condition. The bout began just before 10 p.m.

KID HUBERT.

---

24 *Louisville Courier-Journal*, September 16, 1900; *Louisville Times*, September 18, 1900.
25 *Louisville Courier-Journal*, September 15, 18, 1900.

1 - Hart was the aggressor, leading with lefts that Hubert ducked. Hart got inside a Hubert right and put a left to the face. Hubert eluded some hard swings, displaying cleverness in ducking and side-stepping.

2 - They exchanged rights, and Hart followed with a left to the face. Hart landed a left to the body and Hubert countered with a right to the neck. Hart landed a hard left to the ribs, but the Kid eluded the follow-up right. They exchanged lefts to the body. Honors were even at the bell, and they were boxing clean and fair.

3 - Hart landed his right hard to the body. Hubert missed a hard right swing. Both missed lefts. Hubert landed two hard lefts to the head and Hart missed one. At the bell, they were missing swinging lefts.

4 - The bout really heated up in this round. Both missed rights. Hart missed a left lead, while Hubert landed as Marvin came in. At close range, they exchanged rights and lefts. Both landed rights to the jaw, and in the mix-up which followed, Hubert slipped to his knees. They fought fast and hard, and the crowd was on its feet, for it was a hot round.

5 - The round began with both roughing viciously. Hubert landed a left to the cheek. Both missed lefts. Hart ducked half a dozen lefts. They began slugging again, left and right. "It was evident that it would be only a question of a few minutes before one or the other would succumb."

Hart landed a hard left into Hubert's stomach and the Kid went down to his knees. He rose, but the blow seemed to take all of his steam. Hubert got the worst of the follow-up, and he hugged Hart along the ropes to survive. Referee Hassler found it difficult to break them apart. The round ended with the men sparring. In the corner between rounds, it appeared that the distressed Hubert did not want to continue, and his seconds had to urge him to do so.

6 - Hart, seeing his advantage, rushed matters. They began slugging from the start of the round. Hart landed left and right to the body, and Hubert missed a hard left swing. Hart decked Hubert with a left to the jaw. When he rose, Hart went in to finish, and landed lefts and rights in rapid succession. He finally landed a right to the point of Hubert's jaw, and the Kid went down and out. It was a clean knockout, as Referee George Hassler counted to ten. Hubert's seconds carried him back to his corner. The matter was settled.

The Louisville Times said the fight was interesting from start to finish. "Hubert displayed more science and foot work, but lacked the nerve and gameness of his opponent." *The Louisville Courier-Journal* said, "Hart is a much better boxer than any of his Louisville friends ever gave him credit for." His decisive victory left no doubt as to who was the better man.

In five rounds by steady hammering he had Hubert willing to quit, and in the sixth round finished his man with a right swing to the jaw. Hart was punished some during the fight, and it was by no means a one-sided argument. Hubert was exceptionally clever with his dodging and ducking, and he landed some telling blows on Hart. But he was not made out of the stuff of which Hart is made, and he finally succumbed to the inevitable. ... The fight was fast and clever from start to finish, and everybody left the hall well pleased.[26]

Hart's final fight of his very active first year as a professional in Louisville was on December 17, 1900 in yet another scheduled 20-round bout. Hart's opponent was Peter Traynor. Traynor was a fast, stiff puncher who looked good in sparring against Dave Sullivan, a boxer who had fought for the world featherweight title. A week earlier, Traynor sparring partner Sullivan had defeated Hart's sparring partner Tim Callahan via 18th round disqualification in a great bout.

Tom Williams, John Seitz, Marvin Hart

Pete Traynor could "hit a bit and is not afraid to take a wallop. His best battle was in London. He fought a twenty-round draw with Dido Plumb." Traynor had also fought "Buffalo" Costello 15 rounds (though the same paper on another day said that Traynor had won a 10-round bout). Pete had the experience of many hard contests. He had fought as an amateur as early as 1886. Traynor had defeated former John L. Sullivan foes George Robinson and Professor Laflin, both in 7 rounds. In 1895, he boxed a 4-round no-decision with Jim Hall. At the time he met Hart, Traynor was about 31 years old. He had seen Hart fight Kid Hubert, so he knew what to expect.

In his sparring sessions, Hart had shown improvement in skill. He was very strong and possessed good speed. "He showed well when he boxed

---

26 *Louisville Courier-Journal, Louisville Times*, September 19, 1900. Secondary and semi-primary source claims that the rematch took place on October 12, 1900 are incorrect. For the first time, this book reveals the actual next-day primary source reports of their rematch. Hart and Hubert would meet a third time many years later, in 1908, and fight to a 12-round draw.

Tim Callahan last week." Sparring partner Callahan said that Hart was "quick and had a terrific punch."[27]

Two of Hart's seconds were his former foes, Tom Williams, who had been working with Marvin since he had lost to him, and the recently vanquished Kid Hubert. Hart was listed as 3 inches taller and 15 pounds heavier than Traynor.

There was a debate regarding whether they should fight straight Queensberry rules or whether they should break clean. Under Queensberry rules, fighters could punch in clinches and on the break. They agreed to fight using the unmodified Queensberry rules, and had to protect themselves at all times. A crowd of 1,800 witnessed the bout.

For the first 7 rounds, Hart was the aggressor and forced Traynor about the ring, but Pete fought hard. Marvin attacked both the body and head and demonstrated that he knew how to throw all the punches. It was a fast pace.

In the 8th round, Traynor drew blood from Hart's nose. In the 10th, a Traynor right cut Hart's eye. Undaunted, Marvin continued on the aggressive.

In the 12th round, "Hart put his right hard to the chin, sending Traynor to the floor for the count. Hart landed half-a-dozen hard swings to the stomach, and Traynor went down again for the count. Hart hooked him again to the jaw, and Traynor was again on his knees for the count when the bell rang." Despite three knockdowns, Pete had survived the 12th round.

Hart forced Traynor around the ring in the 13th round, but by the 14th round, Pete had recovered, and they hammered each other.

Hart continued his attack in subsequent rounds, and by the 17th round, he was again forcing Traynor all around the ring. "Hart landed a stiff right swing to the jaw, and Traynor was clearly groggy, but was game to the core, and as Hart came in to finish him he landed a stiff left uppercut on Hart's chin and followed it with a right swing to the jaw which sent Hart staggering." Undaunted, Marvin came in again. They exchanged blows, and "Hart finally clipped Traynor with a hard left-hand hook to the point of the jaw, and Traynor went down and out. Hart had the best of the bout on points up to this time."

Marvin Hart had proven his conditioning and toughness in this one. Although Marvin had the best of it all the way and outpointed Traynor, it was not one-sided. Traynor was always dangerous and competitive. Although Pete was disadvantaged in height, reach, weight, and science, he still demonstrated fine ring generalship, particularly in the areas of ducking and blocking. Hart was complimented for his wonderful improvement, and

---

27 *Louisville Courier-Journal*, December 13, 1900, December 16, 1900.

was said to be "strong, quick and has picked up a considerable knowledge of the boxing game."[28]

Another local paper said Hart had "wonderfully improved his knowledge of the boxing game." Tryanor was game to the core and a good ring general, cleverly ducking and blocking. Pete was a match for about 12 or 13 rounds, but Hart's strength and weight began to tell. Even in the 17th round, Traynor "landed several telling blows on Hart. Towards the end of the round, however, Hart managed to get in a left-handed hook, full on the point of the jaw, which sent the Pennsylvanian down and out."[29]

A third local paper said Traynor displayed more ring experience, but Hart won all the way. Marvin was the aggressor and did the leading. In the 17th round, "Under a shower of blows on the head and body, Traynor went to his knees and fell forward on his face," and the referee counted him out.[30]

In his very first year as a professional, the undefeated Hart had already proven his gameness, power, and conditioning in lengthy bouts against Rogers (14 rounds) and Traynor (17 rounds). Marvin Hart was a fighter, and he fought often, winning all 12 of his bouts. None of his opponents in his first year of boxing had lasted the distance. All of Hart's bouts had been fought in Louisville, Kentucky, as would be all of his 1901 bouts.

---

[28] *Louisville Courier Journal*, December 18, 1900.
[29] *Louisville Evening Post*, December 18, 1900. Oddly enough, earlier the article said Hart wore down Traynor and knocked him out with a right hook on the jaw.
[30] *Louisville Times*, December 18, 1900.

CHAPTER 2

Stepping it Up: Becoming a Contender

Marvin Hart's first opponent of 1901 was Al Weinig, who was considered to be a significant step up in class for Marvin. Both men had reputations for being hard fighters with a good amount of science and the ability to take punishment. Weinig previously had a 1900 KO14 Dick O'Brien (avenging an 1899 LKOby2), LKOby10 Dan Creedon, LKOby1 Billy Stift, KO8 Jim Jeffords (the big 6'4" heavyweight) and KO5 "Chocolate Drop" Jim Watts. Weinig was said to be much cleverer than Hart. He had greater ring experience, was of equal weight and reach, and was slightly taller. Weinig had "fought some of the best middleweights in this country," and as a result, he was expected to defeat Hart. However, Marvin's friend said, "If Hart lands that right on Weing you can bet he will take the count."[31]

The Hart-Weinig bout took place in Louisville on January 21, 1901. As was the case with most all of Hart's bouts, it was a scheduled 20-rounder. For this one, the boxers agreed to break clean. Tommy Williams and Kid Hubert were again Hart's trainers and seconds.

According to the *Louisville Courier-Journal*, they fought like demons. In a fierce exchange in the 2nd round, Weinig obtained first blood by landing a hard left to the nose. In subsequent rounds, they both landed heavily, slugging away. The fight was a corker. In the 9th round, Hart shook him a bit with rights and lefts to the jaw, but Weinig came back with the same. It was a splendid contest that was even up until the 10th round.

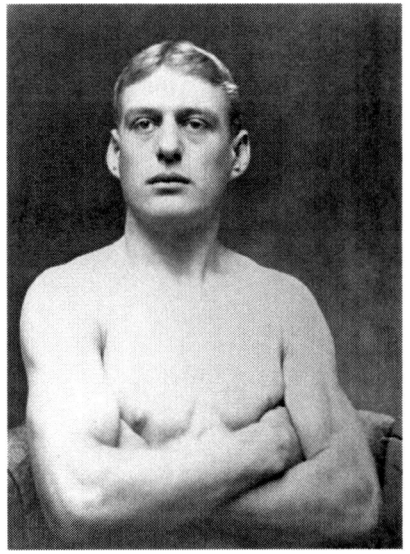

In the 10th round, Hart landed very well to the jaw, and some thought that he did not realize that he could have finished Weinig. However, they

---

31 *Louisville Courier-Journal*, January 13, 1901; Boxrec.com; *Louisville Evening Post*, January 21, 1901.

were both landing at will, and both appeared groggy. *The Louisville Evening Post* felt that Weinig had the points advantage up to the 11th round.

However, in the 11th round, Hart "hooked his right to the jaw and Weinig went down for the count. He arose at nine, and Hart swung at his jaw and Weinig went down again. He got up at the sound of 'three,' only to be knocked down and out, falling across the ropes." It was another Hart knockout victory in a competitive and entertaining battle. Weinig put up a stiff fight, but Hart was faster.

The less detailed *Louisville Times* told its own slightly different version of the end. In the 11th round, Hart dropped Weinig with a stiff left over the heart, his head striking the floor very hard. He arose with great difficulty, only to be floored again with a left to the jaw. Upon rising, a right and left sent him down and out. It was the "hardest test Hart has yet had," but he showed that "he can stand the gaff and keep his head."

The Courier-Journal called Weinig the first real first-class man that Hart had met. "Hart showed that he is a good game man, with a hard punch in either hand and capable of withstanding a world of punishment." It also called him quick, shifty, and a terrific puncher. He maintained his composure even when receiving a grueling. Marvin received the worst beating of his career but was always ready for more, and when the time came, he was able to land the knockout blow. That was Marvin Hart. The only criticism lodged was that he "can not recover quickly after he delivers or misses a punch, but this ability will come in time with experience." At times, Hart had a tendency to be wild or overthrow his punches, although his full commitment to his power was a big contributor to his success.[32]

The Evening Post said that Hart was "no longer in the dub class" and had "clearly demonstrated" that he was a "boxer of considerable ability." It had been 11 rounds of fierce fighting in which Marvin had "received a terrific punching, enough to bring out the yellowness, if it existed, in any man." However, Hart "showed beyond the shadow of a doubt that he has the one pre-eminent requisite for a pugilist, that is gameness, sand, nerve, or whatsoever you wish to call it."

> Hart is by no means a clever boxer. He has yet much to learn of the science of the game, yet this defect can be easily remedied under careful tutelage. He is strong, well built, and has a knockout up his sleeve at almost any stage of the game. In Weinig he met a more clever boxer, a better ring general, and a man his equal in strength, endurance, height and reach, and yet he whipped him. His victory was due simply to the fact that he had the heart to take a thumping without losing his head.[33]

Marvin Hart had the heart of a champion.

---

32 *Louisville Courier-Journal, Louisville Times,* January 22, 1901.
33 *Louisville Evening Post,* January 22, 1901.

The National Police Gazette later reported, "Marvin Hart says he can lick Weinig every day in the week, but will take his time about meeting him again." He knew that he had met a tough cookie.[34]

Sports were in vogue in America at that time. "Socially, it is the correct thing to go in for sport in one form or other, and never in the history of this country did sports and sportsmen in different branches multiply with the rapidity that has been shown in the last few years." Certainly, the good money that boxing offered had attracted many men to it.[35]

Just one month after the Weinig bout, on February 25, 1901 in Louisville, Marvin Hart took on the vastly more experienced middleweight veteran "Australian" Jimmy Ryan, who had over 40 bouts under his belt. Ryan's most significant results included: 1892 LKOby7 Dan Creedon; 1895 KO1 Nick Burley; 1897 KO12 Bill McCarthy, LKOby8 Tommy West, D12 Burley, LKOby5 Tommy Ryan (who in 1898 became world middleweight champion); 1898 D10 Burley, W20 Jim Watts, D6 Creedon and L6 Jack Root; and 1899 LKOby14 Joe Walcott (the black fighter who in 1901 became world welterweight champion), KO14 Bill McCarthy, L20 Jack Root, L20 Young Peter Jackson, D25 George Byers (a top heavyweight black fighter who had an 1898 W20 over Frank Childs), L20 Joe Choynski, KO4 Tom Williams, LKOby7 Choynski, and D20 Jack Finnegan (who would later lose via KO1 to James J. Jeffries). However, in 1900, Ryan had lost his last two fights by knockout, in the 8th round to Dido Plumb for the British middleweight crown, and in the 3rd round to Aurelio Herrera.[36]

Ryan was born in Australia in 1867 and was 33 years old. The local paper said that he had been boxing professionally since 1887, and had defeated all the best middleweight boxers in Australia except Dan Creedon. The experienced Ryan was expected to give young Hart the toughest fight of his career.

There was a stark contrast in experience between Ryan and Hart, as well as opponent quality. At that point, Hart had only been boxing professionally a little over a year. "From a mere novice with the gloves he has developed into a championship possibility within a twelve-months' time."[37]

In preparation, Hart sparred with Kid Hubert and Punch Campbell, amongst others. Campbell said of Marvin, "Oh, my, how he can hit!"

---

34 *National Police Gazette*, April 13, 1901.
35 *Louisville Evening Post*, February 23, 1901.
36 Boxrec.com.
37 *Louisville Courier-Journal*, February 24, 1901; *Louisville Courier-Journal*, June 12, 1900. The LCJ said Hart had over 20 bouts, though his known record only lists 14 to that point. Primary source accounts would consistently vary in the number of bouts reported for Hart. They might have been inflating his record for promotional purposes, or he may have had additional fights. *The Courier-Journal* also incorrectly listed Marvin as being 22 years of age, when he was 24 years old. Ironically, the same newspaper listed him as 23 years of age the year before.

Jimmy Ryan trained with Tommy West. He expected to defeat Hart, relying on his experience and strong right punch, even though he would be giving away ten pounds.[38]

The Louisville Evening Post said the scheduled 20-round bout was an opportunity for Marvin to gain a national reputation. More local interest was being taken in the match than any other fight ever before. "Hart is a local boy and has had a very meteoric career in the ring. From a novice some eighteen months ago he has developed into a fast, scientific boxer."

Despite Hart's local reputation and "meteoric" rise, Ryan was the local betting odds favorite. The locals had seen Ryan fight in Louisville in victories over men such as Jim Watts [W20], James Payne [KO7], Jack McDonough [KO8] and Jim Franey [KO4], and they were impressed. He had been meeting the best men in the country for the past ten years.[39]

1 - According to the *Louisville Courier-Journal*, during the 1st round, a Hart jab to the face sent Ryan to his knees. Later in the round, Ryan hit hard as they broke away from a clinch, and the crowd yelled, "Foul." Apparently, they were supposed to break clean, without hitting on breaks.

2 - 3 - Hart had the best of it.

4 - Ryan landed two stiff rights very low and Marvin rolled over and over on the ground in great pain. However, the referee would not allow the foul, and so Hart rose and continued. He kept away for a bit. By the end of the round, they were hammering each other. It was the only round that Ryan had the better of it, owing to his foul.

5 - Hart took over again.

6 - Hart "landed right and left half a dozen times, and just as the bell rang he smacked a left to the jaw, putting Ryan to his knees."

7 - Both fighters hit in the clinches. Hart went down claiming another foul low blow, but it was not allowed. They hammered one another with hooks until near the close of the round, Hart "copped Jimmy on the right spot and Ryan went down to his knees and was counted out."

Hart had dropped Ryan in the 1st, 6th, and 7th rounds en route to the knockout victory.

Afterwards, Hart said that he was fouled twice in the 5th and again in the 6th, when Ryan struck him in the groin with his fists and his knee. Once again, in the 7th round, Ryan twice swung his fists into his groin. Despite his pain, "I knocked Ryan out with a right hook on the jaw after I had planted three straight jabs on the face."

---

38 *Louisville Times*, February 23, 1901.
39 *Louisville Evening Post*, February 25, 25, 1901. Hart was again incorrectly listed as being 22 years old.

The *Courier-Journal* said that Hart had the height and reach, but Ryan had the experience. Marvin was the aggressor throughout, and beat Jimmy in every round. The only real trouble Hart had was from the constant fouling committed by Ryan, who hit him low, and kneed him in the groin, hurting him badly at least twice. Ryan palpably fouled in the 2nd, 4th, and 7th rounds, and the paper felt that the referee should have disqualified him. Despite the agreement to box with clean breaks, it was a rough-house affair. However, both men took care of themselves by hitting in clinches, butting, striking low, and using their elbows, amongst other tricks. It called Hart a coming man in the middleweight division.[40]

Like the *Courier-Journal*, the *Evening Post* was critical of the referee for not disqualifying Ryan, who committed a number of noticeable fouls which would have justified a disqualification. Regardless, the fight was warm from the start, and Ryan went down and out in the 7th round from a right to the chin.[41]

Unlike its two local counterparts, the less-detailed *Louisville Times* said Hart stopped Ryan in the 8th round, not the 7th. It too noted Ryan's fouls and felt that Jimmy was looking for a way to get himself disqualified. Ryan went down from a swing to the jaw in the 7th. He was on the floor when the gong sounded. The other papers said this was the 6th round. *The Times* said the 8th round was a "case of rough house," and they went at it "hammer and tongs." Hart put Ryan down and out with a hard right to the chin. Marvin Hart was a much better man than previously thought.[42]

That same day, in Texas, Joe Choynski knocked out a future champion, then 22-year-old Jack Johnson, in the 3rd round. Allegedly, a right to the body did the trick.[43]

Just to provide context for the time's racial climate, the same day as the Hart-Ryan fight-report, the *Louisville Courier-Journal* published an article quoting an author criticizing the book *Uncle Tom's Cabin*, saying,

> [The book is] a false statement of the social conditions of the South previous to the war. It was a crime on the negroes to free them. If it had to come, it should have been gradual. 'Uncle Tom's Cabin' largely aided in bringing about this terrible injury to the negroes by falsely representing the conditions of slavery.[44]

Marvin Hart had been impressive enough such that in his next bout one month later in Louisville, on March 29, 1901, he took on yet another experienced and active middleweight title contender, Tommy West. West

---

40 *Louisville Courier-Journal*, February 26, 1901.
41 *Louisville Evening Post*, February 26, 1901.
42 *Louisville Times*, February 26, 1901. Despite the fact that two of three local sources reported this as a KO7 win for Hart, nationally the bout was reported as a KO8, and many secondary sources echoed this. *New York Clipper*, March 16, 1901.
43 *Louisville Evening Post*, February 26, 1901; *Louisville Times*, February 26, 1901.
44 *Louisville Courier-Journal*, February 26, 1901.

had been in Jimmy Ryan's corner in Hart's last bout, so he knew what to expect. This was yet another step up for Hart.

Amongst his many bouts, Tommy West's impressive career included: 1896 LKOby2 Kid McCoy; 1897 W20 Joe Walcott; 1898 LKOby14 Tommy Ryan (world middleweight title); 1899 D20 Dan Creedon, KO7 George Byers, and KO14 Frank Craig; 1900 L6 Jack Root, KO16 Jack Bonner, KO17 Bill Hanrahan, KO11 Joe Walcott,[45] and ND6 Jack O'Brien; and a March 4, 1901 LKOby17 to Tommy Ryan in another bid for the world middleweight title, less than a month prior to West's bout with Hart. Just imagine a fighter today getting stopped in 17 rounds and then being back in the ring for a scheduled 20-rounder just 25 days later. Tom West was a tough dude. Although West had lost to Tommy Ryan, he gave the champion "the worst beating he ever received." Any fighter who could twice defeat Joe Walcott had to be good. Once again, Hart, who had just over a year of pro experience, was taking on a man who had fought over 40 pro bouts.

Marvin Hart was described as a "glutton for work," who "can take a stiff punch and come back for more," and "has a punch that will win if it lands." He was "game," "strong," "willing and confident." Hart was called the best pugilist Louisville ever produced, and a victory over West "would prove that he is championship timber beyond a doubt."[46]

Three days before the fight, on March 26, 1901, in sparring, Hart stopped black fighter "Chocolate Drop" Jim Watts, the local newspaper at one time saying Watts lasted 5 rounds, but at another point saying he only made it 4 rounds. Hart had been sparring former opponent Kid Hubert, but Watts had been added to the training crew.

> Hart today is willing and strong, but he is rapidly outgrowing those stumbling movements that at one time handicapped him. He fires blows...with a quickness and precision that are remarkable. It is all a

---

[45] Walcott retired with an arm injury under suspicion of a fix. *National Police Gazette*, September 22, 1900.
[46] *Louisville Times*, *Louisville Courier-Journal*, March 28, 1901.

revelation to Watts. He cannot understand how a man of Hart's experience has acquired so much knowledge of the game.[47]

It was reported that West would enter the ring weighing 158 pounds to Hart's 162 pounds.[48] If true, at that point, Hart was more of a middleweight than a heavyweight. They agreed to box straight Queensberry rules, meaning they had to protect themselves at all times, including on breaks.

The round by round descriptions made the fight seem quite competitive.

1 - At first, West was the aggressor and it looked bad for Hart, whose nose was bleeding freely at the end of the round.

2 - West dropped Hart with a jolt to the jaw.

3 - Despite being knocked down in the previous round, Marvin's confidence grew in this round. West kept coming, and Hart met him with jabs to the nose and rights to the body. Still, one paper said that during this round, West got inside of a furious right and knocked Hart to his knees with a short jolt to the jaw. Hart rose instantly though and continued being effective. Hart won every round from the 3rd on, though there was plenty of fighting all the time.

4 - West bled freely from the nose. Hart hit the nose repeatedly throughout the fight.

5 - Hart landed a left hook and right uppercut which staggered West. Marvin landed many uppercuts during the round. One paper said it was Hart's fight from the 5th on, for he became stronger in each round. The punishment he administered would have ended it much earlier had it been anyone other than West.

6 - Still, in the 6th round, West hooked his right to the jaw and knocked Hart down again. Hart nevertheless rose quickly and landed a big uppercut. They fought ferociously.

7 - A right staggered Hart, but he came back with two uppercuts.

8 – 11 - In general, over the next several rounds, Hart landed more often, and landed harder. With a four-inch height advantage, he made effective use of his jab and often followed with an uppercut. Marvin battered Tommy's body and face.

12 - Both engaged in rough work in the clinches, including the use of elbows.

---

47 *Louisville Evening Post*, March 27, 1901. Middleweight Jim Watts' career included: 1897 KO4 Joe Dunfee and LKOby4 Tommy West; 1898 L20 Jimmy Ryan and LKOby2 Jack Root; and 1899 LKOby3 Billy Stift and LKOby8 Joe Walcott. Boxrec.com.
48 *Louisville Times*, March 29, 1901; *Louisville Evening Post*, March 29, 1901.

13 - A left-handed low-blow dropped Hart, but the referee did not allow the claim of foul. Hart recovered and battered West.

14 - Hart continued pounding on Tommy.

15 - West was helpless, and he took a terrible beating.

> Hart landed a stinging uppercut with his right hand, and repeated this dose, and caught West a clip on the jaw and staggered him. Then Hart knocked him down with a right short hook and West went to his knees, holding to Hart's legs. He held there about five seconds before the referee got them parted and stayed down nine seconds more. When he arose Hart swung at him with his right, sending him to his knees with a right and left. He punched West all over the ring, and West was groggy and all but out when the bell rang.

Another source confirmed that West was down for fourteen seconds in the 15th round and was only saved from a knockout because he held onto Hart's legs for five seconds before he fully went down.

16 - Hart dropped West with an uppercut. When he rose, Hart knocked him all about the ring. West was repeatedly down. Finally, in the middle of the round, owing to the fact that Tommy was unable to protect himself, his second threw up the sponge to retire him.[49]

> He gave West such a drubbing as even he never received during all his long and brilliant pugilistic career. He whipped West more decisively than Champion Tommy Ryan did, and whipped him quicker. He knocked West down time and time again until it was tiresome to count.

Another local paper said that in the 16th round, West went down four times until his seconds threw up the sponge. A long straight left sent West down the first time in the round. An uppercut dropped him the next time, and after going down twice more, West's seconds realized that their man had enough. A third reporter said that after being floored twice in the 16th, the sponge was tossed up.[50]

Once again, Marvin Hart had proven his toughness, power, and condition, rising from the deck several times (2nd, 3rd, and 6th rounds) to come back to win a lengthy fight by knockout, dropping West twice in the 15th and several times in the 16th round.

According to the *Louisville Times*, other than Hart, the only two middleweights left standing at the top were Jack Root and champion Tommy Ryan. Another local paper agreed. "Hart is now right in line for the

---

[49] *Louisville Courier-Journal*, March 30, 1901.
[50] *Louisville Evening Post*, March 30, 1901.

championship." The only criticism it had of Hart was that he needed to develop further his side-stepping.[51]

When later talking about Hart, Tom West told the *Police Gazette*, "He is not clever, but he can punch like a heavyweight. I think he will trim more fighters than can lick him."[52]

Including some of his early local bouts that were mentioned in a 1900 listing of his record, up to that point, Hart had fought fifteen fights. Despite his grueling battles, Hart continued fighting approximately every month or so.[53]

Marvin Hart was certainly developing some sort of national reputation at that point. *The National Police Gazette* reported, "The friends of Marvin Hart, of Louisville, Ky., are confident that he is a coming champion and that there will be no delays for him. It is now proposed to match the Louisville ex-plumber with Kid McCoy." It later reported that John Burns, Hart's current manager, had issued a defi to Dan Creedon, the old war horse, who was hankering for a fight. Creedon accepted.[54]

Australian Dan Creedon was another experienced well-respected veteran. In late 1893 and early 1894, Creedon had boxed heavyweight champion James J. Corbett in some sparring exhibitions. In an 1894 bid for the world middleweight crown, Bob Fitzsimmons stopped Creedon in the 2nd round. The active Creedon subsequently fought many top opponents, including: 1895 D6 Joe Choynski, D6 Henry Baker, KO1 Bill McCarthy, KO2 Joe Dunfee, and W20 Frank Craig; 1896 KO2 Jem Smith, W20 Baker, and KO9 Dick O'Brien; 1897 KO4 Jim Williams, KO4 Charley Strong, and LKOby15 Kid McCoy (for the world middleweight crown); 1898 D6 Billy Stift, LKOby2 Jack Bonner, and L20 George Green

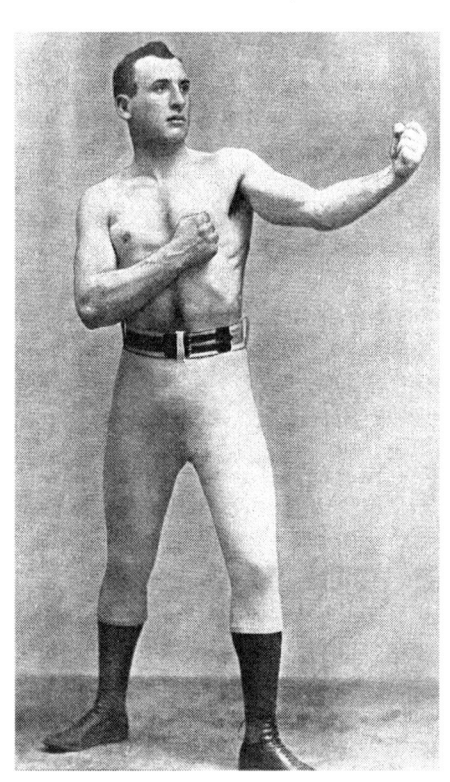

---

51 *Louisville Times*, March 30, 1901.
52 *National Police Gazette*, July 13, 1901.
53 One paper said Marvin had fought sixteen times up to that point. Two others said Hart had fourteen battles. *Louisville Times*, March 30, 1901; *Louisville Courier-Journal*, May 24, 1901; *Louisville Evening Post*, March 28, 1901 (saying thirteen just before the West fight).
54 *National Police Gazette*, April 27, May 25, 1901.

(a.k.a. Young Corbett); 1899 D20 Tommy West, LKOby1 and L20 (twice) Joe Walcott; and 1900 LKOby6 Kid McCoy and LKOby1 Jack Root. In 1901, Creedon scored a KO5 over Billy Stift, who fought Jack Johnson to a 10-round draw that year. In his last bout, Creedon scored a KO1 over Jimmy Handler. Handler had a couple knockout victories over the highly regarded George Gardner, though Gardner had stopped Handler in their third bout. Creedon was 32 years old and had over 50 pro bouts under his belt.[55]

In preparing for the fight, Hart engaged in hurricane sparring sessions with a black fighter named Steve Crosby. A few months later, in August of that year, Crosby would box Joe Gans to a 20-round draw for the colored lightweight title, but would be disqualified in the 12th round of their rematch one month later.[56]

The day before the fight, Hart said that he had never met a man as good as the Australian. However, he also said that Creedon would find that he was hard to catch, and that Marvin had whipped any man that he had ever floored.[57]

Hart fought Australian Dan Creedon in Louisville on May 24, 1901. Tim Hurst refereed. The fight was a scheduled 25-round bout.

The National Police Gazette said Hart weighed 170 pounds to Creedon's 169, so it was a light-heavyweight bout. It called Hart Louisville's "plumber-pugilist." Dan Creedon was said to be a dangerous man, owing to his recent improved condition.[58]

1 - From the start, it was a vicious and bloody battle. Hart was the aggressor. They went at it like bull dogs, pounding away with right and left hooks. They exchanged and landed repeatedly, but equally.

2 - The aggressive Hart had Creedon's left eye closed. However, Creedon hooked Hart repeatedly, and both were weak and groggy at the bell.

3 - They went at it, each trying to knock the other out. *The Police Gazette* said a left hook dropped Creedon in this round, although the local sources did not mention this.

4 - They exchanged vicious blows to the head and body, and both were groggy. Hart landed two rights to the solar plexus, but Creedon landed a right hook and another right swing to the jaw that had Hart hurt and staggering. However, even when almost out, Hart hit Creedon with his own right hook on the jaw that sent Dan sprawling on the ground. He rose and they hammered each other for the remainder of the round. Both were weak at the end.

---

55 Boxrec.com.
56 *Louisville Courier-Journal*, May 23, 1901; Boxrec.com.
57 *Louisville Evening Post*, May 23, 1901.
58 *National Police Gazette*, June 15, 1901.

5 - They continued pounding on each other. Creedon managed to land some hard blows, but was breathing hard. The pace was telling on them both. However, Hart was dismantling him. The bell saved Creedon, while Hart still looked fresh and strong.

6 - They went at it viciously, slugging each other to the point where both were staggering and practically out. Depending on the local source, either a right or a left to the body hurt Creedon. Hart saw his agony and seized his opportunity, going after Creedon like a tiger, landing a series of lefts and rights one after another so fast the blows could hardly be counted. "Finally, a right swing caught Creedon's jaw. The old fellow toppled over on the ropes unconscious and Hurst counted him out."

However, during the ten-count, one of Creedon's seconds, Dave Sullivan, illegally tried to assist Dan to his feet and threw water in his face to revive him. One of Hart's cornermen responded by going over and striking Sullivan. The pro-Hart crowd began attacking Sullivan and a near riot broke out. A couple off-duty policemen tried to restore order by punching at anyone that tried to get into it. Those men and the on-duty police took control of matters, and even had to disarm a man who drew a pistol.

Summarizing the fight, the local *Courier-Journal* and *Times* agreed that Hart failed to show Creedon his due respect, by going at him wildly in an attempt to knock him out from the start, and as a result, the old veteran managed to land many effective counterblows that had Hart groggy. They punched each other so ferociously that they were both hurt quite often and it was anyone's fight throughout. However, Hart demonstrated his ability to take a licking and keep on ticking, for he eventually wore Creedon down and stopped him. Hart was confident that no one could out-slug him.

These papers agreed that Hart could have used his height, reach, and superior weight to avoid punishment, but elected not to do so. As a result, Marvin was on "queer street" dozens of times, but his courage and ability to withstand punishment saved him. When Hart fought wildly, Creedon would "hook his head off." Marvin often reeled about as if he had drunk too much whiskey. He took it all though and still managed to give Creedon the worst beating of his career.

> Hart's greatness was shown in his ability to withstand punishment. He took at least fifty hooks on the jaw, each of which staggered him, and on each occasion Creedon's face wore a look of blank astonishment when Hart refused to fall. Creedon did everything to Hart that he ever did to any fighter, and still Hart knocked him out, and this makes Hart a mighty good middleweight.

It had been an awesome nonstop war. Throughout the contest, both men were hurt and staggering and apparently on the verge of being knocked out. Creedon was more scientific and had the best of it in a points sense, landing numerous hard blows in every round. That said, Hart gave him a pounding as well. It was several hours before Creedon fully regained his senses.

The local *Evening Post* said Creedon had the best of the fight up to the knockout. He had Hart repeatedly groggy from right hooks, almost knocking him out in the 3rd and 4th rounds. Creedon was cleverer, but did not have Hart's recuperative powers and ability to absorb punishment. Hart knocked him out with a right swing to the jaw.[59]

Creedon said that Hart was a great fighter, and that anyone hit by the same punch that Hart hit him with would be knocked out.[60]

In June 1901, the *National Police Gazette* reported that Marvin Hart had gone to San Francisco in search of a match with any of the first-class middleweights.[61] In early August, a fight between Hart and Brooklyn's Kid Carter was announced, but it is unclear as to why the bout did not take place until the following year.[62]

Hart was not able to obtain any matches while out West, including a potential fight with Jack Root. *The Police Gazette*, never shy about needling fighters in order to make a fight, called Root's gameness into question. It severely criticized him for "flunking out" of a match with Hart. Root had refused to face Hart because Marvin would not agree to clean breaks and no fighting in the clinches. *The Gazette* sided with Hart, feeling that the best way to fight was for the boxers to fight themselves loose from a clinch or partial clinch. "It will soon develop then who is inclined to fight and who to hold on. ... This clean break business is only good enough for amateurs, who are apprehensive about having their beauty spoiled."[63]

Boxing officials today should heed the *Gazette's* advice, for the good of the sport. If a fighter won't work his or her way out of a clinch, and insists on continuing to illegally hold, then points should be taken off or the boxer disqualified. Constant breaking by referees ruins the flow of the fight and penalizes the stronger boxer who is trying to fight and not take illegal time-outs by grabbing and using the referee to force the aggressive fighter back and give the other boxer space to move away again.

Unable to make a match out West, Hart returned to Louisville. In early August 1901, manager John Burns matched Hart to fight Bill Hanrahan later that month. Marvin trained at French Lick, Indiana, about 57 miles northwest of Louisville.

Unfortunately, though, Marvin came down with a case of malaria, causing the fight to be called off. In fact, it was said that he was so ill that

---

59 *Louisville Evening Post, Louisville Courier-Journal, Louisville Times*, May 25, 1901; *National Police Gazette*, June 15, 1901.
60 *National Police Gazette*, June 22, 1901.
61 *National Police Gazette*, June 29, 1901.
62 *National Police Gazette*, August 10, 1901.
63 *National Police Gazette*, September 7, 1901.

initially it was believed that it would require at least a year for him to recover.

However, in early October, the *Police Gazette* reported that Marvin was not out of the game for good, and had so far recovered his health that he would be seeking matches inside of four weeks.[64]

The October 26, 1901 edition of the *National Police Gazette* contained a full page photo of Hart, describing him as a famous middleweight. Marvin was obtaining consistent national publicity.

The following week, the *Police Gazette* reported that the sensational Louisville middleweight was again in fair shape after being sick for several weeks. Hart had been boxing regularly, and was getting back into shape to fight again. Chicago's Billy Stift was mentioned as a potential opponent.[65]

The next week's early November edition of the *Police Gazette* said that Hart, "whom all Louisville regards as invincible," was going to fight Chicago's Jack Beauscholte before Louisville's Empire Athletic Club. "Hart was quite ill two months ago, but seems to have entirely recovered."[66]

Hart took on Jack Beauscholte in Louisville on November 1, 1901, five months after the Creedon bout. In 1900, heavyweight Jack Jeffries had stopped Beauscholte in 4 rounds. In January 1901, Tommy Ryan had stopped Beauscholte in 3 rounds. Subsequently, Beauscholte had been sparring with Ryan and Jack Root. He claimed to have won eight consecutive bouts by knockout since losing to Ryan. *The Police Gazette* reported that Beauscholte held a win over Jimmy Handler. He was a young man on the improve and believed that although Hart had fought the better caliber of opponent, his youth would

---

64 *National Police Gazette*, October 12, 1901.
65 *National Police Gazette*, November 2, 1901.
66 *National Police Gazette*, November 9, 1901.

serve him well. He felt that he had as much science as Hart and could hit hard enough to win.

Hart looked lighter than he did before his illness. "There is still some doubt in the minds of the sporting public whether he is as good as he was before his late attack of malaria." They were scheduled to box 20 rounds.[67]

Hart and Beauscholte appeared to be of about equal height and weight, although the specific numbers were not provided. They fought under straight Queensberry rules.

The 1st round work was relatively light. Hart was the aggressor and did all the leading, showing his usual speed. In the 2nd round, Jack hit Marvin several times. However, Hart went after him furiously, and twice stunned Beauscholte. Thereafter, the bout was competitive. In the 5th round, a gash opened over Hart's left eye and it bled freely. Regardless, in each round thereafter, it looked as if the powerful and aggressive Hart would finish him, but Jack lasted and fought back.

In the 9th round, two rights on the chin sent Beauscholte down. He rose and mixed it up. The bell saved him.

They again exchanged blows in the 10th round, Hart landing half a dozen hard ones. Eventually, Hart dropped Beauscholte with either a right or left to the body, depending on the local version. After Jack rose, Hart fired lefts and rights to the body and head until Jack was so weak that he could barely stand. Hart finished him with a right to the jaw that dropped Jack for the count. Another paper said numerous body punches followed by a short right hook to the jaw accomplished the knockout.

Summarizing the fight, the locals said Hart gave Beauscholte a terrific punching. Jack was tough, game, and able to withstand punishment, and therefore it took a while for Hart to take him out. During the fight, Marvin laughed and "kidded" as well, which may have delayed the knockout. Beauscholte was described as a very clever boxer who seemed to lack hitting ability. Hart was not as clever, but "can hit like a mule's kick."[68]

---

67 *Louisville Courier-Journal, Louisville Times,* November 1, 1901; *Louisville Evening Post,* October 29, 1901.
68 *Louisville Courier-Journal, Louisville Times, Louisville Evening Post,* November 2, 1901.

Louisville fans considered Hart to be invincible. All of his bouts to that point had been in Louisville.[69]

In mid-November, James Jeffries successfully defended his heavyweight championship when Gus Ruhlin retired after the 5th round of their bout.

A month and a half after the Beauscholte bout, in his sixth and final 1901 fight, on December 17, the undefeated 17-0 Hart took on "Wild" Bill Hanrahan, who was the former American middleweight amateur champion. Hanrahan was the type of do-or-die fighter who came to win via a knockout or to get knocked out. All of his victories had come by knockout, but he had lost just as many via knockout. Hanrahan had such professional results as 1899 D6 George Gardner and KO4 Patsy Corrigan; 1900 KO12 Kid Carter, LKOby17 Tommy West,[70] KO21 Jack Bonner, LKOby10 Kid Carter, D15 George Byers, D20 Kid Carter, and LKOby12 Joe Walcott; and 1901 L20 Bonner and LKOby5 Jimmy Handler. Less than a month before taking on Hart, on November 25, 1901 in Louisville, Hanrahan won a rematch KO18 over Jimmy Handler. Hanrahan was no slouch in the experience department against top fighters.[71]

Hanrahan and Hart had been matched to fight in late August, but Hart's illness had temporarily derailed the bout. Back in August, in preparation for the Hart fight, Hanrahan had been sparring every day with his former opponent, "Barbados Demon" Joe Walcott. Although Hanrahan had lost to Walcott, Joe "was busy all the time and received a severe slugging. Walcott says that Hanrahan is one of the roughest and hardest hitters he has met, and Joe ought to know." Observers of Hanrahan's work said that Hart was going up against a "mighty tough proposition." Manager Tom O'Rourke was handling Hanrahan. "O'Rourke seldom starts losers,

---

69 *National Police Gazette*, November 9, 1901.
70 Hanrahan's June 1900 fight with Tommy West was a great middleweight battle. Hanrahan was described as big and burly with good height and reach, as well as wild and strong. He led early, dropping West in the 2nd round with a right. West was more skillful though and was able to counter Billy's rushes. In the 10th, Hanrahan almost knocked out West. Billy took over the fight thereafter, but in the 17th round, West knocked out Hanrahan with his right. West went on to be knocked out in the 16th round by Hart in March 1901. *National Police Gazette*, July 7, 1900.
71 *Louisville Times*, October 9, 1900; Boxrec.com.

and he is coming to Louisville confident of victory over Hart." Dave Sullivan said that Hanrahan was a cyclone in the ring.[72]

Since then, the Louisville sports had seen Hanrahan in action defeating Handler. Hanrahan was a highly regarded young up-and-comer whose ferocious style and big punch made him only a slight underdog against Hart. Because both men were so aggressive, strong, and at times, wild, one writer predicted that "a lucky punch may have a good deal to do with the result."[73] One asked, "Has the hour of Hart's Waterloo finally come?" Hanrahan was complimented for his gritty performance against Walcott.

> At the age of nineteen, with little science, but an abundance of strength, he collided with that black whirlwind, Joe Walcott and remained twelve rounds. He knocked the "demon" down, and a knot on Walcott's head made the wearing of a hat a ludicrous spectacle. Walcott, George Gardiner and "Kid" Carter agree that the erratic Hanrahan has a wallop equal to the hardest. Hanrahan says he is certain that he will trim Hart. He expects to do it in a hurry.

The pre-fight analysis prophetically stated, "The first punch that reaches a vulnerable spot will have considerable effect. Hanrahan, because of his marvelous strength, has, in the opinion of many, more than a chance." Bill had a powerful long left jab. He was powerful enough such that if Hart became wild or careless "he may have occasion to regret it." Most experts considered it to be a very good, exciting match-up. One expert picking Hanrahan said, "If he puts one of those 'haymakers' over on Hart the Irishman will cash, and everybody knows it is easy to hit Hart." *The New York Clipper* said Hart was a 5 to 3 favorite.[74]

---

72 *Louisville Times*, August 10, 20, 1901.
73 *Louisville Evening Post*, December 16, 17, 1901.
74 *Louisville Courier-Journal*, December 15, 16, 1901; *New York Clipper*, December 28, 1901.

Hanrahan was expressing nothing but confidence, saying that he would next like to meet any top heavyweight in the world, barring Jeffries. He felt that he was just as strong as Tom Sharkey and just as good as Joe Choynski, saying, "And speaking of Choynski, I feel that I have something on him. When he was training for his bout with Joe Walcott…I boxed with him and loosened his ribs with a wallop." Regarding his bout with Walcott, Hanrahan said that he nearly put Joe out. "Ask anyone who saw the bout. I put Walcott down, and he will tell you today that I am a hard customer in the ring. I was a novice then, only twenty years old, and my knowledge of the game was limited. … I have learned considerable in the last year." Bill knew that Hart was game, strong, and had a big punch, but felt that he was just as strong and had more experience.[75]

Hart expressed confidence as well, saying, "I think I can beat any man in the world weighing no more than 190 pounds." Hart was listed as 24 years of age, though he was really 25 at that point. He had enlisted the just-vanquished Jack Beausholte as his trainer. Hanrahan was said to be 21 years old. Both reportedly stood 5'10 ¼" and weighed about 165 pounds. The fight was scheduled for 25 rounds using straight Queensberry rules.

On fight-night, according to the *Louisville Courier-Journal*, Hart said he weighed 168 pounds, while Hanrahan gave his weight as 165. Hart appeared to be a couple inches taller, despite the pre-fight report that they were of the same height.

4,000 people witnessed the bout. *The Courier-Journal* said it only lasted 1.5 minutes, while the *Evening Post* said the bout ended at 2 minutes and 10 seconds of the 1st round.

According to the *Courier-Journal*, "Hanrahan put his right to the ribs. He put his left to the ear. Hanrahan landed his right and left to the head, and a left clip to the jaw put Hart to his knees." After rising,

> [Hart] made a wild swing with his right and Hanrahan stepped back, allowing it to slip past his nose. Then Hanrahan shot over one of his famous rights which he calls "the Mary Ann." This is a long right swing, the boxer using his right hand as if he were going to throw a baseball. Usually there is no telling where it will land, but on this occasion it caught Hart on the back of his head behind the ear, and dropped him as if he had been hit with a hammer.

Hart rose in bad shape and Bill stepped back. As Marvin advanced, Bill landed a left hook to the jaw and Hart staggered to the ropes. Bill quickly landed a right to the jaw that knocked him down and out. It was Marvin Hart's first loss.[76]

The Louisville Times had a slightly different version. It did not mention the initial knockdown from a left hook that its local counterpart claimed. It

---

75 *Louisville Courier-Journal, Louisville Times*, December 17, 1901.
76 *Louisville Courier-Journal*, December 18, 1901.

agreed that Hart was dropped by the wild right behind the ear, which Hanrahan called his "Mary Ann." It said that Hart "got up groggy, and a few more wallops, the final one in the solar plexus, finished him." It said a body shot finished it, while the other local paper said it was a right to the jaw.[77]

The Louisville Evening Post was similar to the *Times*, but with its own variation. It said a high right, starting from away back, traveling in a semi-curve, landed high on the side of Hart's head, sending him down for the first time. Hart rose and crouched like Jeffries. Hanrahan swung wildly. There was a clinch, and after breaking, Bill rushed again and a swing to the body dropped Hart. Marvin's eye was bleeding. He rose and tried an uppercut that missed. Hanrahan hit the body and roughed him to the corner, "where Hart went over against the ropes from weakness. He pulled himself up and stepped out, only to receive a left hook in the stomach that sent him to the floor for good." Hart looked slow and weak and had been unable to hit Hanrahan.[78]

The Courier-Journal said the truly decisive punch was the swinging right that went over Hart's head and hit him in back of the left ear to drop him for the second time. Hart never landed a stiff punch.

Afterwards, Hanrahan was less than gracious, saying,

> It was easy money for me. I never went up against such an easy 'mark' before…. Hart must have been an awful lucky fellow to beat the people he has. He actually threw up his hands at me like an old woman. I was astonished when he came at me. I thought I was in a trance and everybody was kidding me, including Hart. It looked like a shame to hit him.

In response, Hart called Hanrahan a "big lobster" and said that he had landed a chance blow that he could not duplicate again in a thousand years. "He can hit hard, and I ran into one of those lucky punches that was swung in a half circle." Responding to those who were so surprised at the result that they felt that Hart had thrown the fight, Marvin said, "The contest was upon the level."

Referee Tim Hurst said, "Hart never had a chance to get started…. that wallop back of the ear put him out of the running. Those two punches to the body also did business with him. … Bill used his right straight to the body, and when he does this he is a hard man to stand off."[79]

The Police Gazette said that Hart had been thought of as a contender for the middleweight crown, but Hanrahan whipped him easily. Marvin tried to rise, but only made it to a sitting position.[80]

---

77 *Louisville Times*, December 18, 1901.
78 *Louisville Evening Post*, December 18, 1901.
79 *Louisville Courier-Journal*, December 18, 1901.
80 *National Police Gazette*, January 11, February 22, 1902.

However, in Wild Bill's next fight, in February 1902, colored heavyweight champion Frank Childs knocked out Hanrahan in the 4th round. In March 1902, Joe Choynski stopped Hanrahan in the 5th round. As a result, many were inclined to the belief that Hanrahan's victory over Hart was indeed a fluke. In Hanrahan's next fight, he fought a 6-round draw with Jack Beausholte. It was his final fight, for on April 18, 1902, Bill Hanrahan died from pneumonia.[81]

Undeterred by the loss to Hanrahan, a month after the defeat, on January 20, 1902 at Louisville's Music Hall, the gutsy Hart got back into the ring against another very experienced and active fighter in Chicago's Billy Stift, in a scheduled 20 rounder. The previous year, Stift had fought Jack Johnson to a 10-round draw. Stift's 46-fight-career results included: 1895 W6 Mike Brennan; 1896 LKOby7 Tommy West; 1897 LKOby6 Tommy Ryan (police stopped the bout); 1898 D6 Dan Creedon; 1899 LDQby7 Jack Root,[82] L20 Tommy Ryan,[83] KO3 Jim Watts, D6 George Byers, L6 Jack Root, LKOby13 Kid McCoy, and W6 Jack McCormick; 1900 KO1 Al Weinig, W6 and D10 Jack Jeffries, and L6 Dick O'Brien; and 1901 LKOby5 Dan Creedon, D10 Jack Johnson, KO2 Weinig, W6 Byers, L6 Weinig, and D6 Jack Beauscholte.

The National Police Gazette gave the middleweight Stift a full page photo in its March 3, 1900 issue, so he was a nationally recognized fighter. Certainly, he was an experienced boxer who was not shy about fighting the best, always offering good competition. Hart and Stift boxed with 5-ounce gloves, the standard size for the era's fights.

1 - Stift staggered Hart with a right, and he also hit the ribs often.

2 - They mixed it up and mauled each other in the clinches.

---

81 Boxrec.com; *New York Clipper*, February 15, 1902.
82 In February 1899, Stift and Jack Root fought a good battle. Stift was dropped in the 4th, but he knocked down Root in the 6th and 7th rounds. However, on that final knockdown, Stift hit him with an uppercut while Root was down and was disqualified. *National Police Gazette*, March 11, 1899.
83 World middleweight champ Tommy Ryan easily won a 20 round decision over Stift. *National Police Gazette*, May 6, 1899.

3 - Hart crouched low with his left arm extended. After a couple feints, Marvin sent a long, wild right swing over Stift's head that landed just back of the left ear and dropped him. When Billy rose, the same punch landed in the same place and knocked him out.

Marvin Hart had knocked out the shorter, stockier Stift in the 3rd round, the fastest anyone had ever stopped Billy. One paper said that Stift was a "disappointment" and failed "to give Marvelous Marvin an argument."

However, Referee Hassler said that it was a hard, fast bout, and up to the end, it seemed even. "[T]he two blows that put Stift out were long, right swings from the hip. It looked as if both of them landed in the same place, 'just back of the ear.'" Perhaps Hart had learned something from Bill Hanrahan. Some felt that Stift had laid down and quit, but Referee George Siler, acting as an analyst, disagreed, saying that although Stift had put up better fights, Hart was a hard puncher and too shifty for Billy.

Stift said,

> Hart is undoubtedly a great boxer. I thought I could beat him after the second round, on account of his rushing tactics, by side-stepping and a straight right. Hart is clever with his body, and got away from several short-arm blows that would have done business with him had they landed. I have boxed all the best middleweights in the West, and Hart hits the hardest blow of any of them. He hit me back of the ear in the third round, and it was one of the hardest blows I ever experienced. It knocked me down…set the 'bees roaring' and I could not hear the referee count. … I felt strong and got up… [but] just then Hart landed another blow, harder even than the first one, on exactly the same spot. It floored me and I could not rise at the count.[84]

The Police Gazette reported that Hart had distinguished himself with the 3rd round knockout victory over Stift. Marvin was the aggressor all through, but Billy was shifty and blocked several swings. Stift's blows lacked steam and he had difficulty landing on Hart. They started in to mix things in the 3rd round, and after several clinches, Hart dropped him twice and took him out. Marvin was back on the hot contender trail again.[85]

On April 7, 1902 in Louisville, Hart took on yet another middleweight veteran in Dick O'Brien. O'Brien's over 50-fight-career results included: 1894 LKOby12 Joe Walcott; 1895 D25 Kid McCoy and LKOby1 Walcott; 1896 D6 Walcott, KO4 Dick Moore, and LKOby9 Dan Creedon; 1897 LKOby10 Kid McCoy and KO2 Frank Craig; 1898 LKOby19 Jack Bonner, W15 Moore, D15 Bonner, and LKOby14 Tommy Ryan; 1899 LKOby13

---

[84] *Louisville Times*, January 20, 21, 1902; *Louisville Courier-Journal*, January 21, 1902.
[85] *National Police Gazette*, February 15, 1902.

Jimmy Handler, LKOby14 Walcott, KO3 George LaBlanche, KO2 Al Weinig, and D10 George Byers; 1900 LKOby14 Weinig, KO5 Dick Moore, D15 Byers, L6 Jack Root, W6 Billy Stift, LKOby3 Jack Root, and WDQ4 Sandy Ferguson; 1901 WDQ4 Ferguson and LKOby5 Weinig; and February 7, 1902 LKOby11 Weinig.

The locals said that Dick O'Brien, "while not clever, has a dangerous punch in his right hand, and is a chunky sort of boxer." Hart was called "strong, rugged and hits a terrific punch." The bout for which O'Brien was most noted was his 25-round draw with Kid McCoy. One report said O'Brien was likely to be heavier than Hart.[86]

O'Brien's manager said,

> O'Brien is twenty-eight years old, and has been fighting for thirteen years, ever since he was a kid. He will weigh on the night of the contest 168 pounds, and he is five feet seven inches in height. He has wonderful steam behind his blows, and if he ever lands one in the right place it will be all off with Hart.[87]

For the first 2 rounds of the Marvin Hart–Dick O'Brien bout, it appeared that neither was desirous of doing serious injury to the other. Perhaps they were just being cautious, respectful of each other's power. One local paper said Hart's performance was substandard and that O'Brien gave a poor, amateurish showing. However, the referee thought that O'Brien was stalling and looking for a knockout punch.

In the 3rd round, there was considerable infighting, until a Hart right to the jaw dropped O'Brien. After rising, they went at it, with Hart using right and left hooks. A Hart right uppercut dropped Dick again, and he was counted out. Many were unsure as to where the punch landed. One said the uppercut seemed to land in the chest. Some said it hit the chin. Referee George Siler said it landed on the ribs. All agreed that it was a good, stiff punch.[88]

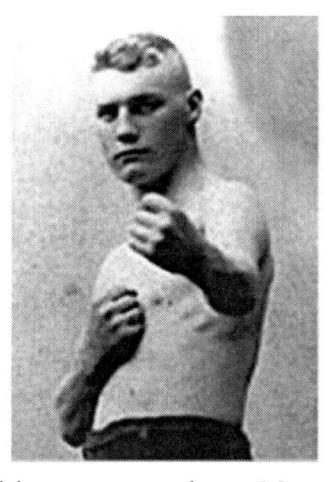

Another local paper said the fight was no match and that "Marvelous Marvin" had O'Brien at his mercy in the final minute of the fight. This version was higher on Hart, saying that he went in to knock out O'Brien right from the start, but O'Brien fought carefully.

> In the third round in one of the rushes Hart landed on Dickey's wind and gave him half a dozen stiff jabs in the stomach as they backed

---

86 *Louisville Courier-Journal*, April 4, 6, 1902.
87 *Louisville Times*, April 5, 1902. A few days before the fight, Hart refereed a local bout
88 *Louisville Courier-Journal*, April 8, 1902.

across the stage, O'Brien leaning on Hart and being supported by the latter. They broke away and Hart rushed his opponent before the latter had time to recover, landing on his stomach with a right-hand punch, and the latter went down for the count. O'Brien fell with force, and struck his head sharply against the floor. He tried to get up, but was unequal to the task, and he was counted out with time to spare.[89]

Hart's successive 3rd round knockout victories over Billy Stift and Dick O'Brien had put him back on track, and showed that his loss to Hanrahan was a mere anomaly.

---

[89] *Louisville Times*, April 8, 1902. Some sources list this as a 4th round knockout, but both local primary sources said O'Brien was stopped in the 3rd round.

CHAPTER 3

The Carter War

On May 3, 1902 in Louisville, Marvin Hart took an even bigger step up in opponent quality when he took on Brooklyn's Eddie "Kid" Carter, who had some significant victories. Earlier in 1902, Carter had knocked out Joe Choynski in the 1st round.[90] This big win came after Choynski's 1901 KO3 over Jack Johnson and 1902 KO5 over Bill Hanrahan (the man who in late 1901 had stopped Hart in the 1st round). In 1900, Carter had scored a KO10 over Hanrahan. Carter also had a 1901 KO7 over Joe Walcott, who was one of the era's best pound-for-pound fighters.

Kid Carter's nearly 60 career results included: 1898 D10 and LDQby10 Jack O'Brien; 1900 LKOby12 Billy Hanrahan, LDQby19 George Gardner, KO10 Billy Hanrahan, D20 Hanrahan, and L6 Tommy Ryan; 1901 WDQ19 Joe Walcott (Carter dominant), D20 and W20 Jack Bonner, LDQ15 Jack Root (Root badly beaten and almost out when knocked down in the 15th, but Carter hit him when down and was disqualified),[91] LKOby18 George Gardner (165-pound Carter put up game fight but Gardner clearly better),[92] KO7 Joe Walcott, and LKOby8 Gardner; and 1902 KO1 Choynski, D20 Jack Bonner, and W6 Al Weinig.

Carter was described as a good boxer and puncher, but lacked coolness, for when he was hit hard, instead of being cautious; he became angry and lost his head.[93] However, another report said, "Carter is considered one of the best lightheavyweights that

---

90 The Carter-Choynski bout was fierce from the beginning. First Choynski landed well, but was then dropped by a series of windmill lefts and rights from Carter. A right swing on the jaw knocked Choynski out. Joe said it was the hardest wallop he had ever received. *National Police Gazette*, April 19, 1902.
91 *National Police Gazette*, July 20, 1901.
92 *National Police Gazette*, September 21, 1901.
93 *Police Gazette*, April 18, 1903.

ever donned a mit. He is one of the three men who ever defeated 'the Black Demon,' Walcott. Though defeated by George Gardner, he beat Joe Choynski in a round."[94]

Carter was said to be looking good in his preparations for Hart.

> Judging by his great work in training, Carter will fight his man from beginning to end. He is a glutton for punishment and never knows when to let up. He fights from gong to gong. His blows carry great force, but are not delivered with a swing. He hits free and easy with both hands and never draws back when he is going to strike. His best blow is a right-hand jolt.... He also has a wonderful left hand and is as quick as a lightning flash on his feet.[95]

During training, Hart sparred with George Grant, a black heavyweight who had lost two 1898 6-round decisions to John "Klondike" Haines, who would subsequently split two bouts with Jack Johnson. In one sparring session, Hart and Grant engaged in a hurricane 3-round mix-up in which Hart dropped Grant in the 2nd round. "Grant's strength, agility and clever blocking availed him little against Hart's rushing tactics. They went very fast for three rounds. Hart repeatedly battered down Grant's guard and gave a lively demonstration."[96]

Former Carter opponent Joe Choynski and former Hart opponent Pete Traynor (a.k.a. Trainor) were also assisting Hart, and were in his corner on the night of the fight. "Hart probably weighed several pounds more than Carter, but the difference in weight, if there was any, was hardly noticeable." They boxed straight Queensberry rules in a scheduled 20-round bout. The fight was to be a memorable war.

1 - Hart staggered Carter with a right, and it looked like the Kid was going to be knocked out, but he managed to survive the subsequent onslaught. It was clearly Hart's round.

2 - Both landed heavily during the round. Carter landed a terrific blow on the stomach. Carter mostly looked to land on the body. Hart drew blood with a right to the nose. Another right staggered Carter, and by the end of the round, one of the Kid's eyes was in bad shape.

3 - The round was again ferocious, but even.

4 - This was Carter's round, as he landed two or three good shots and rushed Hart to the ropes, bringing blood from Marvin's nose. It was anyone's fight from the 4th on, and both took fearful punishment.

---

[94] *Louisville Courier-Journal*, May 4, 1902.
[95] *Louisville Times*, May 3, 1902.
[96] *Louisville Times*, April 30, 1902; Boxrec.com.

5 - Hard rights from each staggered both men. Another right wobbled Carter again. They were rough in the clinches and eager to mix it up, but it was Hart's round.

6 - In this round, they nearly knocked out one another. They "slammed their rights into each other so fast that it was impossible to count them. Carter's face was cut into ribbons, both were staggering and both were all out."

7 - Both were in bad shape at this point and it was still anybody's fight. Staggering Carter with each punch, Hart landed a right and left, and then an uppercut. Eventually, Carter landed a right and left in return, wobbling Hart.

8 - Hart again badly hurt Carter with two rights. They mixed it up.

> Carter seemed to be all but out, and Hart landed right and left almost at will, knocking Carter all about the ring. Carter landed a good stiff uppercut, which also staggered Hart. He then rushed Hart, landing right and left. Carter landed half a dozen lefts to the face. Both men staggered around the ring like drunken men.

Carter was the more punished, but both boxers required assistance to their corners.

9 - Hart began the round perceptibly stronger and tried to end it by raining blows on the jaw. Finally, Hart dropped Carter with a right. After he rose, "Hart timed himself and landed a couple of terrific right jolts to the point of the jaw, and Carter went down for the count." Another version said that after Carter rose from the first knockdown, another deluge of blows knocked him out.

It was a great fight, "unparalleled for viciousness and brutality." It was the fastest ever seen in Louisville, and practically even for 8 rounds. Quite often, both were almost out of it, and it looked as though either might win by knockout at any time. It was a case of survival of the fittest.

> For eight rounds these big fellows battled with the speed of bantamweights and mauled each other almost into insensibility. In the first, second and third rounds Hart had Carter practically out, but the wonderful gameness and vitality of the Brooklynite came to his rescue, and in the fourth, fifth and sixth rounds he had none the worse of the argument.
>
> The last two rounds were simply incomparable with anything ever before seen here in the ring. Hart landed half a hundred right-hand swings...while Carter played a terrific tattoo on the same parts of the local man's anatomy. For a time it looked like both of Hart's eyes would be closed, and his nose had all the appearance of being

broken. One of his jaws was swelled up all out of proportion, while Carter's face looked like he had finished in second place in a collision with a railroad train.

Hart was quick to throw a "terrific straight left hand that was a wonder to behold. At close range he used his right with hooks to the head and smashes to the body with splendid effect."

Another local description said, "Hart landed twice as often as Carter. He used a left jab to the face principally, and he must have made good with it at least thirty times. Hart would follow this jab with a right swing or uppercut to the jaw." At the conclusion of the 8th round, neither knew where his own corner was, and their seconds had to assist them.

However, in the 9th round, Hart attacked ferociously, and Carter was "unable to stand the gaff." Hart hooked in a hard right to the jaw that dropped Carter. He rose, but Hart rushed in and rained in terrific right and left blows to the head and jaw, finally dropping Carter for the full count.

This victory made Hart even more highly regarded.

> Marvin Hart is a really first-class man in the light heavyweight division. While he may not be clever, he has every other quality which goes to make a champion boxer. He took last night more punishment than he had received in all his other twenty ring engagements.[97]

Another local paper agreed, saying, "If there was any doubt as to Marvin Hart's quality as a pugilist, it was removed Saturday night." It was the best slugging match ever seen in Louisville, a supreme test of grit, determination, and ability to give and take punishment. The pace was faster than seen even from featherweights. "Each took an amount of punishment in almost every round which would have put to sleep the average fighter."

Marvin Hart was always entertaining. Such wars have a way of shortening careers, but for the time being, Hart's stock went up. The buzz from this fight lasted several months, and word about it spread across the country.

Afterwards, Carter said,

> I was never surer of winning in my life than I was in the fourth and fifth rounds. I started all right in the sixth and had Hart going when I became overanxious and overconfident. I fought myself out, and at the end of the round, when he made a slight rally, I was too weak to protect myself properly. It was a hard one to lose.[98]

Just two weeks later, Kid Carter unofficially won a 6-round no-decision bout against Kid McCoy, which further boosted Hart. It was said that Hart's decisive victory over Carter was impressive, and the fact that Carter

---

97 *Louisville Courier-Journal*, May 4, 1902.
98 *Louisville Times*, May 5, 1902.

just a short time later defeated Kid McCoy was another feather in Marvin's cap.

At that point, Hart, "the Louisville terror," said, "I have come to the conclusion that I have a chance with any of the fighters, barring Jeffries, and I am willing to take them on. ... I prefer no one. They all look alike." Hart was willing to box any heavyweight in the world, except champion James Jeffries.

Trainer Joe Choynski said that Hart was the world's only legitimate aspirant for stellar honors. Joe had coached Hart for the Carter fight, and subsequently had him under his care and tutelage for a while.[99]

Clearly, Hart felt that he was too heavy to fight as a middleweight, and wanted to fight heavier men. *The National Police Gazette* was again taking notice of him. It said that the clever light heavyweight, through his brother and current manager, Russell Hart, was out with a challenge to meet any man in the world, except for Jeffries.

> Hart's achievements in the roped arena have been phenomenal, and since his victory over "Kid" Carter in nine rounds he has been much sought after, both by club and theatrical managers.
>
> Twenty contests in less than two years and with but a single defeat is a record to be proud of, and in the list of defeated will be seen some of the best men in the light heavyweight class. Hart is but 22 years of age, and good judges who have seen him in action predict that he will some day be champion. Hart shows a marked improvement with each battle and with his indomitable pluck and stamina he certainly has a bright future before him. Built on the lines of a thoroughbred, with powerful shoulders, small waist and trim underpinning, capable of landing a knockout with either hand, no one has more confidence in his own powers than he.[100]

In the meantime, in July 1902, James J. Jeffries knocked out Bob Fitzsimmons in the 8th round, defending the world heavyweight championship.

---

99 *National Police Gazette*, June 28, July 19, 1902.
100 *National Police Gazette*, August 9, 1902. Hart was actually 25 years old.

CHAPTER 4

The 6-Round Road Warrior and the Top Light Heavyweights

The publicity surrounding the Carter bout finally generated a demand to see Hart fight outside of Kentucky. Marvin Hart's very first fight outside of Louisville was a rematch with Billy Stift in Stift's hometown of Chicago. Since being stopped by Hart in the 3rd round earlier in 1902, amongst his many bouts, Stift had lost a 6-round decision to Joe Walcott, a 10-round decision to Tommy Ryan, and Jack Root had knocked him out in the 2nd round. Stift's most significant recent bout results were D10 Harry Peppers and D6 John Willie.[101]

Although Hart was used to fighting in bouts scheduled for 20 or 25 rounds, and his style was designed for the longer distance, the Hart-Stift bout was scheduled for only 6 rounds, the maximum distance allowed in Chicago, Illinois. Boxing was legal and popular in both Philadelphia and Chicago, the most populous cities in the nation other than New York, where boxing was currently illegal, but neither Philadelphia nor Chicago allowed bouts of greater length than 6 rounds. Chicago allowed points decisions, while Philadelphia did not. The only official way to win a bout in Philly was via some form of knockout or disqualification. Regardless of the shortened distance, many fights were taking place in these cities due to the fact that their large populations ensured larger crowds, and therefore larger financial incentives.

Stift's local friends were willing to bet at even money that Billy would last the full 6 rounds. Although many were looking for Stift to do his "trial

---
101 Boxrec.com; Cyberboxingzone.com.

horse" act, trying to stay as long as he could, Stift said he could hit as hard as anyone, and felt that he had as much of a chance to land a knockout blow as Hart did. Stift was sparring and training with heavyweight Frank Childs, who claimed the colored heavyweight championship. Both boxers posted forfeits guaranteeing their appearances for the bout.[102]

The physical advantages were with Hart. Stift could easily make the middleweight limit, whereas Hart was a full fledged light heavyweight. Still, Marvin was weighing in the neighborhood of 170 pounds, while Stift was weighing around 165, so they were of similar size. Hart had the height and reach advantages. However, Stift was accustomed to these handicaps.

> Hart himself is anything but a boxer of the scientific order. He cuts loose with both hands and piles in fiercely from the beginning of things, his one object evidently being to end the fracas in a hurry. This style of milling is just what suits Stift. A vigorous mix-up delights him beyond measure.

Chicago's *Daily Inter Ocean* said Stift had knocked out many a man with his dangerous right, and it was powerful enough that he could do the same to Hart.

It also gave Hart credit for his skill. Although he was a terrific slugger, "Pure strength would hardly win him the string of victories contained in his record." Cleverness was required to defeat the caliber of opponents that Hart had defeated.[103]

The Chicago Daily News said,

> Hart is a slugger from the word go and is far from being ignorant of the finer points of the game. He learned much under Joe Choynski. ... Stift is fighting better and cleverer to-day than he ever did. ... Although Stift possesses a good punch, Hart is decidedly the more dangerous. He is always on the aggressive, punches hard and often and accordingly looks an almost certain winner.[104]

A third local paper said, "Hart is a rugged slugger, of just the sort likely to please a Chicago crowd, and as in Stift he will find another of the same kind, a hard fight is certain." Although Hart was the acknowledged favorite, even Marvin's friends acknowledged that Stift was always dangerous.

Hart knew that Stift was a good opponent and hard to beat, saying, "Stift is always dangerous so long as he is on his feet.... This man rains his blows in from all directions and any one of these chance wallops is dangerous. I am faster than he is, however, and can land just as hard as any of them."

---

[102] *Chicago Daily Inter Ocean*, August 13, 16, 1902.
[103] *Chicago Daily Inter Ocean*, August 17, 18, 1902
[104] *Chicago Daily News*, August 18, 1902.

Some wondered whether Hart might be weakened or diminished in some way by his recent war with Kid Carter, which was called one of the most desperate battles ever seen. Both boxers "were laid up for several days as a result of the mill."

A victory over Stift would make Hart "a prominent candidate for the championship in his class – the light heavy weight division. His knockout victories over Tommy West, Al Weinig, 'Kid' Carter and others leave Jack Root as his most prominent rival for first honors."[105]

On August 18, 1902, Hart and Stift fought their rematch in Chicago at the American Athletic Club. Hart was listed as standing 5'10" and weighing about 170 pounds. A local paper's next-day report said that Stift was listed as weighing 165 pounds, while Hart looked 20 pounds bigger. Most of the betting was on the proposition that Stift would be on his feet at the end of the 6 rounds. Billy was said to be a hard man to put away.

The experienced and well respected George Siler, who refereed the bout, wrote the local *Chicago Tribune's* report. Siler described Hart's stance.

> Marvin's crouched and awkward appearing attitude caused much laughter, but it was a serious matter with him, and he cut loose to knock Stift out of the ring. He extended his long left at full length, sunk his left jaw deep down into his shoulders, and began operations. His position appeared cramped and awkward, but it did not seem to hamper him.

Hart began by firing his left, then following with a powerful right bent on a knockout. "In this he failed miserably, as he invariably telegraphed the coming of his right mawley, thus giving the local man ample opportunity to slip under it." Hart began throwing his right to the body with more success. These punches slowed Stift up and caused him to clinch. Hart outpointed Stift from the beginning, and he had a fair margin by the end of the 3rd round.

The Chicago Record-Herald said neither did much damage during the first 3 rounds. Both swung wildly, with Hart on the offensive and Stift showing clever defense. Although Billy was ducking away most of the time in the mix-ups, he managed to land some blows to Marvin's body and did not allow Marvin much of an edge.

The Chicago Chronicle said that early on, Stift seemed afraid, content mostly to dodge Hart's swings. Hart's best punch was his right to the body that snuck in under Billy's left.

The Chronicle and *Record-Herald* said the 4th round was all Hart's. Marvin tried to finish Stift, hitting him often, repeatedly landing his left to Stift's face, and splitting open a deep cut under his left eye with a right. Hart did the most damage with his right, landing several uppercuts and swings to the

---

105 *Chicago Record-Herald, Chicago Chronicle,* August 18, 1902.

body which slowed Billy up noticeably. At the end of the round, both were swinging wildly.

Marvin still had a slight shade the better of it in the 5th round, and he maintained his lead. Stift was tiring and somewhat the worse for wear.

In the 6th round, Hart continued as the aggressor, but, perhaps encouraged by the fact that it was the last round and he had just a little further to go, Stift fought back hard in the clinches, finally growing more aggressive. Billy sent Marvin back with some good punches, putting up a game fight. Stift did well, and held his man almost even in the round.

Still, Hart had gained a sufficient lead to win Referee George Siler's official 6-round decision verdict. The ruling was well received. However, many were disappointed that Hart had not knocked him out.

Siler called it a slugging match "on the rough house, wild swing and miss order, and in which misses predominated. Hart was never accused of possessing any of the finer points of the game, and as Stift is not letter perfect in science, the contest was bound to be of the scrambling order."[106]

The Chicago Daily News said that although Hart won the decision in a comparatively easy manner, it was a rather poor fight. Stift's persistent holding probably had something to do with it. A cartoon depicted Hart missing a left with the caption, "Hart missed this blow 899 times." Hart had the advantage until Stift finally cut loose in the last round, keeping things even, at least in that round.[107]

The Chicago Chronicle also called the showing disappointing, despite the fact that Hart won the decision. "He got the decision, it is true, but a draw would have been satisfactory to the crowd." The fight featured hard hitting and plenty of clinching.[108]

The Chicago Record-Herald said both men were awkward, but Hart won. It had been 6 rounds of rough fighting. "While it was easily the southerner's fight, but Stift by holding in the clinches, fighting on the defensive most of the way and finishing with a spurt at the end gave his opponent a good argument." Describing Marvin, it said, "He is a big, strong fellow, who fights from an awkward crouching position, and, while he has a left that is always dangerous and last night got in many hard rights to Stift's body, depends largely on wild swings and 'haymakers,' and is awkwardly clever, if he can be called clever at all."[109]

The Daily Inter Ocean merely said that Hart got the decision by being the more aggressive all the way through, although the bout left the impression that Hart was overrated.[110]

---

106 *Chicago Tribune*, August 19, 1902.
107 *Chicago Daily News*, August 19, 1902.
108 *Chicago Chronicle*, August 19, 1902.
109 *Chicago Record-Herald*, August 19, 1902.
110 *Daily Inter Ocean*, August 19, 1902.

Hart's next fight was another rematch, this time against Kid Carter in a 6-round no-decision bout in Philadelphia, the only type of fight allowed there. The press surrounding their wonderful war in Louisville had made promoters eager to see the two in the ring again.

After being knocked out by Hart in the 9th round earlier in 1902, Carter had subsequently clearly "won" a 6-round no-decision bout with Kid McCoy in Philadelphia, so he was well respected there. Although points decisions were not allowed in Philadelphia, the newsmen rendered their own unofficial "newspaper" verdicts. Carter had actually knocked out McCoy with a right at the end of the 2nd round, but McCoy was saved by the bell. In the 3rd round, Carter dropped McCoy three times with rights, and the Kid was again saved by the bell. Carter again dropped him in the 4th round, but McCoy lasted the full 6 rounds and received from Carter the worst beating of his career.[111]

Carter followed the McCoy bout with a KO12 Al Weinig and KO2 Jimmy Handler. However, on September 15, in a bid for Tommy Ryan's 158-pound world middleweight crown, Carter suffered a 6th round knockout loss. Carter was back in the ring again a month later against Hart.

In the days leading up to the bout, Hart trained at the Quaker City Athletic Association. He said he was weighing about 170 pounds. "Hart is a tall, well-proportioned young fellow, with a very pleasant countenance, quiet and gentlemanly in his manners, and a man that is likely to win favor with the public."[112]

Marvin was training regularly every day. In the morning, he did a lot of roadwork through Fairmount Park. In the afternoon, he spent several hours in the Quaker City gymnasium at No. 1913 Market Street. On October 11, after punching the bag and playing several games of handball, Hart boxed 6 rounds with his brother and 4 rounds each with Tom Daly and Jimmy Simister, making a favorable impression in front of the big crowd there. In training, Hart sparred all the local boys who could be coaxed to box with him. Although he was a "very powerful fellow" with a "punch like the kick of a mule," Marvin was careful not to hurt his sparring partners.[113]

Carter had been exercising at Eagles' gymnasium on Broad and Spring Garden streets. However, he transferred to the Penn Athletic Club gymnasium, the fight's location. On the 13th, Carter punched the bag for 40 minutes, tossed the medicine ball for 25 minutes, skipped rope for 2,000 revolutions, and then worked with dumbbells and the wall machines. He ended the day's work by sparring 4 fast rounds with his sparring partner, black heavyweight Bob Armstrong.

That same day, Hart had practically the same routine as Carter. He did his morning run, and began his gym work at about 2 p.m. He boxed 3

---

111 *National Police Gazette*, June 14, 1902.
112 *Philadelphia Record*, October 12, 1902.
113 *Philadelphia Record*, October 13, 1902.

rounds with his regular sparring partner, black welterweight Jim Watts, and another 3 with Kid Husbands. Marvin enjoyed training and was looking sharp.[114]

Local sporting men were divided in their opinions as to the fight's likely outcome. Some banked on Hart's record and prior victory over Carter. Although it would be Hart's first appearance in the Eastern part of the country, "his reputation has preceded him." However, the locals who had seen Carter defeat Kid McCoy liked what they saw, and gave him the edge. "Carter and Hart are well matched as to size and weight, and there is little to choose between them as to skill. Neither man is a fancy boxer, but both are hard hitters and game boxers."[115]

The Hart-Carter rematch took place on October 16, 1902, at Philadelphia's Penn Art Athletic Club on Twentieth Street and Montgomery Avenue.

Charley Harvey, "the golden-voiced orator, announced the events in tones possessed of a little tenor, a little baritone and also a little bass." The boxers fought under straight Queensberry rules, protecting themselves in the clinches and on the breaks.

1 - Hart had the height and reach advantage, and assumed a low crouch in the manner of James Jeffries, his jaw covered by one shrugged-up shoulder, circling to the side, jabbing with his left. Carter was more erect. "Hart's style reminded one of a fellow about to lift a bale of blue grass on a Kentucky stock farm. Carter possessed the better style. The Louisville boy proved from the start that he was there with the wallop, and landed telling rights on Carter's ribs." Hart won the round by landing many a hard blow on Carter's body and head, although he also missed several wild swings, including a big uppercut. Marvin did the forcing, and Carter countered several times, but without effect. Overall, though, both were somewhat cautious, so no significant damage was done.

2 - Hart assumed the Jeffries crouch, but it did not prevent Carter from landing, and he opened up a cut under Marvin's left eye with a clean left. Except for this round, the cut did not bother Marvin much. Both landed frequently on the body. Carter focused on the body and landed hard rights when Hart came in. Carter landed a left and right on the stomach which almost lifted Hart off his feet. Hart landed a clean left on the jaw, and the Kid landed a good right on the ribs. With a right, Hart opened a gash over Carter's left eye. This caused the Kid to fight harder than ever, and he landed some terrific punches on Hart's stomach, as well as the occasional left jab to Marvin's bad eye. The Kid fought the round on even terms. Just before the bell, Hart staggered Carter with a right uppercut on the jaw.

---

114 *Philadelphia Record, Philadelphia Press,* October 14, 1902.
115 *Philadelphia Press, Philadelphia Record,* October 16, 1902.

3 - Two local sources said that during this round, Carter dropped Hart with a right hook to the jaw. Hart was strong when he rose though, and fought hard. A third source did not mention the knockdown, but said that Hart missed a terrific swing, the force of which sent him to his knees, and he stayed down for a count of six. They exchanged lefts and rights to the face and Carter landed a heavy right to the stomach. Hart landed a left swing on Carter's sore eye. Just before round closed, Hart shook up Carter with a stiff right on the side of the head. Carter had the best of the round.

4 - This round was full of mix-ups, mostly at close quarters, the referee having to separate them frequently. Carter landed some great rights over the heart. Toward the close of the round, Hart landed a heavy left to the jaw. When he went to his corner, Carter was bleeding from the eye and nose. However, Carter had the best of the round.

5 - At the start, Hart missed badly, but Carter was too slow to take advantage of the counter opportunities. Hart staggered Carter with a left hook and right to the jaw. The Kid was reeling, but he blocked and held at every opportunity to save himself and avoid being finished off. Hart tried hard to land another good one, but his blows were wild and fell short. Carter recovered rapidly and fought back gamely, but Hart again landed a good left on the neck and another in the face. Hart tried to put him out, but was too wild. In a clinch, Carter, who was not in very good shape, grabbed around Hart's legs and threw him to the floor. When Marvin got up, Carter rushed at him, landing a left to the face as the bell rang. Carter was very tired at the gong. This was clearly Hart's round.

6 - Hart jumped up confidently and landed a left to Carter's bad eye and a right on the jaw. Carter led often and got in a left on Hart's eye and left and right on the body, but his blows lacked steam, for he was somewhat weakened from the hard blow to the jaw that had hurt him in the previous round. He appeared tired, while Hart kept right at him and tried hard to score a knockout. They fought fast. In a clinch, Hart landed a right and left to the jaw which made the Kid unsteady. Marvin landed a left jab to the face and then a left and right to the same spot, as well as a right to the nose, which caused Carter to clinch to save himself. The gong sounded with the men in a fast mix-up. They shook hands warmly.[116]

No official decision was allowed, but the local newspapers each offered their opinions. *The Philadelphia Public Ledger* said the bout between Hart and Eddie "Kid" Carter was "one of the fastest bouts between men of their size that has ever been held in this city. It lasted the full limit, and, while Hart seemed the stronger of the two at the end, both had done hard work all through, and a draw would have been an equitable decision."

---

[116] *Philadelphia Press, Philadelphia Record, Philadelphia Public Ledger*, October 17, 1902.

The Philadelphia Inquirer called it the fastest, hardest, and most evenly contested contest ever seen in Philadelphia. They were both constantly active and attempting a knockout. All their punches were designed for pain and both bled early on.

> There was little to choose between the pair at the little work that was done at long range, but in in-work Hart had the better of the exchanging. He landed short arm punches in the breakaway that did Carter no good, and caused the latter to hug a little more closely than the mandates of the Marquis of Queensberry permit; but at that there was no flagrant violation of the rules.[117]

In the opinion of these two papers, the length of the bout was too short for one of these two fighters to assert clear dominance. They felt it was relatively even, although the overall impression was that if someone had to win, it probably would have been Hart.

Two other local papers felt that Hart had edged the fight. *The Philadelphia Press* said Marvin Hart had a shade on Kid Carter. However, it also said, "It was the impression of ringside spectators that Hart had a shade the better of Carter, but a draw would not injure either man's reputation." The two wasted little time with fancy work, but fought a fast, rattling bout, slugging at close quarters throughout. "Hart and Carter were never accused of being boxers. They are popular with the ring followers for their ability to slug and take a wallop without flinching, and they lived up to their reputations last night." The spectators were pleased. "The crowd turned out to see a fight, and they got what they went after."[118]

The Philadelphia Record said Hart had Carter weak at the finish of 6 hot rounds, and had slightly the best of the fight. The men were evenly matched, and both showed that they can give and take a great deal of punishment. They put up one of the best fights ever seen in the city, one worth going a long way to see. "Had there been a decision Hart should have had it. Not

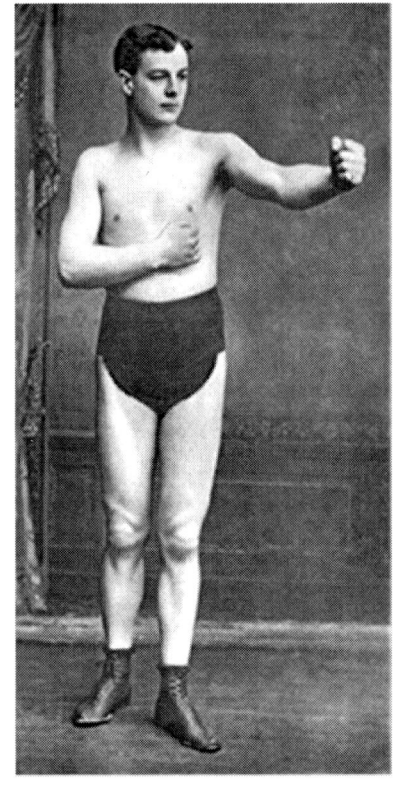

---

117 *Philadelphia Inquirer*, October 17, 1902.
118 *Philadelphia Press*, October 17, 1902.

only did he have the best of the milling, but the bout should have been awarded him on a foul in the fifth round when Carter deliberately grabbed Hart around the legs in a clinch, throwing the Louisville man to the floor." Hart landed several times to the jaw, but he did not land solidly enough to put him out, although the blows shook up the Kid considerably. Hart tried to follow up, but Carter was too elusive, and cleverly got out of tight places with good generalship. Although Carter mostly played for the body, and landed many hard blows there, the well-conditioned Hart took them well.

Of the fight, the *National Police Gazette*'s dispatch report said that such "cyclonic activity, hard punching and equal distribution of punishment has not been seen hereabouts for a long time. Had there been no absurd police regulation forbidding decisions the referee would have called it a draw." The bout was a "tornado of flying fists, with the dull chugging of bodies meeting in rush after rush, the smashing sound of blows sent home with savage intent, with two crimson furies, streaked and flecked and spotted with blood, charging and staggering back and charging again." Neither had more than a momentary advantage, and it was even throughout.

Another *Police Gazette* report that same day said that both were in fine form and went at it "hammer and tongs, demonstrating conclusively their entire ability to give and take any amount of punishment." It too said that the audience unanimously felt it was a draw. "The bout was a combination of science and brawn, with which both men were amply supplied."[119]

Just under one month later, on November 10, 1902, returning to Chicago for another 6-round bout, Hart took a big step up by taking on another top opponent in Jack Root, whose real name was Janos Ruthaly. Root was of Austrian or Czech heritage (or both), depending on the source, but lived in and fought out of the Chicago area. Hence, this would be the second local Chicago boxer that Hart took on in Chicago.

Root's recent results included: 1899 WDQ7 and W6 Billy Stift, and W6 (twice) Frank Craig; 1900 W6 Tommy West, D6 Tommy Ryan, and KO1 Dan Creedon; 1901 KO9 George Byers, WDQ15 Kid Carter, and KO2 Jimmy Ryan; and 1902 WDQ7 George Gardner,[120] KO2 Stift, LKOby17 Gardner[121] and W6 Kid Carter.[122] One paper said the second Gardner fight

---

119 *National Police Gazette*, November 8, 1902.
120 Gardner was the aggressor and Root the boxer in the hurricane battle. Yet, Root was better on the inside as Gardner fought on the outside in a wild and uncertain style. George was never himself after a right in the 2nd round closed his left eye. In the 7th round, in a clinch, Gardner threw a left that landed low and Root went down. Gardner was disqualified for his foul low blow. Some suspected that it was intentional. *National Police Gazette*, February 22, 1902.
121 Both showed speed and gameness under punishment. Root had a good jab, but Gardner focused almost exclusively on the body, weakening his man. Gardner was cut and bleeding, but in the 15th, he dropped Root with body shots. In the 16th round, Gardner dropped Root with a left hook to the jaw. In the 17th, Root was dropped twice by body shots until his corner stopped it. *National Police Gazette*, September 13, 1902.
122 Root was aggressive and Carter clinched. Root was superior in skill and generalship, and equal in power. *National Police Gazette*, November 22, 1902.

was Root's only loss in over 42 fights. The Root-Carter bout took place only 11 days after Carter had last fought Hart, and was just two weeks prior to Root's bout with Hart.[123]

The two had been trying to make a match for a couple years. They had twice almost hitched up, but weight differences, monetary divisions, rules debates and other matters had intervened to prevent the bout.

The two men were opposites in terms of their boxing styles. "Hart is of the Walcott and Carter school of boxing. It is fight with him from gong to gong, his forte being the robust and resolute, the fast and furious." Hart punched hard and often and did not care where he landed.

Root was smaller than Hart, and was expected to box carefully with jabs and stiff straight rights, being careful not to allow Hart's weight and power to tell. Root could box well against bigger men, but he could also punch. Jack Johnson, who had helped train Root for Gardner, "quit dozens of times in [Root's] training quarters before the Chicago champion." Still, Johnson was coming off an October 31 20-round decision victory over Gardner in George's first fight after defeating Root.[124]

Root's recent victory over Carter in Chicago dispelled any speculation that he might be on the decline after his lone defeat by Gardner. Hart said, "I know that Root is the shiftiest, cleverest man I have ever met and it will be a hard contest for me to win, but I intend to make the effort." Hart also said that Root was the best man that he had ever met, but expected to whip him nevertheless. Marvin was willing to bet on himself, feeling that his rugged strength and hitting power would overcome Root's fancy boxing

---

123 *Chicago Daily News*, August 19, 1902.
124 *Daily Inter Ocean*, November 9, 1902.

skills. "I have seen him in many of his bouts, and must frankly say that I think I can overcome his skill."

Marvin knew the bout was very important. He knew that losing a decision would set him back a good deal and interfere with his earning ability. "A victory over Root, on the other hand, will place Hart at the very top of the light heavy-weight division, and insure him a comfortable income for a long time to come." Marvin's brother Russell was looking after his business affairs.[125]

Both Root and Hart were known as two of the country's leading light heavyweights. Hart was said to probably weigh around 180 pounds, with Root about 5 pounds less.

> Hart is principally known for his rushing style of fighting. He depends entirely on a knockout punch to win, and knows much less of the finer points of the game than Root. ... Hart...has never fought as clever a man as Root and the latter is picked by nearly every Chicago follower of the game to win the verdict on points if the fight goes the limit. Hart's only chance to win is conceded to be by the knockout route. With Hart's style of fighting the bout promises to be full of action.[126]

Hart and Root boxed for the Lyceum Athletic Club in its Glickman Theater on Desplaines Street. The arena had a capacity of 3,000. Lyceum president Malachy Hogan refereed the bout. *The Chicago Chronicle* said Hart appeared to weigh about 185 pounds to Root's 170 pounds.

1 - Root kept a good pace, beginning by landing jabs to the head and rights to the body, while the wild Hart had difficulty landing. Root exhibited good defense, and landed a left under the jaw that staggered Hart a bit. Root's left had Hart's nose bloody. However, toward the end of the round, Hart staggered Root with a right uppercut. Another local source said Root had the better of the round, but few effective blows were landed. The round was decidedly tame compared with what followed.

2 - Hart started rushing, and from then on it was a case of hammer and tongs, give and take. Root moved a great deal, but still engaged in a number of exchanges. Many of Marvin's blows were blocked, but many landed too. A right to the body hurt Root, but Jack pressed Marvin to the ropes and landed a number of stomach blows.

They slugged, fighting fiercely until a Root right under the ear, on the jaw, dropped Hart for a nine-count. Upon rising, Marvin appeared groggy, but managed to survive by clinching and dodging several hard blows. Root chased him into a corner, where Marvin stumbled against the ropes and fell

---

125 *Chicago Tribune, Daily Inter Ocean*, November 10, 1902.
126 *Chicago Record-Herald*, November 10, 1902.

down. He was up again at once and clinched. Hart recovered and showed his strength, firing hard blows, but he was wild. Root jabbed away at him. At the bell, Marvin wobbled to his corner. Root clearly had the better of the round. The fierce fighting had begun, and continued to the end of the fight.

3 - At the start of the round, Root outfought Hart, going after him and landing a left to the chin. They exchanged blows until Hart landed a right uppercut to the jaw which momentarily stopped Root. Hart would not be denied. He landed a straight left, and then they exchanged hard body blows. They missed some hard swings.

In a hot mix-up, one local source said Root landed another right hook to the jaw that dropped Hart again. In the process, Root fell on top of him. Other local papers did not exactly call this a knockdown. One said Root landed a right hook and Hart slipped down. Another said that amidst the slugging, both fell against the ropes. When they rose, they went at it hammer and tongs.

Hart recovered quickly enough to land an uppercut. Hart hurt Root with his right to the jaw, for Jack sprinted away out of further danger. Root was bleeding from the nose and looked the worse for wear, although Hart was missing with most of his swings. When Marvin drew close, Root clinched and hung on until both fell to the floor. After rising, a Root miss caused him to run into a Hart punch that shook him. After some clinching, Root banged away and had Hart backing. One said Hart had a shade the better of the round, but Root looked to be in better condition. Another said the fighting was fierce, and both were groggy at the end of the round.

4 - The round opened with fierce exchanges. There were large discrepancies regarding whether or not Hart and/or Root went down from blows. *The Chicago Chronicle* said Root dropped Hart with a right to the head. There was clinching by both, and Hart hit the body. Root landed to the jaw and Hart appeared groggy. Root could hurt Hart but could not finish him. Marvin slipped down in a corner. *The Chicago Record-Herald* simply said that Root was thrown hard against the ropes, but a moment later Hart slipped down. It mentioned no knockdowns. *The Daily Inter Ocean* said that although Root was fresher at the start, Hart landed a wallop that knocked Root down. Root was up quickly and landed on Hart's jaw. Both were weakened from the blows, but Hart was groggier. Marvin missed a lead and fell down in Root's corner.

Root was getting the proper range more with his left, and he kept pumping away with it. A good straight left brought blood from Hart's nose. However, in a mix-up, Root's left cheek bone was cut, and it bled profusely. Hart kept coming despite Root's jabs almost flattening his nose. Hart showed some fatigue, but landed a left to the jaw. Root was landing more frequently, but the strain of battle had taken some of the force from his blows. Both were bleeding from the nose and the blood was smeared all over them. Toward the end of the round, both clinched continually, and swayed slowly around the ring. Still, Root had begun to take a points lead.

5 - The round was fierce. Continually using his left to the face, Root took a more decided points lead in this round. Hart's seconds coached him to play for the stomach, and he landed a terrible right there. However, Root seemed stronger, and in the pulling and hauling that was mingled with the slugging, Root was too strong for Hart. They mixed matters in the ring center. Root landed two rights to the jaw and followed with a right uppercut that made Marvin clinch.

A Root right opened Hart's left eye, causing it to bleed badly. Root planted a left to Hart's right eye that practically closed it, so that Hart fought he remainder of the fight under a disadvantage. Marvin held more during the last part of the round, for he was hurt. His left eye was almost closed, but he still managed to land an occasional hard blow. In a mix-up, Root pounded Hart into a neutral corner. He landed heavily on the body and reached Hart's eye.

Hart showed that even when hurt he had a punch that would win for him if he could land it. He retaliated with a right to the jaw and Root staggered and backed up. For a moment, Root appeared groggy, but Hart was not in a condition to follow up the advantage. Hart's left eye was in terrible shape.

6 - The round "was more like a saloon brawl." When Hart started the round, his left eye was entirely closed. Root went after him at once, and was stronger than Hart was. He used his left to better advantage. Marvin hung on. Hart still had a hard blow though, and once swung himself off his feet when he missed. He got up laughing. Only one local report saw this as a knockdown, claiming that a right hook to the solar plexus dropped Hart, though he quickly rose. Root peppered Hart with left jabs, but Marvin came back rushing and swinging. Jack slipped down to avoid a blow, with Hart falling on top of him. Root landed a right and left to the head, then repeated the dose. A right hook followed by a straight left sent Hart's head bobbing. Regardless, Hart kept plugging away to the end.

Root had the better of the fight, but was glad when it ended. Referee Malachy Hogan awarded Root the decision, which was well received.[127]

The Chicago Record-Herald said it was a hard, fierce battle filled with slugging. Both were covered in blood at the end. Hart's right eye was closed. Root also had a badly damaged eye. However, the Chicago man was more effective with jabs and his cleverness earned him the points victory. That said, from the 2nd round on, "the local man hardly knew when he was fighting cleverly."

---

[127] *Chicago Chronicle, Chicago Record-Herald, Daily Inter Ocean, Chicago Daily News*, November 11, 1902.

Hart's style of milling was insistent and confusing. It caused Root to forget his science and slug with the man from the South. At the slugging game Hart was right there, and several times landed with such force that Root was compelled to back up and recuperate before he accepted any more of the give and take game of his opponent. ...

Root won because his straight blows counted far more than Hart's swings, but it was not a battle that indicated Root's complete superiority over the young pugilist from Louisville. At all stages of the contest Hart had a chance, and at the end of the mill he took the decision good-naturedly and expressed the hope that he might have another try at the Chicago man.[128]

JACK ROOT.

The Chicago Daily News said it was a desperate, fast fight replete with slugging. Root used his left jab and had Hart almost out during the 4th and 5th rounds. Root was clever, but also willing to stand toe-to-toe and mix it up. Root dropped Hart twice, once in the 2nd round with a right to the jaw, and again in the 6th round with a right hook to the solar plexus.[129]

---

128 *Chicago Record-Herald*, November 11, 1902.
129 *Chicago Daily News*, November 11, 1902.

The Chicago Chronicle said that knockdowns were frequent and both were groggy at times. "It was simply a murderous fight of the street corner order." Root won, but "it took his very life to gain the verdict." It said that as a punishment absorber, Hart had no equal. He tried desperately, but a closing left eye hampered him. This was caused by the excellent Root left, which won the fight for him. The decision for Root was "the only fair one that could have been rendered."[130]

Chicago's *Daily Inter Ocean* said that from the very beginning, there was never an idle moment. It was a fast slugging affair all the way, the fiercest fighting seen in many a day. Although Root increased his points lead as the bout progressed, and he had Hart hanging on, Marvin "still had in him a punch that would have put any one away could he have landed it."[131]

The Chicago Tribune's report was not as definitively in Root's corner, but agreed that Root had won.

> While Root's advantage was not marked enough to convince all present that he would win over a longer route, he was clearly entitled to [the] verdict.... Root's margin was that of a straight left jab fighter, who also can hit hard, against one of the swinging type, as represented by Hart.

Root "frequently had Hart against the ropes while pumping in body blows." Although Root could have outpointed Hart with his left, he chose to fight Hart at his own game of "roughing it."

> The only knockdown occurred in the second round, when Hart went down in Root's corner from a left to the neck, taking the count of 'nine' and apparently feigning grogginess as he arose, for at the first opening he pounced in on Root with a series of swings.

This version differed from those that said there were several knockdowns, or that the 2nd round knockdown was from a right.

The Tribune said that as early as the 3rd round, both men were bleeding inside their mouths.

> Root had the better of three rounds, with Hart perhaps having a shade in the third, when he put a blow to Root's jaw which temporarily bewildered the west sider. The other two periods were fairly even.

By the 5th round, both were badly cut about their left eyes. Neither was in danger of a knockout at any time, though. "As to the fight itself, it was the fastest seen in Chicago between big men for many months."[132]

---

130 *Chicago Chronicle*, November 11, 1902.
131 *Daily Inter Ocean*, November 11, 1902.
132 *Chicago Tribune*, November 11, 1902.

Differing from the *Tribune*, the *Police Gazette* reported that Root had the better of it in every round, "notwithstanding that he received a severe drubbing. Hart was down for the limit in the second round, and was saved from a knockout by the gong."

However, another *Gazette* report quoted a Chicago newspaper as opining that the fight was really a draw. "Only one man in ten thousand could have detected any advantage for either man, but fortunately that one was there in the person of the referee, Malachi Hogan."[133]

Marvin Hart was built for longer bouts, and it was clear that he would not do as well in shorter contests against intelligent boxers with superior skill. At least two of the local Chicago newspapers noted that it was not entirely clear that Root would defeat Hart in a bout of longer duration.

Root's victory over Hart put him in a position to next fight for what was advertised as the newly created world light-heavyweight crown, which he would win in April 1903 with a 10-round decision over Kid McCoy. Root would remain a prominent fighter on the scene, and he and Hart would meet again two and a half years later.

Just to give one a sense of the time's racial climate, there was some discussion about the potential repercussions on the sport generated by black world lightweight champion Joe Gans' 15th round knockout victory over white challenger Charles Seiger in Baltimore, Maryland, which took place on November 14, 1902, four days after the Hart-Root bout.

> Believing that the exhibition of the negro pugilist, Joe Gans, mauling and drawing the blood of a white fighter or boxer, has an unwholesome effect upon the rough negro element, tending to make it more disorderly, the police authorities are considering the possibility of refusing to issue permits for contests between white and colored boxers. ... For several years Baltimore has been a haven for pugilists and their exhibitions, but for the above reasons the authorities may decide to put a stop to such contests altogether.[134]

Hence, there is support for the argument that the tradition of legal limitation and impediment upon the sport of boxing is in part based upon race. Keep that in mind the next time politicians try to attack and circumscribe boxing.

Undeterred by his 6-round decision loss to Jack Root, unbelievably, *a mere nine days later*, on November 19, 1902, returning once again to Philadelphia, Hart fought a 6-round no-decision bout with yet another top contender in "Philadelphia" Jack O'Brien (whose original name was Joe Hagen). O'Brien, like Root, would be a prominent fighter on the boxing scene for many years. For the third fight in a row, Hart was on the road fighting a local man in his own hometown.

---

133 *National Police Gazette*, December 6, 1902.
134 *Philadelphia Record*, November 19, 1902.

Jack O'Brien had experience against top middleweights, light heavyweights, and heavyweights. He had been a sparring partner for Kid McCoy before McCoy's August 30, 1900 loss to Jim Corbett. O'Brien's record included: 1898 D10 and W10 Kid Carter; 1900 LKOby13 Young Peter Jackson (O'Brien's only official loss), WND6 Jack Bonner, WND6 Tommy West, and WND6 Jimmy Handler; 1901 KO11 George Chrisp, KO6 Did Plumb, WDQ7 Frank Craig and WDQ12 Yank Kenny; 1902 WDQ5 Kenny, WND6 Joe Walcott,[135] WND6 Young Peter Jackson, WND6 Bonner, KO3 Yank Kenny, W6 Jack Beauscholte, W6 Billy Stift, W6 Joe Choynski,[136] WND6 Peter Maher, WND6 Jim Jeffords, and DND6 Maher ("draw" - O'Brien down briefly in the 2nd). The Maher bout was about three weeks before O'Brien's fight with Hart.[137]

Wins of any kind over Walcott, Choynski, and Maher, three top fighters, were significant. O'Brien had far more experience than Hart, with nearly 70 bouts under his belt, with 59 victories, only one official loss, and 9 draws. To fight such a man only nine days after a brutal and damaging battle with Root shows that Hart was either crazy or one of the most courageous men alive.

Hart had been sparring with big Jack/Jim McCormick, an experienced trial-horse heavyweight. McCormick would become Marvin's trainer/manager.

Hart "fully appreciates the fact that he is going up against a man who far outclasses him in point of cleverness and experience, but…has a serene confidence…. He does not think that O'Brien, with all his cleverness, can stall off his rushes, or evade all his punches." Marvin felt that O'Brien could not hit any harder than Kid Carter, and that all he needed to do was land one solid punch and he would do away with O'Brien.

---

135 There were conflicting views of O'Brien's performance against Walcott. One said it was O'Brien's fight from start to finish. O'Brien's footwork was marvelous and had Walcott bewildered and unable to land. Another account said O'Brien's performance was disgraceful as he seemed more interested in sprinting around and keeping away out of fear. *National Police Gazette*, May 3, 1902.
136 It was a clever battle and both O'Brien and Choynski proved themselves masters in the art of hitting and getting away. O'Brien though had the advantage of youth, and his speed, shiftiness, and better pace, darting in and out with punches, gained him the clear decision. *National Police Gazette*, October 25, 1902.
137 Boxrec.com; Cyberboxingzone.com; *Louisville Courier-Journal*, September 14, 1900.

The speedy O'Brien disagreed with Hart's analysis. After "having withstood Peter Maher's onslaughts, O'Brien cannot figure how Hart can drop him inside the limit."[138]

When Marvin arrived in Philadelphia, he had a pair of black eyes as a result of his recent bout with Root. In speaking of his darkened lamps, Hart humorously said, "You ought to see the other fellow."[139]

The contract weight was 170 pounds, to be made at ringside just before the bout. Hart was 4 pounds overweight and had to lose it at a Turkish bath. O'Brien weighed 166 pounds with his street clothes on. Before the bout, Marvin made 170 pounds, standing on the scale stark naked. They appeared to be about the same height.

The bout was held at the Philadelphia Penn Art Athletic Club, located on Twentieth Street and Montgomery Avenue. They agreed to break clean when told to do so, and mostly lived up to it, although Hart once tried to sneak in a hook when breaking away.

The first 3-4 rounds were rather tame, for both men devoted more attention to defense than to punching, using an unusual amount of feinting. Each assumed a crouching position, even lower than that used by champion James Jeffries. Both were also very active on their feet, so it was very difficult for either to get home with a telling blow. Also, some felt that the weight loss had an effect on Hart, for he did not show the same speed and vigor as in the Carter fight the previous month.

O'Brien won the early rounds. "O'Brien, who is the better boxer, as well as the more active of the two, clearly outpointed Hart in this cautious warfare, and as early as the second round he raised a mouse under Hart's damaged left eye, which at the beginning of the bout still bore the marks of Jack Root's handiwork." A stream of blood trickled down Marvin's face, and from that time on, O'Brien never missed an opportunity to hit the sore spot.

During the 3rd round, O'Brien's belt came off, and he tossed it to one side. Many blows failed to connect on both sides, most going over their heads.

O'Brien got to Hart's nose in the 4th round and made it bleed, in addition to the cut under the eye. Near the end of the round, Hart really went after O'Brien. A terrific right to the heart stopped O'Brien's rushes and took much of the fight out of him. Thereafter, he was not the same, although O'Brien still won the round by a shade. However, Jack went back to the corner looking fatigued, as the fast work began to tell on him.

The local papers agreed that O'Brien had the better of it through the first 4 rounds. O'Brien was the ideal boxer, a master mechanic of the ring. He landed easily, cut Hart's mouth, battered and bloodied Marvin's nose,

---

138 *Philadelphia Inquirer, Philadelphia Press*, November 19, 1902.
139 *Philadelphia Record*, November 15, 1902.

and nearly closed his eyes, striking him with jabs and right and left hooks to the face and body in every round. "The local man's punches had good effect, and bruised Hart's face considerably, but the latter stood the punishment, and waited for an opportunity to even matters with one good punch." Regardless of the punishment, Hart was always coming for more, and punching hard.

In the 5th round, O'Brien landed a hard right to the damaged eye that nearly closed it, and another punch a little later made the blood fly. This aroused Hart's ire, and he threw caution to the wind, attacking ferociously with right and left swings in rapid succession for the head and body. It required all of O'Brien's cleverness to stall off Hart's rushes.

There was a discrepancy in the reporting of the 5th round as to whether or not O'Brien dropped Hart or wrestled him down. *The Philadelphia Inquirer* said, "The Kentuckian rushed in without paying the slightest regard to Jack's jabs. In a clinch toward the end of the round Hart was wrestled to the floor. ... As soon as he regained his pins, however, he went after O'Brien, and handed two wallops on the latter's body."

However, both the *Philadelphia Record* and *Philadelphia Public Ledger* differed, saying that O'Brien dropped Hart. *The Record* said that as soon as O'Brien could steady himself he met the angry Hart with a stiff right on the jaw as he came in, knocking him down. Hart fell on his side, laying there for the count, rising at "9." They clinched and the bell sounded. The Philadelphian's friends shouted themselves hoarse during the minute's rest.

The Ledger agreed that O'Brien decked Hart, but also said that Marvin came back at the end of the round and buckled O'Brien.

> In the fifth round Hart was weak from coming in contact with the local man's stiff punches, and, finding an opening, O'Brien sent in a right hand hook, followed by a straight left, and Hart went to the floor, taking the count. He was perceptibly weak, but just before the gong rang for the end of the round he sent in a right hand punch to the jaw, and O'Brien's knees bent under him. He held on and did not go down.

The Record said Hart came up for the 6th round as good as ever and went right after O'Brien again with wicked right swings. O'Brien cleverly ducked under the vicious blows and twice countered with a right uppercut to the face. Hart suddenly tried his own uppercut that landed on O'Brien's chin, and Jack plunged forward and grabbed around Hart's body trying to prevent himself from going down, but then slipped down to the floor in a sitting position. He got up at 9, but was not quite right when he rose.

Hart sailed in to finish, but Jack grabbed to save himself. O'Brien also landed a hard uppercut and clinched again. Two or three clinches followed and then Jack landed a straight left. Hart smashed in his right to the face and both landed rights. When pushed too hard, O'Brien would hug, and once even had his arm around Hart's legs. They were hard at it when the bell sounded to end the contest without a formal decision. Both the contestants and Referee Crowhurst presented a gory spectacle.

According to the *Inquirer*'s version, in the 6th round, Hart anxiously rushed in and swung wildly.

> O'Brien could not withstand his boring tactics, and lost his guard just for an instant, when Hart copped him with a short right-hander on the jaw. O'Brien went down, and after struggling to his feet went to hugging. Hart again showed too much anxiety, and instead of steadying himself waiting for the chance to land one good punch, swung both right and left around O'Brien's body. These body punches evidently hurt O'Brien, who slipped twice, and on both occasions grabbed Hart about the legs. By this time the house was in an uproar, and for the first time in his career O'Brien was hissed by his home admirers. Hart himself was showing the effects of his hard work, and though he hit O'Brien often about the body and sent his head back with straight lefts on several occasions he could not get in the punch that would have secured for him the verdict.

The Ledgerr's version said O'Brien was still in bad shape to start the 6th round, and made a mistake by taking the fight to Hart. "They fought at a fast pace, and when O'Brien stepped in with a left for the body, Hart met him with another terrific blow, and O'Brien went down." A counter right uppercut had dropped him. O'Brien survived by holding and moving. Hart was too anxious and wild, and O'Brien narrowly escaped defeat.

Two local papers thought the bout was a draw, while two others thought O'Brien had won.

The Inquirer and *Ledger* agreed, "The honors of the bout were about evenly divided." It "would probably be an injustice to either to get anything worse than a draw, particularly when decisions are barred by the authorities." It was O'Brien early, but Hart late, when he began imposing his ferocious power-punching style.

The Philadelphia Press said that from the 4th round on, it was Hart's fight, and many wondered how O'Brien stayed the limit. Hart had decidedly the better of the last 2 rounds, and it was a lucky thing for O'Brien that the contest was only scheduled for 6 rounds. O'Brien appeared to be all in, and resorted to evasive tactics to save himself. The crowd roundly hissed him for his excessive clinching. Once in the 5th round, O'Brien even grabbed and pushed Hart down. "On points O'Brien would probably have received the decision, but it is a lucky thing for Jack that only six-round contests are permitted in Philadelphia." O'Brien was the better short-rounds points boxer, but in a long fight, with Hart's power and ability to absorb punishment, Marvin would have the edge.

The Record, while agreeing with the *Press* that O'Brien had the points edge, did not agree that Hart would necessarily win a bout of greater length, saying, "It is hard to judge what would have happened had the men continued to fight, but from what had already occurred it would seem that O'Brien should have continued to have the better of it."[140]

The National Police Gazette reported that for 5 rounds Hart tried in vain to reach O'Brien with one of his famous knockout wallops. However, in the final round, O'Brien became careless, and in rushing in with a straight left, Hart caught him with a corking uppercut to the chin. O'Brien used the remainder of the round to gather his wits, and was fortunate to escape a finishing blow. O'Brien excelled in short 6-round bouts, whereas Hart's style was designed for lengthy battles.[141]

In January 1903, while training, Hart fractured his right wrist. Initially, he did not realize it was fractured. However, it kept giving him troubles. An examination in February revealed the fracture, and his arm was put in a sling. As a result, Hart was out of the ring for a while.[142]

In late February 1903, Hart again expressed his willingness to fight any man in the world, "barring Jeffries and Fitzsimmons, for a side bet of $5,000."[143]

Marvin Hart's first 1903 bout was back home in Louisville on April 2 against Jack Bonner in a scheduled 20 rounder. Bonner was another very experienced fighter, with a career that contained over 70- bouts. His most significant results included: 1898 KO3 Australian Billy Smith, KO19 Dick O'Brien, KO2 Dan Creedon, L20 Tommy Ryan (world middleweight title), D20 George Byers; 1899 LDQby9 Tommy West, KO3 Dick Moore, D6 Frank Childs, W25 Yank Kenny, D20 Jack Finnegan, and KO2 Harry Peppers; 1900 L6 and D6 Frank Childs, LKOby16 Tommy West, LND6 Joe Walcott, LKOby13 Kid McCoy, LKOby21 Billy Hanrahan, LND6 Jack O'Brien, and LKOby5 Jack McCormick; 1901 W20 Hanrahan, D20 and L20 Kid Carter, and L15 Joe Walcott; and 1902 D20 Carter and LDN6 Jack O'Brien, as well as many more bouts against name

---

140 *Philadelphia Record, Philadelphia Inquirer, Philadelphia Press, Philadelphia Public Ledger*, November 20, 1902.
141 *National Police Gazette*, December 20, 1902.
142 *Detroit Free Press*, February 13, 1903.
143 *Police Gazette*, February 28, 1903.

fighters.[144] Hart called Bonner one of the sturdiest light heavies in the business. Bonner had over 40 victories to his credit.[145]

1 - According to the *Louisville Evening Post*, during the round, Bonner landed his shoulder into Marvin, and Hart called referee George Siler's attention to it. Bonner also led for the stomach but landed low, and Siler cautioned him. *The Police Gazette* said Hart was the aggressor from the start, and followed straight lefts to the face with rights to the body, keeping Bonner on the defensive. Bonner clinched at every opportunity and dug his shoulder into Hart's stomach.

2 - Both took crouching positions, and Bonner's head caught Hart in the groin. Bonner ducked a right and landed his shoulder a little low. According to the *Police Gazette*, Hart had the better of the round and the referee cautioned Bonner for using his shoulder tactics and a low blow.

The Evening Post said that during the round, Hart landed a left uppercut and left hook and Bonner went to his knees, with Marvin falling on top of him. Other local accounts of the knockdown said Hart landed a right to the jaw and then an uppercut, sending Bonner down. Hart landed the most significant blows of the fight during this round.

3 - The referee continued warning Bonner, who repeatedly landed his head into Hart's stomach. Hart kept jabbing, winning the round.

4 - This was also Hart's round, as Bonner clinched incessantly. Siler again warned Bonner after he put his head into Hart's stomach. "This stung Hart and he waded in furiously, and for a few seconds it looked like Bonner was sure to be put out. As they came to a clinch he again struck Hart in the groin with his head, and Referee Siler disqualified him, giving the decision to Hart." The local reports all agreed that after Bonner had once again struck his head into Hart's groin that Siler stopped the fight and awarded it to Hart via disqualification.

The Louisville Evening Post said that the majority agreed with the decision, but a quite vocal minority howled and cried robbery and demanded an explanation from referee Siler. Bonner protested wildly. The police had to protect the ring. Siler had disqualified Bonner for repeated shoulder and head butts to the stomach and groin. He had made bull-like charges with his head and it was quite low when it struck Hart.

The Louisville Times and *Louisville Courier-Journal* agreed that Referee Siler warned Bonner half a dozen times for butting with his head or shoulder. He kept shoving his head into Hart's stomach or groin every time they came to

---

144 Boxrec.com.
145 *Louisville Times*, April 2, 1903.

a clinch, in violation of the rules. Bonner claimed that he was ducking under Hart's rushes and that it was Hart's fault for jumping on his head.

Despite the descriptions of the bout in Hart's favor, these two local sources also said that the bout was fairly even, and it was unclear as to who would eventually win at the time it was stopped. Hart appeared fat and was wild, attempting to end matters early. Bonner was cool, crafty, and relaxed, taking his time. Both agreed that neither had landed many effective blows. Still, Hart had scored the only knockdown, and Bonner appeared more interested in playing defense.

The Police Gazette said that after the fight, Marvin was seen to have bruises on the abdomen below the belt. Siler had cautioned Bonner in each round for hitting low and using his shoulder in the clinches, leading to his 4th round disqualification.[146]

Earlier in the year, the *Police Gazette* said that there was talk of officially creating a new weight class for pugilists who had trouble making the middleweight limit, but who also had trouble fighting above 172 pounds. They were too big to fight as middleweights but felt too small to fight as heavyweights, giving up too much weight to men like Jeffries, Sharkey, Ruhlin, Denver Ed Martin, Bob Armstrong, Jack Munroe, and Peter Maher, all of whom weighed over 180 pounds. Boxers who supported the idea of a new light heavyweight class included Jack Root, Marvin Hart, Kid Carter, Joe Choynski, George Gardner, Kid McCoy, Billy Stift, and Philadelphia Jack O'Brien.[147]

On April 22, 1903, Jack Root won the newly created world light-heavyweight crown, easily defeating Kid McCoy via a 10-round decision (the distance allowed in Detroit), dropping the Kid several times throughout. Demonstrating how well-respected Hart's power was, in early 1903, Kid McCoy had offered to box any man, except for Marvin Hart. He instead fought Root, who held the 6-round decision over Hart. The press looked upon Root as the best man in the country for his weight, having good condition and skill, and terrific hitting powers.[148]

Next up for Hart, on May 3, 1903, was a rematch with Philadelphia Jack O'Brien, once again in O'Brien's hometown of Philadelphia. After Hart and O'Brien's late 1902 6-round no-decision "draw," amongst his important bouts, the active O'Brien scored a 1902 KO4 Jim Watts and 1903 KO12 Al Weinig, WND6 Joe Grim, KO4 Weinig, WND6 Joe Choynski, and D10 Joe Walcott. O'Brien and Hart fought another 6-round no-decision bout just a couple weeks after the O'Brien-Walcott bout.

---

146 *Louisville Evening Post, Louisville Courier-Journal, Louisville Times*, April 3, 1903; *Police Gazette*, April 25, 1903.
147 *National Police Gazette*, February 14, 1903.
148 *National Police Gazette*, January 31, 1903; *Philadelphia Record*, May 3, 1903.

The Philadelphia Record said that Hart had almost knocked out O'Brien in their previous contest, but this time, Marvin could not be so foolish as to wait until the 4th round to cut loose, as he did in their first contest. "O'Brien boxed so fast that he seemed to bewilder Hart for a time, and it was not until Marvin dropped all effort to box cleverly that he was able to do O'Brien any damage. Clever as O'Brien is, as an aggressive fighter he is not at all skillful in defensive work, easily losing his head." Marvin said he would do his best to knock O'Brien's head off his shoulders.

Jack Johnson was in town, looking to fight Joe Butler. Johnson advised Hart that he could whip O'Brien easily if he would fight him "with stiff arms."

The conditions were the same as when they met the previous November, which was that both men would have to weigh 170 pounds or less at ringside, just before the fight began. However, as the bout approached, Hart was overweight. The day before the fight, he thought that a night in the Turkish bath and a little road work in the morning would put him at the agreed-upon weight.[149]

The men weighed in at 9 p.m. the night of the fight, at the Penn Art Club, the fight venue. However, Hart was 12 ½ pounds over the agreed-upon weight limit of 170 pounds at ringside, tipping the scales at 182 ½ pounds. He was a heavyweight. Clearly, Marvin was growing and finding it increasingly difficult to maintain a lower weight. O'Brien easily made weight and then some, weighing 158 ½ pounds. At first, O'Brien said there would be no fight, and claimed Hart's $250 forfeit.

However, O'Brien then made the offer to Hart that they proceed to fight, but with Hart contracting to stop Jack in 6 rounds or forfeit his end of the receipts. That is, if O'Brien was not knocked out at the end of 6 rounds, Jack would be entitled to Hart's end of the receipts. Hart balked at first, but finally reluctantly agreed, realizing that he was not in the best negotiating position, given his failure to make weight. He would have to knock out O'Brien in order to earn any money. Hart would have a 24-pound weight advantage, but O'Brien had the advantage of fast hands and feet, and the fact that it was a short rounds fight.

---

149 *Philadelphia Record*, May 3, 5, 1903.

1 - O'Brien forced the contest early on and landed frequently with lefts and rights on Hart's body and face without a return.

2 - O'Brien continued his aggressiveness, catching Hart with right and left uppercuts, which bloodied his nose. O'Brien kept it bleeding. Toward the end of the round Hart became vicious and started forcing, landing one left to the stomach, but Jack cleverly evaded most of his blows by side-stepping.

3 - Marvin began the round clinching, trying to use his superior weight and strength. After they exchanged uppercuts, the fighting became fast and furious. O'Brien staggered Hart with a left to the chin. However, Hart landed a right to the solar plexus which almost doubled up O'Brien. Jack used his cleverness to escape further punishment. Hart's nose was bleeding. He took chances in attempting a knockout blow, while O'Brien was more careful.

4 - Jack was more wary of Hart's power and avoided rushes with side-stepping and running around the ring, which disgusted some of the spectators. Hart was still the stronger man, but O'Brien was quicker and busier. O'Brien landed several blows to Hart's one, both on the inside and outside. Still, Marvin landed a hard punch on the nose and then "forced Jack to the floor." After rising, Jack landed six blows to Marvin's one.

Overall, O'Brien had the best of the first 4 rounds, giving a wonderful exhibition of boxing, pressing the action, having the best of the exchanges. Hart's left eye was almost closed, there was a big gash under his right eye, and his nose bled profusely. However, the tide changed.

5 - According to the *Philadelphia Inquirer*, Hart's "wind jabs in the fifth changed the complexion of things." He dropped and nearly stopped O'Brien with a "terrific right and left to his stomach."

The Philadelphia Press said of the round that O'Brien jabbed easily until Hart drew him into some infighting and landed his hard left to the body. Jack was jarred but came back with an uppercut to the nose that started the blood flowing again. Hart missed a left but in a flash twice landed his right to the heart. "Jack was nearly all in as a result and hung on to Hart's hips." The referee forced them apart and Hart landed a left to the body that dropped O'Brien. Jack rose and then feinted a punch, but took two more lefts to the body before clinching. Jack staggered back to his corner.

The Philadelphia Public Ledger said Hart dropped O'Brien twice in the round, first with a right to the body, and then with a punch on the jaw. Jack was in great distress and clinched at every possible opportunity. O'Brien staggered to his corner and his seconds had to assist him to his chair.

The Philadelphia Record said the bell saved O'Brien, after a punch on the jaw had him on Queer Street. "He just managed to reach his corner, and would have fallen headlong had not his seconds caught him."

6 - *The Inquirer* said Jack began the round in poor shape, and Hart rushed in like a mad bull. Another smash "in the slats" dropped O'Brien again. *The National Police Gazette* reported that Hart dropped O'Brien with a left uppercut. *The Inquirer* said, "From that time until the final bell it was nothing but a mess of wild exchanges." After the bell, Jack fell into his corner with a thud.

The Public Ledger disagreed, saying that Jack had recovered to start the round, and despite Hart's efforts to land a knockout blow, O'Brien surprisingly gave as good as he received. This article did not mention any knockdown in this round.

The Philadelphia Press said Jack had recovered, but went down once to avoid punishment. He rose and landed both hands to Hart's jaw. "It was really anybody's fight at the finish."

The Philadelphia Record said Jack was in bad shape during the 6th round, and had to resort to hugging to survive, and once went to his knees without receiving a blow in order to get out of harm's way. Still, Jack rallied and rushed Hart to the ropes and smashed him on the cheek with a right, cutting a gash, from which the blood flowed in a stream. Despite this, O'Brien was in bad shape at the end of the round, while Hart was still strong.

Hart had contracted to knock him out, but failed to do so. Because O'Brien lasted the distance, Jack came away with all of the money, and Hart with nothing. There was something less than $2,000 in the house.

Once again, it was not clear who would win a fight of a longer distance. Although O'Brien was the cleverer boxer, Hart had a dangerous punch which could win the fight for him at any time, especially if he had enough rounds to wear O'Brien down. This bout was similar to their first fight. It was essentially a draw.

The Philadelphia Press called it a draw. *The Philadelphia Record* said O'Brien outpointed Hart, but took the worst beating of his career in order to do it. O'Brien had all the best of it through the first 4 rounds. He fought Hart with rare skill, fairly smothering him with fast work. Jack was in and out, jabbing and cutting him with short right hooks, and displaying great superiority. Hart fought with all his strength and skill, but Jack was inside his guard, continually hitting him. O'Brien slipped down a few times during these early rounds, but they were only slips, and he was up like a flash. Hart tried to get to him, even adopting the "stiff arm" tactics Jack Johnson suggested, but it was all to no avail, until the last two rounds.

In the 5th round, Hart caught O'Brien on the jaw, which brought him to his knees, with his arms around Hart's legs. Hart tried to finish him, swinging left and right, chasing Jack continually, landing a few blows that seemed like finishers, but Jack survived and came back for more. Still, O'Brien was down often in the last 2 rounds, taking the count twice. "Some of his falls were very peculiar and were the results of tripping in stopping Hart's terrific blows, which were of the kind that end fights with a single punch." Jack showed more evasive tactics than ever before, and he needed to do so. Despite being hurt, O'Brien emerged from the contest without a mark.[150]

The Louisville papers' perspective was that Hart had the better of the fight. *The Louisville Evening Post* expressly reported that Hart had defeated O'Brien, but lost the purse owing to the fact that he had agreed to knock out the shifty Philadelphian in six rounds. Still, he came within an ace of pulling it off.

The next day, the Louisville press reported that the Philadelphia reporters admitted that Hart whipped O'Brien, but gave O'Brien the credit anyway for putting up the best battle possible given the weight disparity. "O'Brien outpointed Hart. Hart almost knocked out O'Brien. This states in a nutshell the outcome of the battle." Jack had the best of it for 4 rounds, but in the last two, he was only able to avoid being knocked out by wonderful gameness and judgment.[151]

The following year, when discussing the bout, Hart said,

> I found that O'Brien didn't have the punch I expected him to have. He is there with a peculiar left. It doesn't stab or sting you. He kind of smears it down like a brush. It tears the face instead of cutting it. I had O'Brien down hanging to my knees for about five seconds when I shook him off and asked the referee to count. It went nearly to ten when Jack got up. The bell came then.[152]

---

150 *Philadelphia Public Ledger, Philadelphia Press, Philadelphia Inquirer, Philadelphia Record*, all May 6, 1903; *Police Gazette*, May 23, 1903.
151 *Louisville Times, Louisville Courier-Journal, Louisville Evening Post*, May 6, 7, 1903.
152 *Chicago Daily News*, January 25, 1904.

CHAPTER 5

Derailed By a Hand

Amazingly, *only eight days after* the Jack O'Brien rematch, on May 13, 1903 in Louisville, Marvin Hart took on the very experienced and well respected George Gardner (sometimes spelled Gardiner). The middleweight-sized Gardner had an 1899 6-round draw with Billy Hanrahan, and according to the *Police Gazette*, had once knocked out Hanrahan, though a primary source account of his record does not reveal this.[153] Gardner had suffered an 1899 LKOby18 to Jimmy Handler,[154] but scored a 1900 KO3 win over Handler to avenge the loss. Gardner sandwiched a 1900 14th round disqualification win over George Byers between two 15-round draws with him fought in 1899 and 1900.

Gardner defeated the well respected Kid Carter four times, including 1900 WDQ19, 1901 KO18[155] and KO8, and 1902 W6.[156]

In 1900, Gardner won the middleweight championship of England with a WDQ4 over Frank Craig, who clinched throughout and threw Gardner down.[157] Gardner lost a 1901 20-round decision to Joe Walcott,[158] but avenged the loss with a 1902 20-round decision victory over Walcott.

---

153 *Boston Herald*, January 4, 1904.
154 *National Police Gazette*, November 4, 1899.
155 "Gardiner showed that he is a cleverer, a cleaner, harder puncher, and by far the better ring general." Gardiner dropped Carter 8 times over 18 rounds. Both weighed less than 165 pounds. *National Police Gazette*, September 21, 1901.
156 The Carter fight was rough and fierce, but Gardner had the advantage in each round. Gardner cut him up, staggered him with uppercuts, and almost had him out in the final round. *Anaconda Standard*, December 30, 1902.
157 *National Police Gazette*, October 6, 1900.
158 Gardner weighed 158 pounds to Walcott's 146. One report said it was a close fight all the way and many felt it should have been a draw. *Los Angeles Express*, September 28, 1901. Another report gave the

Gardner had a 1902 LDQby7 to Jack Root but avenged the loss that year with a KO17 over Root. However, Gardner then suffered a 20-round decision loss to the larger heavyweight, Jack Johnson.

Gardner also had a 1902 W6 Billy Stift, 1903 4-round no-contest with black heavyweight Bob Armstrong, KO7 Al Weinig, and, one month before taking on Hart, Gardner knocked out Peter Maher in the 1st round. Gardner had over 40 bouts under his belt.[159]

The press felt that the Hart-Gardner bout was an even match-up. Gardner was unofficially being called the light-heavyweight champion of the world, owing to the fact that he held a knockout victory over Jack Root, who had just recently won the newly created crown. Gardner's victories over Root, Carter, and Walcott were his signatures. A native of Ireland, but living in Lowell, Massachusetts, the 24-year-old was described as "cool, crafty, a two-handed fighter, carrying a wicked punch in either fist, clever enough to engage in long range boxing with the best of them, and rugged, strong and willing to mix it up at any stage of the game." Another report said,

> Anyone who has never seen Gardner box has no idea what a wonderfully clever boxer he really is. He is without doubt the best man of his weight in the world when it comes down to science and strength combined….
>
> Gardner is a magnificent two handed fighter, moves free and easy without displaying any great effort. His coolness in delivering a blow and his alertness in blocking a return compares favorably with the wonderful work of Young Griffo when he was in his prime.

Again, Marvin Hart had to be nuts or have serious confidence and guts to take on such a fighter a week after he just went 6 hard rounds with O'Brien.

A number of days before the bout, Gardner was weighing around 165 pounds. He had been sparring with Mike Schreck, another top fighter. Despite his ability, some felt that Gardner would not be able to fight his usual style against Hart. Jack Root's manager said,

> Gardner can do no good standing away and pecking at a man. His game is to wade in and force the fighting from the tap of the bell. This is exactly to Hart's liking, and in my opinion, any man who mixes it up with Hart at close range is undertaking a dangerous proceeding.

Hart was described as "big, husky and an in-fighter for fair. Never a fancy performer, in the early stages he can take a grueling punishment and still be strong enough to polish off his opponent in jig time once the

---

impression that Walcott was the aggressor, dropped Gardner once early, and finished more strongly. *National Police Gazette*, October 19, 1901.
159 Boxrec.com; Cyberboxingzone.com.

fighting becomes fast and furious." Hart's only two losses were explained away. The press felt that based on Hanrahan's subsequent performances, he had been lucky against Hart. Root had only won a 6 rounder, a distance for which Hart's style was not built. His recent bout with O'Brien was said to have "boomed his stock considerably, and goes to show that the local man can not only hit, but that he is fast upon his feet also."

Hart was initially said to be weighing in the neighborhood of 180 pounds. Later, Hart said that he expected to enter the ring weighing about 175 pounds. "His daily bouts with 'Big Jack' McCormick are rough-and-ready sort of affairs." Hart and Gardner were scheduled to box 20 rounds under straight Queensberry rules.[160]

On May 10, Hart sparred Jack McCormick at his training quarters at St. Matthews. Marvin landed some stinging body blows that made McCormick grin and declare that the "boy has the stuff in him that will put Gardner to

---

160 *Louisville Courier-Journal*, May 10, 1903, May 11, 1903, May 12, 1903, May 13, 1903; *Louisville Times*, May 12, 1903.

the bad." Hart weighed 175 pounds. Marvin was happy with the way his face wounds had healed.[161]

The Louisville Evening Post said the battle would likely prove to be the hardest of Hart's career. Gardner would be the slight odds favorite, although there was not much to choose between them on form. Gardner was the cleverer fighter, a hard hitter and a severe punisher. Therefore,

> If the fight goes the limit [Gardner] will undoubtedly be the victor, but if he fails to cover his vital points thoroughly he may fall in the way of one of Hart's sledgehammer blows and then there will be nothing to do but count him out. Hart is a terrific hitter. He is one of the very few fighters who can hit with either hand from any position, but he is not a clever fighter, and he will find it a hard matter to land on Gardner. Hart, because of his strength, staying qualities and wonderful hitting proclivities is a fighter who always has a good chance, no matter whom he meets. He will have ten or fifteen pounds the better of the weight, but he is meeting a well-trained, corking good fighter, who may be able to shoulder this handicap.[162]

In short, Marvin Hart was a fighter ideal for the fight to the finish, but also one whom the cleverest men could outpoint in limited-round contests.

The day of the fight, on May 13, some were questioning the prudence of taking on a high class fighter like Gardner only a week after Marvin's grueling bout with O'Brien, where he "received a terrific punching. ... A good deal of his vitality and strength has been taken away from him, to say nothing of the cuts and bruises." This was a big fight for Hart. A local writer opined that if "he bests Gardner tonight, under the conditions, sporting men generally will agree that the only man which stands between him and the championship of the world is that California 'bear catcher' – James J. Jeffries." Hart was obviously game and willing, taking on two top fighters only a week apart.[163]

The bout was held at the Louisville Auditorium under the auspices of the Southern Athletic Club. Tim Hurst refereed. The day before the bout, Hart was weighing 178 pounds. On fight night, Hart claimed to weigh 176 pounds, while Gardner said he was 164 pounds. *The Police Gazette* said Hart weighed 178 pounds to Gardner's 168. They fought for a $4,000 purse.

1 - Hart began on the aggressive, never giving Gardner a chance to do his own work.

2 - Gardner hit Hart with a vicious uppercut.

---

161 *Louisville Evening Post*, May 11, 1903.
162 *Louisville Evening Post*, May 12, 13, 1903.
163 *Louisville Courier-Journal*, May 13, 1903.

3 - Gardner was in distress during the round. A series of hard swings, along with a few hard punches in the side, weakened George. Hart landed a right to the back of the ear which staggered Gardner. George was clearly groggy, but was saved by the bell.

4 - Gardner bloodied Hart's nose. George landed a stiff left to the mouth and right to the jaw that made Hart appear groggy, and he was forced through the ropes. He hung on and recovered. Both appeared tired.

5 - A Gardner left hook staggered Hart. However, Marvin hooked hard with his right to the side of Gardner's head and then staggered him with a right to the ear. George held on, for he was once again in trouble. Marvin rushed in with punches. Hart's rushing tactics again told on Gardner, and nothing but his skill saved him from defeat. Both men seemed a bit groggy at the bell.

6 - Gardner avoided punishment by a series of clever clinches. Hart kept after him and made George break ground, but Gardner kept jabbing his nose, from which a stream of blood was flowing. Gardner rights and lefts drew blood. Hart kept swinging. Marvin did jab occasionally, but it was a weak punch and Gardner made no effort to avoid it, concerned with Hart's other blows. Gardner was always careful to step inside of Hart's right and allow it to land on his back or the back of his neck. In the meantime, Gardner would hit Marvin's stomach with both hands. Hart clinched and turned his side to these punches. Still, like a piece of iron, Hart took all the grueling punishment that Gardner could offer, never wincing, showing his remarkable strength. It was a great fight up to that point and "honors were practically even."

7 - There was some wrestling and pushing, and Hart staggered George with a straight left on the neck.

8 - A left to the jaw again wobbled Gardner. Gardner hung onto Hart to prevent being knocked out. However, from that point on, Gardner did well with his jab and footwork, although his arm strength was no longer there. Still, he avoided Marvin's swings. They mixed it up at close range, with both landing well. A hard straight left nearly knocked George down. Marvin followed with a shower of blows, including a stiff uppercut. One of Gardner's seconds threw water on his man. Gardner was weak toward the close of the round and Hart was all over him.

9 - There was a lot of close range work. George came back and won the round.

10 - They mixed it up, exchanging blows. When Gardner missed, he threw himself almost through the ropes.

11 - Hart rushed, swinging hard rights and lefts. He seemed to have the better of matters. Apparently, though, Hart claimed that he broke his hand in this round.

12 - Hart rushed Gardner about the ring. Both landed and wrestled. When the bell rang, Marvin went to his corner and told his seconds that his right hand was gone. His second informed the referee that his man could not continue, and the bout was given to Gardner on a retirement.

The injury was legitimate. "Hart's hand after the contest showed evidence of having been broken." After Hart removed his hand bandaging, two doctors examined the hand and determined that three small bones in his right hand were fractured. One of Marvin's backers said it was an old injury going back on him.

Hart said that that he had fought too much and would rest his hand until it had completely healed. He first injured his hand over a year ago, while training last February, and he again re-injured it in his bout the previous week with O'Brien. When he entered the ring, the hand was painted with iodine.

Marvin said that he injured the right hand in the 11th round when he swung and hit Gardner on top of the head. "You can see this big lump here and it was utterly impossible for me to do any good with my right hand after the eleventh round." Hart told another reporter that he was depending on the right for a knockout, and without it, he knew he had no chance of winning. "I don't know just when or how I did it, but the pain was awful when I came into my corner at the end of the eleventh round." He tried to fight the 12th, but after the round concluded, he realized that it was no use. Hart thought that he would have eventually won by knockout if his hand had not been injured. "I had Gardner weak and he was not hurting me much with his punches only when he landed on my sore nose."

Naturally, Gardner said that he was about to knock out Hart, but that Hart, "instead of taking his medicine quit." Gardner looked tired, but did not have a mark on him. He claimed that he would have won with a knockout, and was confident throughout, even though at times he might have seemed tired. "Hart is a big, strong, tough fellow who has an awful wallop, but I think I can beat him if ever we meet again."

The Louisville Courier-Journal said it was a fast, stubbornly contested bout all the way, but that Gardner had the best of it on points. Gardner "withstood the panther-like rushes of Hart, the ferocious lunges and the terrific swings of the local man." Gardner jabbed, stung and cut Hart. However, with bulldog determination, Marvin kept after his cleverer opponent and took all he had to give. Hart was the aggressor, springing at Gardner and raining blow after blow on his face and body. He ignored Gardner's punches and waded in.

During his career, Gardner's style was usually aggressive, but in this one he showed respect for Marvin's punching power, and was more patient. In several rounds it appeared that Gardner was hurt, but he used his craftiness and recovered well. George landed counter hooks that staggered Hart. Most of the time, Gardner was busy keeping Hart away from him. "In this respect he showed as much cleverness as Fitzsimmons, Corbett...or any of the other scientific boxers that the writer has ever seen." George was able to block punches with elbows, shoulders, wrists or the back of his neck, and returned short right and left hooks that made Hart's lips swell, his cheeks puff out, and his eyes discolor. The press agreed that Gardner would have a chance with any man in the world, except for Jeffries.

The Louisville Times complimented Gardner's science. "All the vicious swings which Hart has used to defeat his opponents were side-stepped by Gardner, and when it looked as if Hart would win Gardner would come in with a straight jab which would land almost every time, then swing his left and come to a clinch." Hart took punishment gamely. Gardner emerged unscathed.

The Louisville Evening Post said Gardner had the decided advantage during the last two rounds. It was Gardner's cleverness and ring generalship which won him the fight. He was one of the greatest defensive fighters in the world, marvelously avoiding the terrible swings and hooks Hart sent at him. His keen eye and judgment of distance kept him from being knocked out. It was apparent from the outset that Hart's one chance at victory was by knockout. For the first 8 rounds, he brought the fight to Gardner, willing to take the jabs just for a chance to land a right swing. The pace was terrific, without any breathing spells. Gardner was very careful, and did not force the fight, satisfied to use his cleverness and jabbing when Hart rushed. Although hurt on occasion, he managed to get himself out of trouble and recover.

It also opined that Marvin was not in as good a shape as he had been in against Kid Carter, and the blood Hart was losing from his nose had a weakening effect. Had he not broken his hand, and been in perfect condition, he might have eventually worn Gardner down; for once George lost his nimble footwork it would have been over for him. However, under the circumstances, as things stood, had Hart continued with his broken hand, he probably would have lost a decision to the man with superb generalship. It is one thing to ask a man to fight for several rounds with a broken hand in a short fight, but quite another to ask him to fight the full distance in a 20-round bout with the handicap of his most powerful wing being crippled, when up against a top fighter.[164]

The non-local *Philadelphia Public Ledger* reported,

---

164 *Louisville Evening Post, Louisville Courier-Journal, Louisville Times*, May 14, 1903; *Police Gazette*, May 30, 1903.

Hart was strong and vigorous, but Gardner was much faster. ... It was still anybody's fight in the twelfth, in spite of the fact that Gardner was the cleverer. He hit Hart as often as he desired, but his blows lacked steam. Hart surprised the crowd by claiming a broken right hand and his seconds threw up the sponge.[165]

Hart's hand injury was quite serious. Three pieces of broken bone were surgically removed. "It will be a year before the Louisville man will be able to do any boxing at all." Some felt the hand would never be the same again. This could be a big handicap for a fighter who used his fists to administer powerful knockout blows. Marvin wound up being out of the ring for six months.[166]

Although George Gardner was claiming the light-heavyweight championship crown, most believed that Jack Root first won that title with an April 1903 10-round decision over Kid McCoy.[167] Of course, Gardner had already knocked out Root in August 1902, so he may have had the superior claim. No matter, because Gardner went on to win or solidify his claim to the world light-heavyweight title with a July 4, 1903 KO12 over Root.[168] Jim Corbett held Gardner "in great esteem and he thinks the Lowell man is one of the cleverest fighters in the business at his weight."[169]

Gardner had stopped Root twice, via KO17 and KO12. He was the only man to have beaten Root. Footage exists of one of their bouts, although it is not entirely clear which one it is. The footage reveals that Gardner was taller, with longer arms. Gardner threw sharp, quick punches, and utilized his height and reach well, both when moving back and when attacking. Root was a tough fighter also, throwing hard combination punches, looking his best when advancing, putting up a competitive fight. However, eventually, Gardner came over with two consecutive rights that dropped Root. Gardner dropped him again with a right off a double jab. George again attacked with a series of quick rights and lefts to drop him a third time. Root just missed beating the count.[170]

Twice Hart had twice been deprived of potential opportunities at the light-heavyweight title as the result of losses. Root went on to defeat McCoy for the vacant title after he defeated Hart in a 6-round decision, and

---

165 *Philadelphia Public Ledger*, May 14, 1903.
166 *Police Gazette*, June 13, 1903.
167 Root easily handled McCoy, dropping him in almost every round. *Police Gazette*, May 9, 1903.
168 Gardner decisively defeated Root in 12 fierce rounds. Gardner hit harder, was more aggressive and had speed. Gardner's body attack was impressive. When Root attempted a left in the 12th, Gardner's right went inside it and dropped him. He rose but was too weak to proceed and the referee stopped it. *Police Gazette*, July 18, 1903.
169 *Police Gazette*, July 25, August 8, 1903. The Root-Gardner fight was successfully filmed by polyscope.
170 Contrasting the footage, the *Police Gazette* said only one knockdown took place in their second bout. It is possible that the footage was actually of their previous bout, when the *Gazette* said three knockdowns took place in the 12th, although if true, it erroneously reported that body shots led to the knockdowns and that Root's corner stopped the bout.

Gardner went on to defeat Root for the world title after George had defeated Hart, owing to the hand injury.

After Gardner won the championship, Bob Fitzsimmons scheduled a world light-heavyweight title challenge against champion Gardner. Hence, the hand injury loss to Gardner may well have also cost Hart a payday against Fitzsimmons.

When Fitzsimmons tipped the scales at 203 pounds in late July, Gardner insisted that Bob make 168 pounds for their fight, and Bob agreed.

Fitzsimmons sparred with heavyweight champion James Jeffries, helping prepare Jeff for his upcoming title defense against Jim Corbett. On August 14, 1903, James J. Jeffries scored a KO10 over Jim Corbett to defend his world heavyweight title.

On September 30, 1903 at Philadelphia's Washington Club in a scheduled 6-round tune-up bout, Bob Fitzsimmons took on "giant" Irish heavyweight Con Coughlin.[171] As was often the case in a Fitzsimmons fight, the bout did not last very long. For 30 seconds, Fitz feinted, trying to draw a lead, but Con was wary. Fitz feinted him back into a corner and in a sharp exchange that followed; Fitz dropped him with a vicious left flush to the jaw. Con barely beat the count.

A right to the body dropped Coughlin the second time, but he got up quickly at three. Fitz again backed him to the ropes, and after landing another pair of left-handed wallops, Con looked like he had enough. Bob held his hands high above his head to call attention to the fact that he thought it should be stopped, but Con would not quit. Fitz landed a left to the body and Con went down again. Bob had him at his mercy, and since it was apparent to all that another blow would put Con into dreamland, his manager humanely gave up the contest on behalf of his man, throwing up the sponge. It was over at 2 minutes into the 1st round.[172]

In another 6-round tune-up bout, on October 14, 1903 at Philadelphia's Southern Athletic Club before a crowd of 5,000, Fitz met Italian Joe Grim. Grim was a trial horse known for his durability. Although he usually lost, he almost always lasted the distance.[173]

Fitz made a good showing, and although Grim was badly punished and floored at least nine times, he lasted the 6 rounds. Bob dropped him in the 2nd round with a left to the wind. In the 3rd, Bob dropped him with a right to the chin. He arose bleeding from the nose. In the 4th, Bob rained blows upon him and had Grim groggy. A solid punch to the face dropped him. Twice more he was sent down, but Bob could not finish him. In the 5th, Bob knocked Grim down twice in succession, and again at the bell Grim

---

171 *San Francisco Evening Post*, July 25, 1903. Heralded as the Irish champion, Coughlin had fought an amateur heavyweight tournament in Philadelphia. He won a decision over Jack McCormick on a foul, but lost in the finals. Joe Butler subsequently knocked him out, quite some time ago.
172 *Philadelphia Inquirer*, *Philadelphia Public Ledger*, October 1, 1903; *Police Gazette*, October 17, 1903.
173 Grim's record included newspaper decision losses to Jack O'Brien, Bob Thompson, George Cole, Kid Carter, and Joe Walcott, and a DQ3 loss to Peter Maher.

was floored with a right under the heart. The final round was exciting, with Grim landing a hard right that almost dropped Bob. A second later though Fitz landed a right that dropped Grim again. He made it to the final bell.[174]

In late October, Fitzsimmons said he was weighing 176 pounds, and would make the 168-pound limit for the late-November Gardner title fight without trouble.[175]

---

174 *Police Gazette*, October 31, 1903.
175 *Chicago Tribune*, October 23, 1903.

CHAPTER 6

Solidifying Contender Status

Despite his hand injury setback, Marvin Hart was still highly regarded. *The Police Gazette* said Marvin Hart was "One of the Few Fighters Who May Become Champion."

> [Hart] gave every indication of developing into an ideal type of the heavyweight fighter. Even today he is one of the best built among the fighters....
>
> In the ring he is a fighter from the first tap of the gong. He is an aggressive fighter, always coming in, always leading, always dangerous. ...
>
> Hart is crafty, clever and game, and studies his opponent from the toes up, as the saying goes, always looking for the weak spot that may be taken advantage of. His forte is hard hitting, and it is a fact that there is not another man in the ring who has as clean a record of knockouts as has Hart. Out of the twenty-four ring fights of importance in which he has engaged, he has won sixteen by knocking out his opponent. Several of the others were no-decision bouts in Philadelphia, two he won on the decision of the referee, and only three out of the whole number he actually lost. ...
>
> When Hart is fighting he can hit as hard with the left hand at long range as any man of his weight. His position is as peculiar as that which Tommy Ryan taught Jeffries. He crouches somewhat and shrugs his left shoulder up so that it entirely covers his jaw. His head ducks down behind that shoulder for protection just as the head of a turtle bobs back under its shell. His left arm he keeps extended to nearly full length. His right hand is drawn back in a position where it is ready for a drive at the body. At short range his body blows are nearly as dangerous as those of Fitzsimmons. ....
>
> Hart is a bigger man these days than many people think. When he knocked out "Kid" Carter he weighed about 180 pounds. In fact, he was as big, within a couple of pounds, as Jim Corbett.[176]

With his hand injury healed much faster than anticipated, Hart returned to the ring six months after the Gardner bout. Despite being out of the game for a while, true to form, Hart did not take a soft touch in his first

---

176 *Police Gazette*, June 27, 1903.

fight back. Instead, he took on the well-respected veteran Joe Choynski. Choynski was a skilled and powerful fighter who, though middleweight and light-heavyweight sized, had fought the best heavyweights of his era, both black and white. Choynski was 35 years old and had been fighting professionally for about 15 years. During that period of time, he had fought about 70 bouts.

Choynski's lengthy career included fights with men who eventually became world heavyweight champions: LKOby27 Corbett (1889); D/LKOby5 Fitzsimmons (1894); D20 Jeffries (1897); and KO3 Jack Johnson (1901). He had sparred with John L. Sullivan and Peter Jackson. He had even coached Hart for Marvin's May 1902 bout with Kid Carter, and trained and likely sparred with Marvin for a short while thereafter.

Choynski had also fought bouts with men such as Joe Goddard, Mick Dooley, George Godfrey, Dan Creedon, Frank Childs, Jim Hall, Tom Sharkey, Joe McAuliffe, Peter Maher, Gus Ruhlin, Kid McCoy, Steve O'Donnell, and Joe Walcott.

Following his 1901 KO3 over Jack Johnson, in 1902, Choynski stopped Bill Hanrahan in 5 rounds. However, an aging Choynski thereafter had sketchier results, including: 1902 LKOby1 Kid Carter, KO6 Al Weinig, L6 Jack O'Brien, and W6 Frank Childs; and 1903 KO2 Peter Maher, LND6 O'Brien, and a June LKOby2 Nick Burley. After losing to Burley, Choynski said, "When a dub like this fellow Burley can beat me I think it is about time I retired from the ring." However, in his last bout before taking on Hart, Choynski scored a KO7 over Burley in a rematch. In recent years, increasingly Choynski had been mixing in more losses with his wins, but he was mostly fighting top fighters, and he was still able to defeat good heavyweights. Hart was pretty gutsy to take on a top veteran like Choynski in his first fight back after a lengthy layoff due to a broken hand.[177]

---

177 *Police Gazette*, July 18, 1903.

Hart's only losses to that point were to Hanrahan (LKOby1), Root (L6), and Gardner (LKOby12 retirement owing to the hand injury). Fellow fighter Jack McCormick, the Philadelphia heavyweight, was training Marvin.[178] McCormick had lost an 1899 6-round decision to Choynski.[179]

Hart and Choynski fought a 6-round no-decision bout in Philadelphia on November 16, 1903. The fight was held at the Washington Sporting Club. William Rocap refereed. *The Philadelphia Record* said Hart looked much heavier, but the extra weight appeared to be rolls of fat. A match-up of two punchers such as these was bound to be exciting, and it was.

1 - Hart crouched and started at Joe, making a number of wild swings. Joe kept nimbly running around the ring out of his way. Choynski eventually "met Hart's rough rushes" with "cleverly timed left hand jabs which jolted" Hart. Finally, Marvin landed several hard shots to the body. Joe landed two left uppercuts, but could not stop Hart, who rushed him to the ropes. *The Philadelphia Inquirer* said Hart had the better of the round but "it was plain that he was making too much use of himself." *The Philadelphia Public Ledger* said the round was even.

2 - They rushed to a clinch. At long range, Hart landed some jabs. Choynski landed three times without a return. They then mixed it up savagely. Joe ducked several blows, and the crowd cheered his cleverness. Neither man moved much. Hart was again rough, leading with right jolts that eventually landed to the jaw, but Joe got in his left again. Joe landed a good right. Hart landed right uppercuts. Joe landed a couple stiff jabs. Hart came back with two stiff rights that hurt and staggered Choynski. Hart rushed Joe into the corner and was forcing him down with repeated blows when the bell rang. The round had been fierce. It was Hart's round.

3 - Both were tired at the start of the round. Choynski's blows were cleaner, but Hart would not be denied. He came back for more every time and landed some stiff swinging blows. One local source said Hart dropped Choynski with a punch to the jaw. However, the other local reports did not mention this. Joe avoided Marvin's rushes with speed and generalship.

The last minute of the round was very exciting. Neither boxed, but simply swung their arms to the body and head, landing frequently. Joe threw cleverness to the winds and mixed it up with his rugged opponent. It was give and take by both, and they beat each other all over the ring. Both were attempting a knockout. The crowd was continually on its feet, enjoying the fast fighting. This was Hart's game, though, and a couple hard rights to the stomach and a right to the heart hurt Joe. A wild left staggered Choynski, but he came back with a left to Marvin's jaw, which shook him

---

178 *Police Gazette*, October 31, 1903.
179 Cyberboxingzone.com.

up. At the end of the round, both men were very weak and fatigued, and they staggered to their corners.

4 - It was a remarkable round. Choynski paid no attention to his seconds' advice, and waded right into his younger and stronger opponent, exchanging lefts and rights. According to the *Philadelphia Press*, Hart landed on the jaw and staggered Joe, and while Choynski was trying to stop a right, he collided with Hart and went down. Both the *Philadelphia Record* and *Philadelphia Inquirer* said of this sequence that Hart rushed at Joe and missed a punch. In the clinch that followed, Hart threw Joe to the floor. Choynski took the count on one knee.

After Joe rose, Hart beat him all over the ring and nearly knocked him through the ropes, but could not finish. Again, Hart rushed and forced Choynski against the ropes. However, Joe rebounded off the ropes and landed several hard blows. His courage was up, so he attacked. Choynski brought the crowd to its feet by landing a left and right to Hart's jaw that rocked him, and also by swinging his right hard over Hart's heart. Marvin swung back wildly, but Joe got inside the blows.

At the end of the round, both threw their arms in aimless fashion, landing about as often as they missed. Hart made a big effort to take Joe out, but Choynski used all his cunning to stop Marvin's efforts. When the bell sounded, both were so tired that they could hardly stand. Hart was bleeding from the nose, while Choynski's left eye was badly cut.

5 - Choynski started with a rush and landed several hard jabs. Hart was weakening, but Joe's own exertions were telling on him as well, so he could not land a decisive punch on Marvin. Both were bleeding from the nose. They lunged in with punches, and then fell up against each other, taking a rest.

Hart punched Choynski on the jaw and staggered him. His left cut Joe's left eye. Blood flowed from both optics. However, Choynski's skill soon came into play, and he started blocking or eluding Marvin's wild swings, smartly getting inside of them.

Both the *Philadelphia Press* and *Philadelphia Public Ledger* said the round was even.

6 - Choynski again threw science to the winds and waded in to mix it up. They "both cut loose and tried for all they were worth to win a decision. Hart had Choynski staggering around the ring in the first half of the round, but the latter gave a marvelous exhibition of recuperative power, and by well timed right and left hand leads met Hart as he came in." Hart had forced the fighting for a while and had won the first half of the round, but a few Choynski blows to his stomach, including a hard left hook to the body, took the steam out of Marvin's punches and turned things Joe's way. Hart had no guard and Joe landed a half dozen times on his jaw, but there was only enough steam in the blows to wobble Marvin's head. They forced each

other around the ring, both being weak and shaky on their legs. Joe had a nasty cut over his right eye. At the end of the round, the house was in an uproar as they were mixing it up in wild fashion when the gong sounded. The crowd cheered to the echo.

The local papers agreed that they had fought to a fierce 6-round draw, although since it was Philadelphia, it was technically a no-decision. If an official decision could be rendered, "Anything worse than a draw would have been unfair." Another said, "It was the general opinion that the battle was the best seen here in a long while and that the verdict should be a draw." *The Philadelphia Record* said it was one of the hardest contests ever seen in the city. Hart had the best of the first 3 rounds, but Choynski did such good work in the latter part of the contest that he evened up matters. *The Philadelphia Press* said the men punched each other to a standstill. Choynski's superior science got him an even break against Hart's youth and slugging ability, making it a draw.

One said that with the exception of Fitzsimmons-Ruhlin, it was doubtful if two big men had ever boxed 6 harder rounds. *The Philadelphia Inquirer* said, "There were stages of the contest when it looked as though Choynski must succumb, but just when he appeared to be going he would make a rally, and then it would look as though Hart would be the one to go out." They fought so hard that each would take turns growing fatigued.

The fight was so good and well matched that if they were to fight again, everyone who saw it would want ringside seats. The crowd was hoarse from cheering. Although recently on the wane in his career, Choynski had put up a remarkable showing.[180]

When discussing the fight, Choynski said,

> Somebody had evidently told Marvin Hart to batter my ribs. Consequently, he went after them. In every round, he would rain punches on my sides, leaving me free to polish up his countenance in beautiful fashion. When he shifted to the head he had me going several times, but instead of keeping after my jaws, the poor, misguided boy would return to those ribs. ... When the fight was over, the few blows I had received around the face had marked me up some, as you can see, but the 200 or more punches shot at my ribs had not even jarred a sinew.[181]

Once again, Marvin Hart had given the fans their money's worth in an exciting battle, having been matched with another fan favorite who was a respected veteran of the game, and again Marvin had proven that he could fight on even terms with the best in the business.

---

180 *Philadelphia Record*, *Philadelphia Press*, *Philadelphia Public Ledger*, *Philadelphia Inquirer*, November 17, 1903.
181 *Police Gazette*, December 12, 1903.

CHAPTER 7

Three-Time Champion

The big fight of late 1903 was the world light heavyweight title fight between Bob Fitzsimmons and George Gardner. Fitz was going for his third world title in three different weight divisions at a time when there were only a small handful of weight classes. The fight garnered a great deal of interest, discussion, and debate because it was considered to be a very good match-up. The bout certainly had a big fight atmosphere surrounding it.

Although initially the legendary Fitzsimmons was the 10 to 6 betting favorite with the public, most of the boxing experts were picking Gardner to win. Fitzsimmons was 40 years old, and many thought he was even older. They figured that no man, no matter how great, can defeat father time. Bob seemed a bit lackluster in his sparring with 220-pound Joe Kennedy and 180-pound Sam Berger, showing the wear and tear of many years of boxing. He was "anything but the Fitzsimmons of old." Bob would have a good day and a bad one. Some wondered whether the beating he endured in the last Jeffries fight would affect him. Furthermore, for the first time in nine years, he was compelled to make weight, 168 pounds at 3 p.m. on the day of the fight. He had been weighing 190 pounds just a few months earlier, and some wondered whether the removal of all that weight might have drained him, and would affect him in a 20-round bout. Bob had been doing a great deal of running to lose weight, and his feet were badly blistered and sore. He had been suffering from colds. His legs were noticeably lean, and even his wondrous shoulders did not look as formidable as they did a few years ago.

On the other hand, Gardner was just as tall, and actually had a one-inch reach advantage at 76 inches. The young but fairly experienced Gardner was looking bigger and better than at any time in his career. He had speed, power, skill, footwork and condition. He was on a 6-fight win streak, including victories over Stift, Carter, Weinig, Maher, Hart, and Root.

Spider Kelly was sure Gardner would win. Tim McGrath said Gardner could beat clever men as well as sluggers. DeWitt Van Court said Fitz had met his match in a young, clever, dashing man. Eddie Hanlon said Gardner looked too big and strong, and was a man who could take an awful punch and still keep going strong. Aurelia Herrera said George would wear Fitz out. Toby Irwin said Gardner had speed, condition, and good hands, and Fitz would not be able to keep up the pace. There was a feeling that

Gardner would wear Fitz down. Bob McArthur said Gardner was the coming wonder for sure.

Sandy Ferguson had once been a Fitzsimmons sparring partner for 14 weeks. He had recently sparred with Gardner, so he was well equipped to assess the match-up. Ferguson was sure that Gardner would win. "This fellow Gardner is the fastest fellow I ever sparred. I look to see him knock Fitz out inside of ten rounds."

Alex Greggains, who was training and sparring with Gardner, said Gardner would be the only man in the fight. Alex said George was very fast, trained to the minute, very confident, and with every reason to be. He had improved wonderfully during the past year and grown 10 pounds bigger. Greggains had sparred with Fitz many years before, when Bob was preparing for the Maher fight in New Orleans, so he knew how to coach Gardner on the pitfalls that he needed to avoid. Alex said Fitz was only human, and was past his best. "I believe that Gardner, in his present shape, would have been a match for Fitzsimmons the best day the Cornishman ever saw and I think Gardner will put Fitzsimmons away in a few rounds, because Fitzsimmons is only an imitation of the Fitzsimmons that was fighting a few years ago."

George Gardner had seen Fitzsimmons box, and said that he was not afraid. "Now don't you think that Fitzsimmons is going to walk up and bang me the way he did Jeffries the last time. He is not going to do it, for I won't let him." He had a great coach, and had the advantage of having seen Fitz fight, whereas Fitzsimmons had never seen him box. "I have seen Bob fight and made a study of his style, but he has never seen me box."

Regardless, age had never been a detriment to Fitzsimmons. In the past, he could look so-so in training, not feel well, or be dealing with injuries or ailments, but perform at a high level in the actual fights and still find a way to win. Bob said, "I have something the matter with me every time I fight. I really think if I went in the ring feeling right once I might kill some one." No one had defeated him other than heavyweight champion Jeffries.

> The rules which apply to other pugilists and other athletes do not seem to apply in his case. ... Fitzsimmons is a creature of surprises. ... His opponent may appear to be having all the best of the argument and Fitz may be staggering around and seemingly ready to fall when he will turn the tables completely with one little shift or jolt that may be sent in so covertly and from such short range that two-thirds of the crowd will fail to see it.

There were some who said that although Gardner was a very good, well-rounded fighter, Fitz was special, the best of his weight alive. Bob's sparring partner Sam Berger said Gardner had never met a man like Fitz and would not touch him at all. "You may think him old but watch Gardner when Fitz lands either hand. It's the worst wallop in the ring still."

James Jeffries picked Fitzsimmons. "I have fought him and know that he is a great fighter. In fact, I think he is the hardest proposition I have ever encountered. He is a wonderful hitter, and is on to all the tricks of the game. He is an excellent ring general." That said, even Jeff admitted that like other professions, a fighter cannot always last. Fitz's hands were not what they once were, and he had endured many hard fights. Still, Jeff said, "I know of no other fighter who can hit a harder blow than Fitzsimmons."

A couple days before the fight, Gardner money was pouring in, bringing Fitz to just a 10 to 9 favorite. James Corbett said he was betting at least $500 on Gardner. Gardner predicted that his strength would wear Bob down. He had bet several hundred dollars on himself. The day of the fight, he said he was in perfect condition and confident that he would stop Fitz within the limit. "I know that Fitzsimmons is a crafty ring general, but I am sure that I know his style and his favorite punches, and that I can cover up for his attacks, and give him some punches that will be new to him." He also said, "If I am successful in winning from the old man, as I know I will, I will issue a challenge to Champion Jeffries."

TRAINING QUARTER "SNAPS" OF GEORGE GARDNER AND ROBERT FITZSIMMONS, BOXERS WHO ARE TO BATTLE FOR THE LIGHT-HEAVYWEIGHT CHAMPIONSHIP.

On the other hand, Fitzsimmons said the odds were about right. His body was stiff, but he would do his best regardless. He was not predicting victory, but that he would give anyone who bet on him a run for their money. "I can't say how long the fight will last, but as long as I am on my feet those present will admit that they saw a fight."

Gardner insisted on soft surgical bandages, not hard bandages, fearful that he would be cut-up the way Jeffries was in his last bout with Fitzsimmons. He was going to have a man with Bob when he put the bandages on, and would also examine them in the ring to make sure they were all right. "Bandages sometimes harden up when they are on too long." Gardner wanted to make sure Fitz did not use any surgical plaster the way he did with Jeffries.

Referee Eddie Graney said Fitz liked to use surgical tape, and Gardner had agreed. The men agreed to break when ordered to do so, but would protect themselves while breaking. The contest was set to begin at 9:20 p.m.[182]

---

182 *San Francisco Bulletin*, November 10, 11, 20, 24, 25, 1903; *San Francisco Examiner*, November 17, 20, 23-25, 1903; *San Francisco Chronicle*, November 24, 25, 1903; *San Francisco Call*, November 25, 1903.

A little over a week after the Hart-Choynski bout, on November 25, 1903 at San Francisco's Mechanics' Pavilion, 40-year-old former middleweight and heavyweight champion Bob Fitzsimmons took on world light heavyweight champion George Gardner. Both weighed 168 pounds, neither causing the scale's balance bar to move. They agreed to ordinary surgical tape, without the application of collodion or any liquid which would have a hardening effect.

It was anticipated that before the men were introduced in the ring that Philadelphia Jack O'Brien would climb through the ropes to challenge the winner. However, his actual challenge was to fight any man at 158 pounds. He did not want to go out of his weight class, at least not at that point.

Fitzsimmons approached the ring at 9:05 p.m. He entered the ring first, wearing purple trunks with a belt of American flag colors, and lavender socks. He put on green gloves. Bill Delaney, Sam Berger, Joe Kennedy and Johnny Croll, Jr. assisted him. He was the crowd favorite, for it gave him an ovation.

Gardner came on after Bob. He wore emerald trunks, green belt, with a bathrobe over his shoulders, and green socks. Alex Greggains, Billy Pierce, Harry Foley and Dave Barry advised him. Jack Johnson was in attendance.

They agreed to fight straight Queensberry rules. Announcer Billy Jordan let the crowd know that the men would protect themselves in the breakaway and break at the referee's order. He then howled out his well known "Let 'er go," and the gong sounded.

1 - Each tried to feint the other into leading. They sparred cautiously. Gardner danced and ducked in lively fashion. The fighting was slow, both exercising great care. Gardner seemed very nervous, while Bob was cool. George was a bit more aggressive, though, and slightly opened Bob's eye with a left jab. Fitz appeared to be bothered with a cold. However, Fitzsimmons landed a stinging jab to the jaw; another left to the jaw and right to the stomach, and then sent Gardner's head back with a left hook to the jaw. One opined that honors were even. Another said the advantage was slightly with Fitzsimmons.

2 - Both were cautious again, with little vim. Gardner rushed Bob to the ropes with a series of body blows. Bob puffed, and his motions were slow. Gardner was rushing Bob around the ring. There was not much force to most of the blows landed, though. Bob was content to defend, elude, and counter. *The Call* said it was a comparatively even round, with the advantage, if any, being with Gardner.

3 - Fitz did not appear to be trying hard. However, near the end of the round, Fitzsimmons suddenly woke up to the fact he was in a fight and stopped Gardner's rush with a fierce left to the face and a terrific smashing right to the jaw. Bob had finally decided to let Gardner taste his power. After a clinch, they exchanged some hard blows and Bob rushed him to the

ropes with a series of short-arm smashes. Bob was no longer sparring, but firing in hooking blows. He landed a left to the face and a right to the body. Fitz had given a flash of his old fire. He drew George on, and Gardner fought back hard. It was Fitz's round.

The Examiner and *Bulletin* said the contest was even through the first 3 rounds. Bob's right to the jaw in the 3rd round was the fiercest punch of the fight thus far.

4 - Gardner worked Fitzsimmons to the ropes, forcing matters. A right to the body seemed to hurt Bob, for he clinched to save himself. However, Fitz finally acted like himself and suddenly rushed at him and showered in the hard blows.

Fitzsimmons landed a left hook and right to the jaw that dropped Gardner like a log. George took an 8-count. Bob pounced on him with right and left short-arm swings to the body and head, rocking Gardner's head from side to side with his savage hooks, beating him back to the ropes. Gardner reeled about the ring like a badly beaten fighter. The audience was in an uproar. Gardner saved himself by clinching.

While in a clinch, Fitz half wrestled and half punched him to the floor with a vicious right. After Gardner rose, Bob doubled him up with a left to the body and continued battering him along the ropes with frightful blows. Gardner was all but out on the ropes but was saved by the bell. The audience tumult for Fitz was tremendous.

Afterwards, Bob said he badly hurt his left hand in this round.

5 - Bob kept a good pace for the first minute. Gardner was still dazed from the previous round. Fitzsimmons floored Gardner with a short left hook on the jaw. Bob landed the punch with so much force and forward momentum that he fell forward and Gardner in attempting to grab in part pulled Bob down over himself as George went down in a heap onto his back. Fitz jumped up at once. Gardner was down for 8 or 9 seconds. He rose appearing hurt and weary.

After Gardner rose, Fitzsimmons mauled him with left jabs and rights that had steam. Fitz did all the hitting, doubling him up with savage digs in the stomach and beating his head from side to side with short snappy hooks. Gardner was hurt, but moved around the ring and clinched repeatedly in order to survive. He held on until he recovered. Gardner's nose was badly bleeding.

Fitzsimmons grew tired from his own exertions, and his blows became taps. Some thought that Fitz appeared to be playing with Gardner as a cat does a mouse, and allowed him to recover. They could not understand why Bob began waiting. He even let George hit him, and did not try to hit back. Fitz was laughing and stalling, and some thought he was trying to create the impression of being tired. Others thought he was actually fatigued. Gardner rallied and began roughing it in the clinches and hitting Bob's body and kidneys. George took the offensive, but his blows had little force and did no damage. Bob had the crowed guessing as to whether he was shamming or actually tired.

The Bulletin said Bob had broken one of the knuckles in his right hand in the previous round. He did not reveal this until after the fight.

6 - Both seemed tired. Gardner slowly and steadily walked towards Fitz, throwing leads. Fitz contented himself with moving or walking away, or covering up, grinning over his shoulder, as if to show how easy it was to get away from Gardner's leads. Fitz was inclined to rest, reserving himself. Still, Gardner was ducking and clinching at every feint, obviously concerned about Bob's blows. The crowd hissed the tameness of the fighting. With a left shift, Fitz cut Gardner's right eye. George clinched. His eye began to swell and it became discolored. Gardner was following Fitz around, but was cautious. Most of his blows were directed at the body. Bob's lips began to puff up a bit. The bout had become slow. This continued for several rounds.

7 - Fitz was fiddling and feinting, moving around and then moving away, stalling. Gardner stood away, landing body punches and the occasional clip on the face, but there was no punishment in his blows, although Bob's lips began bleeding. Both looked tired. The crowd jeered and urged them on. Fitz appeared to be losing his speed and seemed content with acting more on the defensive.

8 - Bob backed away, allowing George to do the leading. However, Fitz would occasionally spurt with hard punches. Bob's rallies would jar Gardner. Bob landed a left and right to the jaw, and then left to the jaw and right to the body. When Bob bothered to punch, he put Gardner on the defensive, and George would clinch to save himself. However, the round was mostly slow, with Fitz dancing away.

One paper said Fitzsimmons improved in this round and the advantage was his.

9 - They sparred cautiously, Fitz backing away, bent on resting. Gardner half-heartedly advanced and led. The crowd grew angry at the bout's tameness, and hissed and called on the men to fight. Gardner's straight lefts puffed Bob's lips and caused the blood to well from the mouth, but his blue eyes showed no distress. The pace was very slow. Bob landed a left hook to the jaw and danced away. Gardner chased, but did not land. Fitz suddenly waded in and forced George back. Fitz slowed up considerably, but was evidently waiting for a moment to land his famous knockout punch. He would rest for a while, then suddenly lash out and test Gardner.

The Chronicle said there was little to choose from the 9th to the 13th rounds. The rounds were poor. Fitz's shifts were the only redeeming features. However, he was not leading at all.

10 - Bob backed away and contented himself with blocking leads. He took some blows with a view of getting in a good return. Bob occasionally landed a good jolt. He landed a left hook on the mouth that caused Gardner to spit blood. Gardner's nose began bleeding as a result of the rights and lefts that occasionally came from Fitz. When Bob wanted, he could work his shifts at will, but he picked his spots. Blood came from Fitz's lips and Gardner's nose. In a rush, Gardner slipped down to the floor, partly from a right cross to the jaw and partly from clumsiness. This round was a trifle more gingerly.

11 - Fitz quickened up but his spurts were short, and between them, there was a lot of inactivity. Gardner blocked several blows. His own punches lacked force. Bob jolted him with a straight left to the stomach. Fitz took most of the light blows, but blocked the harder ones. Gardner sent in a right to the face, but Bob sailed in with a left hook to the jaw, staggering Gardner. The gong rang. Bob had the advantage of the round.

12 - Fitz was winded, breathing heavily. As usual, he backed away, but landed a nice right uppercut to the chin. The pace again slowed up and the

crowd yelled at them. Gardner's blows were very light. He had yet to land a telling blow.

The fighting was very commonplace during subsequent rounds. Fitz was stalling a great deal. He would occasionally let out and mix it for a few seconds, but he spent most of the time gliding around and keeping out of encounters. Gardner pressed, but not hard enough to do anything effective.

13 - Although Gardner was less afraid to punch, infusing more ginger into his work, landing some lefts to the face, he still was not doing much effective work. Halfway through the round not a solid blow had landed. Gardner kept pegging away, but could not land. What did land had little force.

At the end of the round, when Gardner rushed, Fitz suddenly held his ground and landed another mule-kick overhand right to the jaw below the ear that sent Gardner down to his knees, just as the bell rang. Gardner rose in a couple of seconds, though, and seemed okay physically, although he had a look of distress on his face.

14 - Fitz feinted with a right and sent in two lefts to the jaw. He followed with a hard left hook to the jaw and a hard right to the body.

Fitzsimmons landed a stiff right to the chin that sent Gardner down for 5-7 seconds. He got up groggy. Fitz tried to finish him, but the Lowell man moved, covered up and held. Bob's blows were a bit wild. Bob was blowing hard, but he was punishing Gardner. Fitz landed a hard right cross and right uppercut to the chin which staggered Gardner. Blood streamed from George's nose.

However, Bob slowed again and allowed Gardner to make the pace. George began rushing again, but could not land. Gardner was the aggressor, but in a half-hearted way. The excitement of the contest and/or the fear of the dreaded Fitzsimmons wallop had left Gardner weak. Fitz's manner left the impression that he had no fear of Gardner's punches. The balance of the round was uninteresting. Both were tired and did little effective work. Gardner went to his corner appearing groggy, while Fitz coolly smiled at his friends.

15 - Bob kept away from George's rushes and jabbed him with the left. Fitz fought carefully and made his blows count. Bob jarred him with a hard right to the jaw and left hook to the body. Gardner again stalled with movement and clinching. In the clinches, Bob hit George with right uppercuts that distressed him. Gardner's face was covered with blood. It was Fitz's round.

Rounds 16 through 19 were tame, and neither scored heavily. Gardner did most of the leading, while Bob moved about the ring. Fitz did not seem to be trying. Gardner was short with his blows to the face, but landed several good blows to the body.

16 - Fitz nursed his strength carefully and made no unnecessary moves. Gardner's fight had been disappointing, with no strength.

17 - The round was mostly desultory sparring. Bob did some clever blocking. Gardner landed a hard right at the end, but not hard enough to bother Bob, who went to his corner smiling.

18 - Fitz acted as though he was mighty tired. He clinched frequently. Gardner hit his body. George forced Fitz about the ring, missing swings. Both landed some good blows.

19 - Gardner went after Bob, ripping in a number of body shots that hurt and troubled him. Bob wrestled George to the mat. Fitz complained that Gardner was hitting low. The claim was not allowed, though the referee cautioned George. Gardner landed a good left to the stomach that brought a look of pain on Bob's face. Fitz kept covering and grabbing tightly. He occasionally let out and drove George off. Bob was too clever to allow Gardner to land anything like a knockout punch. The round ended in a lively mix. George landed several short lefts to the stomach, but they had little power. One said honors were even, while another said Gardner won this round, as well as the 20th, but it came too late to do him any good.

20 - Gardner feinted and Fitzsimmons danced around. Fitz acted almost entirely on the defensive, defending Gardner's blows. Fitz blocked and took body shots, and though tired, did not seem worried. Still, near the end of the round, Bob had enough strength left to send his left to the head and body, staggering Gardner, who clinched. Gardner held on, and the referee could not separate them. The bell rang ending the bout.

When Referee Ed Graney pointed to Fitzsimmons as the winner of his decision, the crowd stood and cheered the new champion. They wanted a speech, but all Fitz would say was, "Haven't I done enough for one night?" He was tired, but happy. Bob had a puffed lip. Gardner's face was badly swollen and he had a cut over his right eye.

Graney said that although it was a slow affair, this was wise strategy on Fitz and Delaney's part. If Bob had mixed it too much or too long, he might have worn himself out or left himself open to Gardner, who at all times was dangerous. Gardner had the better condition and was strong, but he failed to take enough chances until the last few rounds. He seemed afraid of Fitz's heavy punch. Graney said Bob was tired at the end, but held his own in all but a very few rounds. His knockdowns counted a long way in his favor. All of his punches carried sting, whereas "Gardner could not hit hard enough to break a pane of glass." Although Bob rested and moved away a lot, stalling for time, Gardner did nothing worthy of mention, despite being more active. He forgot to bring his punch. Fitz was too strong for him. However, Bob was out of condition. "Had he been the old-time Fitz he would have won in three rounds."

Fitzsimmons said if his hands had not gone out on him, he would have stopped Gardner in 5 rounds. He said he broke his right early, and disabled his left in the 13th round. Still, he gave Gardner some credit. "There is a great deal of praise due to Gardner, for he fought a game, hard fight. He was always ready to come back into the fray after he had been hit hard, and he mixed it when the opportunity was afforded."

Bob's hands really were injured. It was necessary to cut the gloves from his hands. In the dressing room afterwards, a physician examined Bob's right hand and confirmed that the knuckles of the thumb and first finger were fractured. Bob's left hand was swollen to twice its natural size. Later, he could not handle a knife or fork to eat.

Still, although agreeing that hurt hands might have affected his ability to put Gardner away, most felt that the predominant reason was that Bob was no longer what he once was. Even Fitzsimmons recognized that he was past it. "I did well for an old man, but my ring days are over."

> Tonight's battle ends my career in the prize ring. I will never fight again. I am getting old … Why a week ago I wrote George Dawson that I would be lucky if I won, and I tell you now that I am a lucky fellow. I was a sick man, I tell you, and I can easily feel the effects of Gardner's punches, even though they were not very hard ones.

Bill Delaney said Fitz showed that he was getting old, but Gardner never stepped close enough to land a big punch. Bob mostly bluffed his way through the bout, save for the flashes of his old-time form. He gave Gardner credit for taking the punching he did and getting up off the floor and coming back again. Gardner was aggressive, but not confident. When he finally showed some confidence at the end, his strength was gone. Still, taking those punches showed he was gritty and game.

Gardner said Bob's heavy blows staggered him early and took a lot of the fight out of him. Still, he noted that Fitz weakened, and during the last part of the fight did nothing but stall, so he felt that he was entitled to the decision or a draw. His coach and trainer, Alex Greggains, said Gardner should have won the decision. He was the aggressor from the 13th round on, following his opponent about and forcing the fighting. Still, he admitted that George did not fight up to his standard. He was slow and his blows lacked force.

Robert Edgren said Fitz seemed slow throughout, but at times showed amazing bursts of speed. Gardner used left jabs to the face and body to hold Bob off.

All of the local newspapers agreed with the decision.

However, all reporters also agreed that Fitz's best days were past, and that Gardner would have been an easy mark for Fitz when Bob had been at his best. The reporters felt that it had been a relatively poor fight, the poorest of Fitz's career. It was slow and spiritless. Some said the fight was pathetic, while others said the bout was good and bad in streaks. Fitz's statement during training that he was not in his old-time form was proven correct. Age and a lengthy career were clearly telling on the war-worn veteran. Some said Fitz could no longer punch like he once could, while others said he still had a punch, but fatigued quickly. Many thought Bob should retire. *The Chronicle* opined that this version of Fitzsimmons would never land on Jack Johnson.

Bob was tricky and clever as ever, but he "does not work his fists so rapidly and the sting is gone out of his shifts and swings." A short time ago, the same punches would have meant knockout. At present, he "tires very easily," "cannot lash out in the rapid style of the old days," and "there is not half the poundage in his punches." One said Fitz was slow and weak compared to what he once was.

Fitzsimmons fought well in spots, but he would alternate flashes of power with fatigue. He knew when and where to hit, and was not slow in starting to punch, but he was quick in stopping, looking to kill the clock after striking hard blows. His wind was not good. When he had Gardner groggy and going, Bob was too weak to take the chance of rushing in to finish, but instead would fiddle and stall for the balance of the round. Fitz no longer had the same vim, and it was inability and not unwillingness that held him back.

He had Gardner down on the floor twice in the 4th and once in the 5th rounds. After failing to knock out Gardner, Bob seemed to realize that his steam was lacking and paced himself. He was content to outpoint Gardner. Bob rested up frequently. Although his hands were hurt, it also appeared to be the case that sheer weariness affected Fitz and not just crippled fists. Still, Bob's flashes of hard punches won him the fight. Gardner was down again in the 13th and 14th rounds. To some, it seemed that Bob was just toying with Gardner. For round after round, it seemed that Fitz could have ended matters whenever he wanted to, but he allowed Gardner to recover.

Bob won because he scored all the knockdowns and his hitting was much cleaner and more forceful, and he had generally handled Gardner, who could not hurt him. Even with two hurt hands, Bob managed to stall off the younger and faster man. Bob was too experienced, crafty, and powerful for him. Fitz had the class, and had used his veteran generalship with flashes of power to win, despite his age, poor condition, injured hands, and fact that he had been suffering from a cold. "Fitz showed the most consummate ring generalship. His every move seemed to have been studied out and he hardly wasted a blow."

Gardner was a disappointment. He was too nervous and overly cautious. He seemed to be a victim of stage fright. He did not show the form he had in training or in his fights with Walcott, Carter, Hart, and Root. Gardner mostly fought at long range, and ineffectively. His blows, when they landed at infrequent intervals, had little sting to them, and had no impact on Fitz, who mostly just warded them off on his arms and elbows.

After making a flowery showing at the start, despite the fact that Fitz had broken hands and had grown fatigued, Gardner had a wholesome respect for Fitz's wallops. He seemed unable or unwilling to get in close enough to be effective. The spectators were amazed at Gardner's poor performance, given his previous showings.

Gardner lost his courage after he was knocked down in the 4th round, and he never really regained it. "It was rarely after that that he made anything like a determined effort to beat the Cornishman down." Gardner rarely took real chances.

From the 5th to the 18th rounds, although Gardner carried the fight to Bob, he did it in a half-hearted and ineffective way. George's condition was first class, but when Fitz worked in his shifts and right and left blows, Gardner seemed to go to pieces. "Toward the close of the fight he kept tapping tired Mr. Fitzsimmons on the midsection with his left. He caused the impression that he was trying to create an opening which never came." Gardner's battling spirit was low. He did not make a showing until the end of the bout, when he did some good work in the last 2 rounds when his courage revived and he stung Fitz with some good body blows. It was too little, too late.

The total gate receipts were $16,435, which was allegedly split between the fighters and the club. The fighters split the purse 75% winner, 25% loser. Hence, Fitz earned $6,163 and Gardner $2,054. Apparently, though, Bob also had an understanding with the club wherein he received 10% of the gross receipts as a bonus. That brought his earnings to $7,500.[183]

---

183 *San Francisco Chronicle, Examiner, Bulletin, Call*, November 26, 27, 1903.

CHAPTER 8

Settling Matters

A week after the Fitzsimmons-Gardner world light heavyweight title fight, and just over two weeks after his 6-round war with Joe Choynski, Marvin Hart's final 1903 fight was a third match against Kid Carter in Boston, Massachusetts.

After being stopped in the 9th round by Hart and fighting him in a 6-round no-decision bout, Kid Carter's subsequent results included: 1902 L6 Jack Root, KO2 Peter Maher, and L6 George Gardner;[184] and 1903 W15 John Willie, LKOby11 Sam McVey, KO1 Joe Butler, W6 Joe Grim, ND6 Jack O'Brien,[185] LND6 Gus Ruhlin,[186] and L15 Joe Walcott (twice).[187] McVey, Butler, and Walcott were all black, so Carter was not one of those boxers who drew the color line.

There was a demand for a third Hart-Carter bout owing to the fact that their two previous fights had been highly entertaining. The local Bostonians had seen Carter lose to Walcott, but were impressed enough with his creditable performances that they wanted to see him go at it with Hart.

The Boston Post called Hart the Louisville wonder, who was considered to be a championship possibility. He had been doing grand work until typhoid fever forced him to rest some months ago (interestingly, not referencing the hand injury). Big Jack McCormack/McCormick, the man who had a

KID CARTER

---

184 The Carter-Gardner fight was rough and fierce, but Gardner had the advantage in every round. *Anaconda Standard*, December 30, 1902.
185 One report said O'Brien used his lightning footwork to outbox Carter. Another said O'Brien might have had a slight advantage, but a draw would have been proper if a decision had been rendered. *Police Gazette*, July 18, 1903.
186 Ruhlin-Carter was a fierce give and take fight all the way through. The 200-pound Ruhlin had as much as a 25-pound weight advantage and scored a knockdown in either the 4th or the 5th round. *Police Gazette*, September 26, 1903, October 10, 1903.
187 Boxrec.com.

knockout victory over Kid McCoy, was training him.[188]

The third Hart-Carter bout was held on December 1, 1903 at Boston's Criterion Athletic Club. *The Police Gazette* said they fought at catchweights.

Typical for Hart's bouts, the fight was called the greatest battle seen in Boston in years. It was yet another vicious war. The fight was scheduled for 15 rounds, but it did not last quite that long.

1 - Hart began the contest landing hard rights and covering his own chin with his shoulder. He landed body and head shots all through the round, while Carter focused on the body. Hart appeared to be too strong for Carter.

2 - Carter landed some damaging punches. He scored often with his left jab. It was his round by a slight margin.

3 - Hart nailed Carter with right and left hooks, the sequence ending with a right that floored the Kid. He rose quickly, but Hart landed powerful rights to the jaw that weakened Carter. By the end of the round, Carter was almost out.

4 - Hart hurt Carter again, but the Kid revived and got to Marvin's body very well. Carter's clever jabbing offset the advantage Hart gained earlier in the round.

5 - *The Boston Herald* said Hart's superior weight began to tell. However, the *Boston Daily Globe* said the round was even.

6 - Carter's body shots slowed up Hart. A straight left caused Marvin's nose to bleed. This was another even round.

7 - Honors were slightly in Hart's favor, though Carter hit Hart's body often and staggered him with a hard right cross on the jaw. Until the 9th round, it was give and take.

8 - Carter staggered Hart with a right, but Marvin quickly recuperated and was stronger at the end.

9 - It was an exciting back and forth round, both landing left hooks to the body and rights to the head. Carter almost dropped Hart at the start.

However, Hart hit the jaw with his right and dropped Carter. Carter recovered quickly, attacked, and had Hart hurt by the end of the round.

10 - Hart slowed up a bit. The round was even, with Carter having whatever advantage there was. However, towards the end, Hart got to Carter often.

11 - At the start of the round, Hart dropped Carter with a right. A left to the body and right to the head forced Carter to hold in order to keep from going down again.

---

188 *Boston Post*, November 29, 1903.

However, after some exchanges, Carter sent in a stiff left hook to the cheek that opened it up and sent Hart down to the mat. Blood spurted from the cut under Marvin's eye. Hart was forced to take the defensive for the remainder of the round. Carter forced him about the ring but could not finish him. Hart was hurt, but the gong saved him.

12 - *The Herald* said Hart came back well, which forced Carter to stall. However, the *Globe* said the round was slightly in Carter's favor, jabbing repeatedly and landing almost at will.

13 - Their boxing was fast and fierce. Three uppercuts dazed Carter. Hart banged him around the ring until a right to the jaw floored Carter. Although almost helpless, Carter managed to get away and survive.

However, a series of hard rights and lefts to the jaw, ending with a right, sent the Kid down again at the bell. Carter was carried to his corner.

14 - It was another back and forth round. Hart came after Carter with "wonderful speed." The Kid fought back gamely. A Hart right dazed him. Just when Hart seemed to have things well in hand, Carter landed a right that badly hurt Hart. Carter had him all but out.

True to form, Hart came back and dropped Carter with a right. The Kid "was all to the bad when the gong sounded" ending the round.

15 - From the start of the final round, Carter was weak and had the appearance of a beaten man. Hart smashed him often with both hands, at first to the head, then to the body. He chased the Kid around the ring, smashing and pounding away. Finally, while on the ropes, Carter's hands dropped down to his sides. He was helpless, unable to punch back or defend himself. Quickly seeing that he was all but gone, fearing for his safety, the referee stepped in and stopped the fight, with just under a minute remaining in the round.[189]

Marvin Hart almost always managed to be in a good fight, and the *Boston Daily Globe* called the southern light-heavyweight champion "a revelation." The crowd got their money's worth. Carter was quite tough, showed great grit, administered a lot of punishment, and demonstrated an ability to take it and come back, but in the end was outclassed by the stronger, 15 pounds heavier Hart.

Hart "usually emerged from his corner in a crouching position, his jaw well protected with a high left shoulder and his right hand always in a position to unloose at any time." Sometimes though, Marvin would disregard Carter's punches and move right in, firing away.

The local *Boston Herald* said, "Several times, with driving rights to the head and occasional jab or a left hook, Hart had Carter in a bad way. Six

---

[189] *Boston Herald, Boston Daily Globe*, December 2, 1903; *Philadelphia Public Ledger*, December 2, 1903; *Police Gazette*, December 19, 1903.

times he put him to the mat." However, Carter would quickly come back and hit Hart hard and often, mostly to the body. "Five times Hart went down." However, its round by round description only describes Carter going down five times to Hart's once.

Combining the local round by round descriptions, Carter was dropped in the 3rd, 9th, 11th, 13th (twice), and 14th rounds, while Hart hit the deck in the 11th, a round in which both were down.

Making Hart's victory over Carter all the more impressive, the following month, Kid Carter scored a KO1 over Joe Choynski.

The much smaller Joe Walcott issued a challenge to Hart. However, Marvin only replied, "Tell Mr. Walcott that I am a Southern gentleman." *The Police Gazette* reported, "Now it is Marvin Hart who has drawn the color line." Hart had sparred black fighters, but he had yet to fight one.[190]

After the Carter fight, Marvin had been training in Philadelphia.

Bostonians had liked what they saw of Hart, and wanted to see more of him. Typical of his constant fighting clip, Hart returned to the ring only a month after his 15th round victory over Kid Carter.

In his first 1904 bout, on January 5, once again in Boston, Marvin Hart fought a rematch with former world light-heavyweight champion George Gardner, the man against whom Marvin had retired owing to a broken hand suffered during their bout the previous year. Clearly, Hart wanted to avenge the loss, insisting that he would have won but for the hand injury. Gardner's subsequent results were KO12 Jack Root and L20 Bob Fitzsimmons in world light heavyweight title fights.

Gardner was from Massachusetts, so once again, Hart was fighting on his opponent's home turf, a fact not insignificant in the sport of boxing, which has a history of favoritism for locals when it comes to decisions. Even local reporters would often, but not always, favor the local man in their presentation and analysis of the bout.

Both Hart and Gardner were called big, strong, clever, fast, and terrific hitters. Hart's performance against Carter in

---

190 *Police Gazette*, December 19, 1903.

Boston had advanced him considerably. He had shown his ability and willingness at all stages to be in the midst of battle. "Hart is a good, big, healthy, strong, willing young man who is indifferent about a punch and who is willing to stand many punches from an opponent to get in one for himself." Marvin was constantly after his foes. Although he was not especially clever, he was gaining more science and experience all the time. Hart said he would go right after Gardner with the hope of wearing him down.

However, Gardner, who was from Lowell, Massachusetts, was a slight favorite to win. Gardner combined remarkable cleverness, generalship, and good blocking skills with punching power. He was shiftier than Hart, relying on speed and science. Hart was more reckless, willing to take one to give one. "Naturally the fellow with the wallop and the cleverness would be figured as the winner, but the young Kentuckian has time and again proven that when he puts his famous punch on, the other fellow forgets his science." As a rule, Gardner was cautious and only aggressive when compelled to be so. Newsmen felt that he would have to be both defensive and aggressive to beat Hart.[191]

The fight took place at the Criterion Athletic Club. The crowd was the biggest that the Club had ever handled. There was not a vacant seat in the auditorium, and hundreds of members who had waited to pay were turned away. Amongst the crowd was Tom Sharkey, who had come from New York to see the fight. He was in training, preparing for his fight with Jack Munroe.

The Boston Post said their unofficial weights were announced as 175 pounds for Hart and 167 pounds for Gardner. Both looked to be in good condition. They fought straight Marquis of Queensberry rules.

1 - They started off at a rapid clip, leading hard and clinching immediately after every mix-up. Hart landed a short right to the jaw, while Gardner returned with a straight left to the mouth. Both landed heavily in a hard mix-up. Gardner landed a hard left jab to the jaw, blocked Marvin's rush and again served him with a left. Gardner used his left with precision in repulsing Hart's vicious rushes. He clearly was attempting to box defensively and to avoid mix-ups. Gardner had a slight advantage in the round, which was the tamest of the fight.

2 - Hart rushed Gardner to the ropes and landed two telling body shots. "As Gardner squirmed out of the corner, evidently much distressed, Hart swung his left and it landed squarely on the jaw." Gardner's feet flew from underneath him, his body landed on the floor with a thud, and his neck landed on the lower rope. Some locals reported that it was a right to the jaw

---

191 *Boston Herald*, January 4, 1904; *Boston Post, Boston Globe*, January 5, 1904.

that had dropped Gardner; some said it was a left hook that did the trick; while others said it was both a right and a left.

Gardner rose quickly in a daze. Hart rushed him around the ring with right swings. George managed to survive by moving, blocking and grabbing. Hart rushed him to the ropes, smashed right and left to the head and body, missing as much as landing due to his wildness. Gardner stalled through the round.

Hart went after Gardner so hard that he tired himself out from his own exertions, trying to break down an impregnable defense. Gardner allowed Hart to punch himself out. After that, Marvin was too tired to do any execution.

Gardner recuperated, and after a clinch and break, George attacked and landed several punches that hurt Marvin. By the end of the round, Hart was in some distress. Still, Hart had won the round. Gardner had shown great cleverness in getting out of a bad spot, something he had done with Fitzsimmons.

The Boston Herald said that thereafter, Gardner was cautious for several rounds.

3 - Because Hart had fatigued himself in the previous round, and Gardner had recovered during the minute's rest, Gardner had the advantage in the round. At first, honors were even as they mixed it up. Hart landed a hard left jab to the nose. Gardner ducked and stalled cleverly, fighting for the body, which Hart did not like. Gardner drove Hart to the ropes with a right to the stomach. Hart landed a vicious left uppercut to the chin. Gardner got in a right to the stomach and then crossed it hard to the jaw. The pace was very fast. Gardner scored with his straight punches. It was Gardner's round.

4 - Hart struck a hard right to the ear and they clinched. Gardner was cautious and worked the stomach in the clinches, crossing his right to the head. Hart caught him coming in with a right uppercut, clinched and pounded the body. Hart connected with right and left to the jaw. They exchanged jabs. In a mix-up, Hart landed a heavy right to the jaw. Both showed the effects of the pace. It was an even round.

5 - Hart scored a right to the heart. In a clinch, Hart landed an uppercut to Gardner's chin. Gardner landed both hands to the body. Hart staggered him with a fierce uppercut. He plunged his right to the body and left to the jaw. George was doing all his execution at close quarters with stomach blows. The pace was slowing up a bit. Hart easily won the round.

The Boston Post said that Hart had discovered that Gardner could not stop his left, and using it to advantage, won the 5th through 7th rounds with it.

6 - Gardner drove Hart to his corner with body punches. Hart drove him back with a hard right to the head. Gardner rocked Hart with a right to the jaw, and Hart clinched and hit the body. Hart landed three hard blows to

the ear without a return. Hart was forcing the fight and had Gardner weak at the end. It was Hart's round.

7 - Hart was the aggressor, and he caught Gardner with a hard right to the nose. He landed another hard short-arm jolt to the nose. Gardner was tired. Gardner worked the body, but Hart was outpointing him with straight punching. Hart's left connected with the jaw hard. Hart stabbed Gardner with his left jab and uppercut him with his right.

8 - Gardner landed a left to the jaw and right to the stomach and Hart clinched. Hart stabbed the chin with his left and landed his right uppercut. A straight left to the chin rocked George. Gardner stabbed the mouth with his left and then swung a right to the jaw and they clinched. George again hit the stomach. Hart came back by landing right and left swings. Gardner clinched. They were at it furiously when the bell rang. The round was even.

9 - Hart landed a straight left and three rights to the jaw. Gardner clinched and went for the body. He was doing a lot of holding on and appeared tired. Hart landed a hard straight right to the jaw. Marvin seemed quicker in every mix-up, and his blows were more effective. It was easily Hart's round.

10 - They started off more tamely. Hart hit him with a straight left and right to the jaw. George landed a left to the nose which hurt. Gardner hooked a right to the jaw and drove Marvin to the ropes. Hart was back in a flash, though, and gave Gardner more than he sent. Hart was forcing the pace, while Gardner was weak. It was still all Hart, although neither man seemed to have the strength to score a decisive knockout at that point.

11 - Hart rushed and landed a hard right to the jaw. Gardner was stalling and working body punches. Hart landed a left jab. Gardner landed on the jaw with a hard left. Hart landed his right uppercut. Gardner smashed his right to the stomach. Hart returned with the same blow. Both worked the body until the bell. Both were tired. The round was even.

12 - Hart landed a right to the ear and a left uppercut. Gardner rushed and landed a right to the jaw. Hart came in with a fierce right uppercut, and then another while in a neutral corner. Hart smashed in a hard right to the mouth. Gardner ran into a left jab and Hart jabbed him again. Hart rushed him to the ropes and smashed in right and left uppercuts. Gardner drove him across the ring with two right swings, but did no damage. It was Hart's round.

13 - Hart landed his right to the jaw. George stabbed the face with the left and went to the body in the clinch. Then there was a furious mix-up, with honors even. In the next clinch, both fought for the body. Hart's uppercuts at close quarters seemed to worry Gardner. Hart twice stabbed with his left. Gardner drove him back and had the best of a fast bit of close work. The round was even.

14 - Hart went in viciously but Gardner clinched. Gardner landed both hands to the stomach. Hart landed hard left jab. They fought at a furious pace again. Gardner landed a hard left swing. Hart stopped his rush with a hard left to the nose. Hart got his left to the jaw. They went at it intensely. The round was the fastest of the bout, with Hart having the advantage.

15 - According to the *Boston Post*, Hart made his victory seem certain in the final two rounds. He carried the battle to Gardner. Both threw science to the winds in the last round and slugged, trying to knock the other man out. Both got in some telling work. Hart was better able to stand the gaff, and although he received heavy punishment, he sent back more than he got. When the round was half over, Gardner was all in, and his strength was gone. All he could do was lead wildly and fall into a clinch. Hart would get loose, rush in again and Gardner would again hang on. At the end of the round, Gardner was receiving such punishment that only the bell saved him. It was all Hart. The referee's draw decision was a big surprise, for most everyone thought Hart had won.[192]

The Boston Post said, "Referee Buckley's decision was not liked by the crowd, and it is fair to say that Hart should have had the decision, for he outpointed Gardner in nine of the 15 rounds, was even with him in four and Gardner had the advantage in only the first and third rounds."

It had been a fast and satisfactory bout. "Hart is the most willing boxer of the heavier men that has ever been seen in this city, and his style is always pleasing." Owing to the fact that Gardner had previously defeated him, Hart's showing was a surprise, and despite the fact that Gardner was well-known locally, as the bout progressed, Hart's advantage was so clear that the crowd was with him. "The decision was distinctly disappointing, and it is safe to say that nine out of ten of the members who saw the bout disagreed with it." The crowd and newsmen knew that Hart had won.

Although well known for his right, Hart's left hand had won the bout for him. "He landed it on Gardner's face so often that one could not keep count, and there was steam behind those jabs, too."

Marvin carried the battle to Gardner all the way. He was on top of him all the time, and Gardner was usually the one who clinched. In every mix-up, George closed in as soon as he could and played for the body at short range. This was about all he could do - push and hit the body.

Hart was not so defensive. He was willing to take one to land one. Still, Gardner landed cleanly very few times. At close quarters, Hart would uppercut Gardner, straightening him up and driving him back to the middle of the ring. He jabbed George at will.

---

192 *Boston Post, Boston Herald, Boston Globe,* January 6, 1904.

Although outclassed from beginning to end, Gardner showed some cleverness by eluding knockout blows, stalling cleverly, showing some effective work inside, and blocking fairly well, except for Marvin's left.

The Boston Daily Globe said that after suffering a knockdown in the 2nd round, thereafter, Gardner was much more cautious and defensive, and was fighting on nerve, not appearing to be the same. That said, he "fought a wonderful uphill battle."

> During the middle of the fight Gardner showed much of his anticipated cleverness, and he jolted and jabbed and hooked with his left in an amazing manner, but there was little steam behind the blows, and Hart's triphammer smashes easily offset the comparatively light counters of Gardner.

Gardner was "indeed a lucky fellow to earn a draw." Hart fought with confidence throughout. He depended upon his "wallop" and had a way of slipping in his right uppercut, which jarred Gardner every time it landed.

> The decision was not a particularly popular one, as many thought that Hart had a shade on the ex-champion…and while Hart did seem to show the most ability, generally speaking, it must be remembered that Gardner once had him tired and willing to hold at every opportunity.

The Boston Herald said that several times after the 10th round, Hart had Gardner "in a bad way, but George kept his left out straight or else jabbed. Both played for the body."

The Herald saw the last round differently than did the *Post*. Gardner swapped punches in the 15th and final round, and though he was hurt early in the round, George mixed it up in a fast round and got the better of it. "This alone probably saved him from having the decision given against him." Apparently, because he still fought well in the last round, the referee ruled it a draw.

Still, the *Herald* agreed that Gardner was lucky to get a draw, for he showed poorly, and just missed being knocked out after getting dropped. Gardner swung wildly, like a novice, and "reeled almost like a drunken man." George recovered slowly, and landed some stiff long lefts and rights, but then he tired badly, and relatively early on.

The crowd hissed the decision, and cheered Hart, the out-of-town boxer. It is saying something when a draw decision is deemed to benefit the local man and is booed by his own local crowd. It was generally conceded that Hart had won.

The Herald's perspective on how Hart fought was a bit different than one might think, for it said that he was not aggressive enough. Hart depended almost entirely on countering in the early rounds. After George jabbed, Marvin would throw right uppercuts and move in for a clinch. He also often landed right and left hooks to Gardner's body.

Had he gone to Gardner and swapped punches with him, it is doubtful if the bout would have gone the distance. Hart was easily the harder puncher and the steadier boxer. He made the grave mistake of allowing Gardner to set and jab. Here Gardner was good, for, with the advantage obtained by his tremendous reach, he simply jabbed Hart about the ring as he pleased, at times, and rushed the Kentucky boxer to the ropes repeatedly with straight left jabs to the face and right crosses to the head and body.

Once on the ropes, Gardner beat Hart heavily about the body in the early rounds, but when he tired after half the contest had gone he grew so weak from his own exertions and wild swinging that his punches had almost no effect on the healthy southerner.

Back home, the *Louisville Times* reported that nearly every man in the crowd thought that Hart should have been given the decision and that the audience and Hart vigorously protested. Hart had Gardner almost out on several occasions, but George managed to survive by clinching. Hart was able to elude his jabs with his crouch, and what blows George did land lacked steam and did little damage.[193]

Hart later gave his own version of the fight, claiming that he was robbed of the decision.

> The decision in my fight with George Gardner was a clear steal. I beat him easily, knocking him down repeatedly, and had him all but out several times. The referee seemed to be a Gardner man, as in the clinches he continually put his weight on me and was always wrestling me away, while Gardner was getting a chance to steady himself and rest a bit. I must concede that Gardner is a good man, but I think I am his master.[194]

He was also quoted as saying, "When I fought Gardner I used a crouch on him. He stung in his left and I came up under it and met him. I hit him once and he went to the floor like a log, only his head hit the lower rope and that threw him forward."[195]

Because Hart was considered to have had the better of the fight, the draw did not hurt him, but rather served to erase the previous retirement loss to Gardner. Marvin was boosted by a de facto victory over the former world champion.

The Louisville press said that champion Bob Fitzsimmons was all that stood between Hart and the championship, and that Hart would have a great chance against Bob, who had aged a great deal.[196]

---

193 *Louisville Times*, January 6, 1904.
194 *Chicago Tribune*, January 25, 1904.
195 *Chicago Daily News*, January 25, 1904.
196 *Louisville Times*, January 7, 1904.

Speaking of decisions, one writer at that time complimented top referee George Siler for his perspective in rendering decisions, of which more of today's judges should take note:

> He does not stand for slapping, which is nothing else than a whack with the open glove. This is not fighting, but merely a trick. It is easier to land this way than with the glove closed. Lots of fighters indulge in these tactics, and although they score continually they are not declared the winner, at least by Siler. To the average spectator such methods may be legitimate.... He is not the winner by any means, but a lot of referees are easily fooled and base points on just such tactics.[197]

Marvin Hart was no slapper. As will be seen in several future close bouts, Hart's propensity to attack and land crisp shots with the weight of his body behind them helped Marvin when it came to referee decisions.

---

[197] *Chicago Tribune*, January 24, 1904.

CHAPTER 9

Hanging With the Heavyweights

Just twenty days after the Gardner bout, on January 25, 1904 in Chicago, Marvin Hart took on Chicago's John Willie in a 6 rounder. Willie was a local Chicago heavyweight. He was husky, tough, strong, and hit hard enough to make a fight of it against anyone, but was not considered to be in Hart's class.[198] That said, he did have some good experience, which included: 1901 W6 Jack Beausholte and L20 Al Weinig; 1902 W6 Jimmy Handler, D20 Weinig, D6 Billy Stift, W6 Weinig, and W6 Young Peter Jackson; and 1903 L15 Kid Carter, LKOby4 Tommy Ryan, and another W6 Jackson.[199]

Hart felt better than ever. He said that he was weighing 180 pounds, but some thought he was closer to 190. "His square, muscular figure is devoid of superfluous fat." His hands were in good shape. "I have my punch stronger than ever and really believe I am twice as clever as I used to be. At any rate they are not hitting me as often." Marvin was in town with his wife Florence, as was manager Jack McCormick.[200]

Hart had come from Philadelphia, where the previous evening he was going to box, but the club had been unable to find a suitable opponent. Hart said that he had not boxed there because "the club could not find a white man to meet me. I do know that colored men are on the fighting map. There are plenty of them around there about my weight but I wouldn't dare go back to Louisville if ever I got in the ring with one of them."[201] Hart drew the color line, fearing that he would be ostracized back home if he crossed the line.

---

198 *Chicago Tribune*, January 24, 1904.
199 Boxrec.com.
200 *Chicago Tribune, Chicago Herald, Daily Inter Ocean*, January 25, 1904.
201 *Chicago Chronicle*, January 25, 1904.

Hart had been tentatively scheduled to meet Fitzsimmons in Boston on February 22, but the authorities had closed down the fight game there, so the fight was off. Marvin thought he had a good chance to defeat Bob.

A local paper said that the last time Hart was in Chicago; he had made a strong fight with Root but lost by a narrow margin. "Hart and Root would make an attraction worth going nine miles on hands and knees through the snow to see." Since then, Marvin had been making a great name for himself against some of the toughest men in the light heavyweight division.[202]

Willie intended to belt Marvin in the midriff. He was in good shape, having been training steadily for three weeks. Marvin said he did not know anything about Willie.

The bout took place at the Watita League Club. Abe Pollock refereed. Hart looked to be 15 pounds heavier than the local man, but there was no official weigh-in.

1 - Hart forced the fighting. Willie seemed nervous, and paid particular attention to his defense, blocking and clinching at every opportunity. Hart rushed, using straight lefts to the face and attempting a right cross to the jaw, but with little effect.

Willie momentarily opened up and hit Hart with a right that sent him to the ropes. He also hit Hart with a left and right that staggered him. Marvin evened matters up with several right uppercuts to the body. The rest of the round was a series of clinches and roughing in close quarters, where Hart was superior.

2 - They would lead, clinch, pull and maul. Both violated the rules - Hart with his forearm and Willie with his head and shoulders. Willie scored the greater number and cleaner blows, but neither did very much good work. Hart's uppercuts caused Willie's mouth to bleed.

3 - Willie gained confidence and began mixing it up, hitting the body with both hands, which slowed Hart up a little. John hit low once and drew a caution. Hart kept trying for the jaw, and although he landed several stiff rights to the head, they landed too high to hurt Willie to any great extent. Hart mostly missed his punches to the head, so he switched his focus and went to the body with his right uppercuts. Willie had the better of the round.

4 - Hart was stronger, landing solid uppercuts on the breakaways, one of which landed on the nose and mouth, drawing blood from Willie's mouth. Marvin made up some lost ground. Willie mostly slipped and ducked, and occasionally landed a left or right lead to the head.

The Daily Inter Ocean said the 4th and 5th rounds were fairly even.

---

202 *Chicago Herald*, January 23, 1904; *Chicago Daily Inter Ocean*, January 24, 1904.

5 - This round was similar to the others, with Hart attempting a knockout and Willie content to sneak in an occasional blow when there was an opening. There was also the usual cinching and rough-house work, making the contest less than satisfactory.

6 - Both started with vim, and a couple quick rallies ensued. Willie hooked Hart on the jaw with his left and smashed hard on the body with his right. Hart kept rushing, landing rights and lefts to the head in quick succession. Willie kept at the body. There was a lot of rough work in the clinches, both hugging continually. Willie scored several times in the breakaway, but Hart had much the better of matters at long range, owing to his superior reach. Although Hart's nose bled, aside from this, practically no damage was done and both finished the bout almost unmarked.

The referee declared it a 6-round draw.

The Daily Inter Ocean said there was little to choose between the pair at the finish, but felt that perhaps the local man Willie had a slight shade on points. "The general opinion was that had the local man not been afraid to lead at the beginning of the bout he would have secured the decision."

The Chicago Record-Herald said Hart and Willie swung and clinched their way through 6 unsatisfactory and slow rounds to a draw. Both were heavy and awkward. It said Hart had a little the better of Willie in the clinches, but on clean blows, the shade was with the comparatively unknown local boxer. The crowd was with Willie and cheered his efforts, but most critics agreed with referee Abe Pollock's decision of a draw.

George Siler, writing for the *Chicago Tribune*, was critical of Hart, saying he had failed to show improvement. It was an unsatisfactory bout from either a scientific or a slugging standpoint. It was a continual hit-and-clinch performance, with rough and at times illegal work in the clinches. Willie was the cleverer and his leads more accurate and effective. His defensive work was better as well. Hart was wild and missed many times. His best punch was a right uppercut to the body, which in conjunction with his aggressiveness and short-arm work in the clinches secured for him the draw.

The Chicago Daily News called it a poor showing by Hart. "The fight was slow, neither landing more than two effective blows in each round, and clinching was frequent."

The Chicago Chronicle said Willie could have won if he had done more leading, but he seemed afraid and kept out of reach. Although Willie landed many blows, he did not land with much effect. Hart did not land very effectively either. It said the draw decision was well received but that many were of the opinion that Willie, the local man, had won.[203]

---

203 *Daily Inter Ocean, Chicago Record-Herald, Chicago Tribune, Chicago Daily News, Chicago Chronicle*, January 26, 1904.

The Police Gazette said Hart received a setback with the draw against a second-rater whom Marvin outweighed by 15 pounds. It was a poor fight with few clean blows landed and mostly holding, wrestling and mauling in the clinches.[204]

John Willie had graduated from the wrestling world and moved into boxing. He had used his knowledge of the former to keep the bout tame. Given that Marvin Hart was usually in good, exciting bouts, it was likely more Willie's fault than Hart's for the bout being boring. Hart and Willie would eventually meet again.

On March 16, 1904 at the Whittington Park Athletic Club in Hot Springs, Arkansas, Marvin Hart took on John "Sandy" Ferguson, a true heavyweight, the largest opponent of Marvin's career. Ferguson was a big, tough, durable, and experienced white boxer who was willing to take on the best black and white fighters. He stood 6'3" and typically weighed around 220 pounds. Ferguson had been a Fitzsimmons sparring partner in 1901.[205] His recent pro record included: 1902 KO3 Yank Kenny and LKOby5 Denver Ed Martin; and 1903 D8 George Byers,[206] KO4 Dick O'Brien, W12 Byers, L10 Jack Johnson, KO6 Dick O'Brien, D15 Gus Ruhlin,[207] ND6 Jack Johnson, KO1 Bob Armstrong, W15 Joe Walcott, L20 Jack Johnson, W6 John "Klondike" Haines,[208] and February 6, 1904 ND6 Jack Johnson.

(Photo by Chickering.)
SANDY FERGUSON.

Victories over Bob Armstrong, George Byers, Joe Walcott, and Klondike Haines, and a close and competitive draw with Gus Ruhlin proved that Sandy Ferguson was a top fighter and a tough test. Tim McGrath said he had seen Ferguson "play with 500 pound iron dumb-bells as if they were so much wood." Ferguson had gone the distance with Jack Johnson on several occasions, and their bouts were competitive. He had even managed to drop Johnson in the 7th round of their 20-round bout. It

---

204 *Police Gazette*, February 13, 1904.
205 *National Police Gazette*, June 15, 1901.
206 It was a draw per agreement because there was no knockout. It was a poor and unsatisfactory contest, but Byers seemed to have the better of it. *National Police Gazette*, February 21, 1903.
207 The clever Ferguson appeared to have outpointed Ruhlin, but he was not as aggressive. *Police Gazette*, June 13, 1903.
208 It was a miserable bout and Ferguson defeated Haines through sheer weight and strength, demonstrating little cleverness. *Police Gazette*, January 16, 1904.

was said that "Ferguson's awkwardness bothered the negro." Ferguson knew a few things about boxing.[209]

Hart weighed in at 185 pounds to Ferguson's 197, which was very svelte for Sandy, proving he was in top shape. Hart was either a 1 to 2 or 7 to 10 betting favorite, depending on the source. The bout was scheduled for 20 rounds. The local and national round-by-round reports were relatively sparse, poor, and inconsistent, with contradictory reports regarding knockdowns, but here is an amalgamation.

1 - Even round.

2 - *The Louisville Times* said a hard swing dropped Marvin for a five-count. Hart rose and rushed Sandy, and as they were both swinging simultaneously, both went to the floor, and then quickly rose. They were eagerly trying to finish each other. Most other accounts did not mention any knockdowns in the 2nd round. *The Louisville Courier-Journal* said a stomach blow made Ferguson weak at the end.

3 - This was a repetition of the first two rounds. Both were groggy at times. Hart slipped and took a count.

4 - According to the *Louisville Courier-Journal*, Hart hit Ferguson twice on the jaw, making him groggy, but Ferguson rallied and a left swing to the jaw dropped Marvin. Some reports noted this knockdown, while others did not.

5 - They mixed it up.

6 - Both exchanged hard blows, Sandy getting the best of it, with Hart appearing groggy. After Hart landed a right to the ribs, Ferguson said, "You're trying to make me quit."

---

[209] *Police Gazette*, September 19, 26, 1903, December 26, 1903. One unconfirmed report said Jack Munroe had defeated Ferguson. *Louisville Evening Post*, March 16, 1904.

7 - Ferguson landed many jabs and in a fierce mix-up sent Hart to the floor with a vicious right. Hart was down for 7 seconds. Some reports mentioned this knockdown, while others did not. Ferguson was unable to follow up his advantage.

After that, for the rest of the fight, the landing was fairly even, except that Hart was the aggressor. Hart fought fiercely and landed many telling kidney blows, face and head swings, and uppercuts. Ferguson boxed mostly from the outside, landing many jabs.

12 - Sandy broke through Hart's guard and forced him to the ropes and landed a hard right to the jaw, but failed to follow up the advantage. Marvin landed a left to the jaw and right to the kidney that hurt Ferguson. Marvin was not able to finish him, though.

13 - Hart landed a couple of hard punches to the jaw and followed up with a hard right to the kidneys that hurt Ferguson.

14 - Another right caused Marvin to fall against the ropes, and he then went into a clinch and was saved by the bell.

In subsequent rounds, Ferguson met Hart's rushes by keeping his jab in his face. This caused Marvin's nose to bleed. Ferguson "engaged in a kidding match with the spectators throughout the entire fight." However, Marvin kept up the pace, throwing vicious punches throughout.

20 - Hart attacked like a mad bull and forced Ferguson back, landing some hard swings. Both were exhausted by the end of the round. Hart was more damaged, having a discolored eye and puffed lip. Ferguson was unmarked.

The Louisville Courier-Journal said, "Referee Early was at sea for a few minutes as to who should be given the honor of winning the contest, but finally decided in favor of Hart. This was a signal for many of the admirers of Sandy to hiss."

Although the referee awarded Hart the 20-round decision, most thought that Ferguson at least earned a draw, and some thought that Sandy had won the bout.

Ferguson was heavier and had the longer reach, which he used to his advantage, but the difference in styles aided Hart in the decision, because Sandy laid back and countered more at long range, mostly using his jab, whereas Hart made the fight and attacked with vicious blows, which might have given him the edge with the referee. *The Courier-Journal* said Hart did all of the leading and was the fresher of the two at the end.

The Louisville Evening Post said Hart was the stronger of the two at the finish. Marvin had done the leading and was the aggressor throughout, but Ferguson's effective left had drawn the blood from Hart's face. Hart was dropped for 7 seconds in the 7th round. However, Marvin punished Sandy severely throughout the bout, although he was not able to shake him.

Ferguson was able to assimilate Marvin's powerful right, which seemingly had enough steam to crush bones. They had fought on such even terms that Referee Early hesitated before awarding Hart the decision. When the decision was announced, there were hisses and jeers. "The general opinion seemed to be, according to the dispatches, that the bout should have been declared a draw."

> Ferguson was alone deprived of the decision by his allowing Hart to be the aggressor. He fought with fully as much skill, his footwork was superb, and both in his offensive and defensive work he showed his admirers that when he beat Joe Walcott that it was no chance victory.[210]

The Louisville Times also reported that many thought it should have been a draw. Ferguson was described as a fighter with a stiff punch and the ability to withstand punishment. Its "special from Hot Springs" said Ferguson had an enormous height and reach advantage and was about 15 pounds heavier. Ferguson clearly won the early rounds. They alternated between boxing and occasional exchanges of swings. Referee Pat Early "based his decision on the fact that Hart was at all times the aggressor and did nearly all the leading in the last eleven rounds."

The Little Rock Arkansas Gazette said, "Ferguson had the better of the contest in the early rounds and was still in good condition toward the close. The decision did not meet general approval." *The New York Herald* reported that the 20-round decision for Hart was "vigorously hissed, many of the spectators believing that Ferguson had won."

The New York Journal reported that the referee did Ferguson an injustice when he awarded Hart the decision. Ferguson clearly outclassed Hart and had him on Queer Street several times.

Up to the 7th round, the fight was even. Hart had done most of the leading and had landed more often than Ferguson, but had received some telling smashes.

In the 8th, Hart landed a hard right to the body and Ferguson countered with a left to the jaw and Hart went down. He got to his knee and listened to the count. He rose at seven. Hart immediately rushed at Ferguson. Sandy grew wild and missed as Marvin moved his head. Hart fought well thereafter, and they fought evenly until the 12th round, when Hart was in trouble again, but saved by the gong.

However, in the 13th round, Hart administered the punishment, and he had Ferguson in trouble and staggering, but Marvin could not finish him. From then on it was a back and forth battle.

Ferguson's weakness was his inability to follow-up advantages. Hart forced the pace throughout, and it was on this ground that he won the

---

210 *Louisville Evening Post*, March 17, 1904.

decision. He landed a number of telling blows, but only had Ferguson in trouble once, in the 13th round.

The spectators thought Ferguson had won. "Had the referee announced the affair a draw the chances are everyone would have been satisfied."

The Chicago Tribune said,

> The decision was questioned by many, who seemed to think Ferguson at least deserved a draw. All the way through the battle Hart forced the fighting, but several times Ferguson had him groggy. His use of his left in jabbing the face worried Hart, but the Louisville man fought back gamely, even when smashed the hardest. If Ferguson could have used his right more effectively the story would probably have been different. Hart was bested several rounds, but in the latter part of the bout he fought fiercely, landing many kidney and body blows, with not a few face and head jabs and swings.[211]

The Chicago Daily News reported that Hart was the aggressor throughout, landing on the jaw and body several times without a return, but some spectators thought Ferguson should have had a draw because he dropped Hart in the 4th round and brought blood in the 7th. However, from that point on, Hart forced the fighting.

The Police Gazette said that the referee by awarding Hart the 20-round decision did Ferguson an injustice. He outclassed Hart as a boxer, hit where and when he pleased, and several times had Marvin hurt. Hart landed a number of telling blows throughout the fight, but only had Ferguson in trouble in the 12th round.[212]

As was the case throughout Hart's career, and as will be seen in at least one very significant future fight, aggressiveness and leading counted a great deal in the scoring of bouts. Those who made the fight and took risks were given a bonus/edge in the scoring because they were the ones who generated the action. If both fighters were cautious and laid back, waiting for their opponent to lead or step forward, there would not be much of a fight. Hence, the risk-taker got the edge. Plus, the thinking was that if you are the better fighter, then you should not be afraid to lead and be aggressive. This scoring method served Hart, an extremely aggressive fighter, very well.

Despite having just been in a tough 20-round bout, the typically active Hart was right back in the ring again just a month later against the "Akron Giant," Gus Ruhlin, who was another big name heavyweight contender. Once again, Hart would be fighting a larger man. Ruhlin at his best typically weighed 200-210 pounds. Against James J. Jeffries in 1897, Ruhlin had

---

211 *Chicago Tribune*, March 17, 1904.
212 *Louisville Courier-Journal, Little Rock Arkansas Gazette, Louisville Times, Chicago Daily News, New York Journal*, March 17, 1904; *New York Herald*, March 18, 1904; *Police Gazette*, April 2, 1904.

fought a 20-round draw. Ruhlin's more recent results included 1900 KO4 Jack Finnegan, KO15 Tom Sharkey, and LKOby6 Bob Fitzsimmons; 1901 LKOby5 Jeffries (world heavyweight title); 1902 KO2 Peter Maher and KO11 Sharkey, and 1903 D15 Sandy Ferguson and W6 Kid Carter.[213] Gus had also been a Corbett sparring partner. Ruhlin had experience with two former heavyweight champions, the current champion, and had twice knocked out the next toughest customer out there in Tom Sharkey. This made him a real threat and test for Hart.

On April 20, 1904, Marvin Hart fought Gus Ruhlin in a 6-round no-decision bout in Philadelphia at the National Athletic Club. They agreed to box until ordered to break, and to step back without hitting while breaking away. Hart looked small next to Ruhlin, and the crowd was on his side.

1 - Hart opened with a couple rib roasters. Ruhlin landed a light left to the face. *The Philadelphia Press* said Hart did nearly all the work, but except for a hard right to the body, the blows had little steam behind them. Ruhlin scarcely landed a punch. *The Philadelphia Record* said the round was pretty even, neither man doing much damage.

GUS RUHLIN.

2 - Hart missed the head but landed terrific right swings to the ribs. Ruhlin was kept busy trying to defend his body. Gus occasionally landed a jab, but his rights missed. Ruhlin jabbed several times, and in a few mix-ups, landed to the head and body, but the blows were not well timed. At the end of the round, Ruhlin walked back to his corner looking rather tired. One said Marvin had the better of the round, while another said both did good work.

3 - Both continued the same tactics, except that Hart at times varied his right swings for the ribs by sending in his left to the nose and mouth. Hart landed hard to the body. Gus got in a stiff facer. There were two or three spirited exchanges, with both landing left and right. However, this round was also in Marvin's favor.

The Philadelphia Public Leger said that for the first 3 rounds, Hart hit Ruhlin's body, while Ruhlin mostly clinched.

4 - This round was marked by fast fighting. Hart was out to finish him and nearly succeeded. Marvin drew blood from Ruhlin's nose with a jab and right uppercut. Hart followed this with a straight left to the face. Both

---

213 Boxrec.com.

landed rights to the jaw. Hart feinted with his left and drew Ruhlin on. Marvin smashed his right to the jaw, staggering Gus.

A hard mix-up followed, when Hart dropped Ruhlin with a short right on the jaw. Ruhlin was groggy upon rising at the count of nine. When Hart went in to finish, he was so wild that he missed badly. Hart was too anxious to finish, throwing at random, instead of taking his time and trying to measure his man. Gus hugged to survive.

One punch did catch Ruhlin on the side of the head and he reeled from it, but he managed to clinch. Hart also staggered Ruhlin with a left uppercut to the mouth. Gus fought back hard, but most of his blows were wild. Eventually, Ruhlin improved and landed a couple hard stinging facers. Ruhlin ended the round with a bleeding nose and nasty abrasion over his left eye. *The Record* said this was a disastrous round for Ruhlin.

5 - Hart opened the round with two hard rights to the ribs. However, Hart let up a bit, and allowed Gus to make up lost ground. Gus landed nearly all his blows, but they were so light that no damage resulted. Hart worked the body. There was a great deal of clinching as well. Gus landed two left jabs that sent Marvin's head back. The only significant punches Ruhlin landed were two or three straight lefts to the face and one left swing to the mouth. Hart landed hard, driving Ruhlin back, and Gus seemed bewildered, turning around and looking back at his corner. Marvin kept up his body attack. Ruhlin used some good jabbing before the round ended. *The Public Ledger* said the round was even.

6 - Ruhlin attempted a strong finish, but his blows did no damage. Also, Hart was as good as Ruhlin at evading blows, and fought back in a vicious manner, which caused Ruhlin to back up. Ruhlin landed his straight left a couple times, but other than knocking Marvin's head back a bit, the jabs had no visible discouraging effect.

Hart rushed in as if to finish him, but was wild and missed. A little while later, he landed a couple stingers which made Ruhlin run away. Several hard exchanges followed, each landing. They clinched, and after breaking, Ruhlin landed hard to the face. Marvin came back and forced the fighting. He would not be denied, and during the last minute, he had Gus holding repeatedly.[214]

Hart was cheered at the end, while the fans hissed Ruhlin as he left. An unofficial victory over Gus Ruhlin served to further boost Hart's reputation.

The local *Philadelphia Public Ledger* said Ruhlin was "practically outclassed" despite advantages in height, reach, and weight. Hart was the aggressor in 4 of the 6 rounds. Apparently, Marvin had an injured left hand,

---

[214] *Philadelphia Record, Philadelphia Public Ledger, Philadelphia Press, Philadelphia Inquirer*, April 21, 1904.

and primarily used it to feint, doing most of his leading and countering with his right.

The Philadelphia Record said Hart had won the hard 6-round bout that was full of action all the way. Hart's left was not of much use, and he rarely threw it. Most of his left hooks went around Ruhlin's head. However, Hart did most effective work with his right, landing to the body and ribs quite often, and some of the blows hurt. He missed many rights for the jaw, but one that landed plumb on the jaw in the 4th round sent Ruhlin down for a nine-count. Gus was groggy and in bad shape upon rising, but managed to avoid the finishing blow. Ruhlin had the physical advantages, but that did not matter, because he did not properly use them.

The Philadelphia Inquirer said Ruhlin "never figured seriously in the milling." The popular verdict went to Hart. Ruhlin was simply not willing to mix it up, "clinching at the slightest excuse, and once Hart, with arms high in the air, carried his bulkier opponent about the ring." Except for a brief time in the 5th, Gus never took the initiative, and mostly stalled. "In the fifth and sixth rounds Ruhlin was clearly out of it." Ruhlin's punches were more like pushes in these rounds. He was "given a roast by the spectators." *The Inquirer* was critical of Hart as well. "Hart himself did not show the form that was expected of him. His eye for distance was noticeably bad." Marvin's best punches were to the body.

The Philadelphia Press said Hart had slightly the better of Ruhlin. During the early rounds Hart displayed his superiority over the big heavyweight, and in the 4th round had Ruhlin nearly out. It was a lively round, the only one of the bout that the large crowd of spectators truly enjoyed. However, Hart failed to follow up in the 5th and Gus recovered from the punishment. Ruhlin became aggressive in the last 2 rounds, but he was too slow. He landed a majority of his blows in the 5th and nearly all of them in the 6th, but they had no sting, and only one or two had any effect on Hart.

GUS RUHLIN.

Hart was scheduled to fight Kid McCoy in a few weeks, and the Kid was at ringside for the Ruhlin bout. For whatever reason, the McCoy fight did not materialize. Perhaps McCoy did not want to fight another fighter like Tom Sharkey, who had knocked him out.

His reputation having taken a hit by the Hart bout, Ruhlin wanted a rematch, and Hart was willing.

Exactly one month from their previous bout, on May 20, 1904 at Baltimore's Eureka Athletic and Social Club at the Germania Maennerchor Hall, Hart and Ruhlin fought a rematch scheduled for 12 rounds. The larger Ruhlin was listed as being 15 to 20 pounds heavier and about 10 years older. In Hart's corner were Jack McCormick, Kid Howard and Jim Donnell. Ruhlin had manager Billy Madden and Jake Kilrain.

The local *Baltimore Sun* provided its take on matters. They mixed it up from the beginning, with Hart being the more aggressive and quicker, having a shade the best of it in the first 2 rounds. Ruhlin stopped Hart's rushes with jabs that kept things relatively even.

Ruhlin became aggressive in the 3rd round, cutting Hart with a left that landed below the right eye. The cut was deep and partly crossed the nose. Hart was dazed and the blood blinded him. Marvin managed to survive the round, as well as the 4th round, by clinching often. "Hart bled like a stuck pig." Marvin began fighting desperately. Ruhlin tried to finish, but Hart shot out right and left blows to the head that sent Gus staggering back.

For the remainder of the bout, Hart was handicapped by the cut under the eye. Regardless of the cut, Hart was the more aggressive fighter in this fierce bout. He "fought like a fiend in spite of the blood that poured from a cut just below his right eye."

From the 5th to the 8th rounds, Ruhlin would manage to reopen the cut, but whenever it looked like it was over for Marvin, Hart would fight like a tiger, landing again and again, beating Gus back.

In the 7th round, a Hart jab dropped Ruhlin. Gus quickly rose and attacked like a mad bull. They fought hard in the clinches.

Before the 9th round began, Hart had a messenger announce to the crowd that although he looked bloody, he was as strong as ever and not seriously hurt. Marvin wanted it to be known that appearances could be deceptive.

Regardless, Hart seemed a bit weakened from the 10th to the 12th rounds from the loss of so much blood. However, the fast pace also told on Ruhlin, who was fatigued. Ultimately though, the fight finished with both fighting hard and seeming as if they could keep it up for many more rounds. Referee Eckhardt's decision of a draw was considered satisfactory.[215]

---

215 *Baltimore Sun*, May 21, 1904.

The Baltimore Morning Herald said it was a fierce battle in which the honors were even, for both boxers were fresh at the end. "While the decision gave general satisfaction to the crowd which packed Germania Maennerchor Hall, it appeared to many of the old devotees of the prize ring that Ruhlin had a shade the best of it. He came out of the bout apparently without a mark, while Hart was cut up considerably about the face." Although Ruhlin tried for a knockout, "Hart blocked and ducked the powerful blows of Ruhlin, and for his cleverness was loudly applauded." It said that Marvin's blows had little effect on Ruhlin.[216]

Ruhlin had put up a much better fight than in their previous encounter. *The National Police Gazette* called it a "hurricane battle from start to finish, with Hart the originator of all the fast work." From the beginning, Hart rushed in and threw right swings to the head and an occasional uppercut. Ruhlin landed a number of hard punches to the body and head. The infighting in the 4th round was fierce, when Gus landed a right that cut Marvin's nose. Rounds 5-7 were fast but even. By the 11th, both were a bit fatigued. Ruhlin pushed Hart over the ropes, causing the spectators to cry foul. Hart fought back hard and landed well. In the 12th, Gus landed a left, but Hart countered with a right that dropped Ruhlin. After Marvin missed two right uppercuts, Gus staggered him with a left. Both were fighting in close at the conclusion. The referee's decision of a draw was met with cheers.[217]

Newspapers across the nation reported that it was the most vicious, fiercest, bloodiest, and hardest fought battle ever to take place in Baltimore. It was a slam-bang affair from start to finish, and the 3,000 spectators shouted themselves hoarse. Ruhlin was 20 pounds heavier that Hart, but nevertheless Hart forced the fighting throughout. In the 3rd round, Marvin's face was badly split between the nose and left eye. Ruhlin's left eye also received an ugly cut. They fought like bulldogs all the way, and the ring looked like a butcher shop. Both were strong at the finish. Referee Eckhardt's 12-round draw decision met with spectator approval.[218]

The New York Journal reported that Hart was cut over the left eye in the 3rd round by an uppercut, and the claret flowed freely and annoyed Hart. However, it did not deter him from forcing the fight. The aggressive Hart went after Gus like a mad bull from the start of each round. Gus, however, used his skill to protect himself from the rushes. Both men slugged, and it was a hammer and tongs argument until the end of the bout.

In the 9th round, the club's manager became scared, owing to Hart's bloody appearance, and was about to stop the bout. However, Hart beseeched him to allow the contest to continue, and assured him that it was only a trivial injury of no material consequence.

---

216 *Baltimore Morning Herald*, May 21, 1904.
217 *Police Gazette*, June 4, 1904.
218 *Chicago Tribune, New York Herald, New York World, Louisville Courier-Journal*, May 21, 1904.

When the contest ended, Ruhlin was unmarked, while Hart's face was cut up. However, Marvin appeared to be in good shape and said he could have gone 20 rounds.

Many said it was the best fight ever seen there. The spectators were loud in their praises. "It proved that Hart is one of the gamest men in the ring and glories in being cut up. Blood streaming down his face only makes him fight harder." The bout also proved that Ruhlin was not a short rounds fighter because he was not aggressive enough; preferring to use cleverness, jabbing, and a careful defense, punching only when he has a man sized up and can avoid being hit.[219]

Hart was given credit for his two performances against a top heavyweight. In late June 1904, the *Police Gazette* contained a full page photo of Hart with a caption that said, "Sturdy Light Heavyweight Boxer Who Recently Surprised the Fistic World By His Battle with Ruhlin and Who Will Probably Meet Fitzsimmons."[220]

Hart had become more confident and ambitious, saying that he wanted to fight anybody, including heavyweights, but Jack Munroe in particular. He saw Munroe defeat Peter Maher and thought the victory was a fluke. Marvin was no longer excepting champion Jeffries from his list of possible opponents. "If Jeffries is never able to fight again I think I will claim the heavyweight championship and defend it....If Jeffries recovers and defeats Munroe I will tackle him. I want to fight."

Hart was anxious for a match with Fitzsimmons, but claimed that Bob passed him up for a match with Jack O'Brien. He also said that O'Brien wanted no part of him. "O'Brien refused to fight me any more. I came near putting him away on two occasions. He claims now that I am too heavy and out of his class."[221]

Bob Fitzsimmons scheduled a 6-round no-decision bout with Philadelphia Jack O'Brien, set to take place at the Philadelphia Ball Park on July 8, 1904. "With the possible exception of Tommy Ryan, Fitzsimmons is the greatest general that ever stepped into the ring. His capacity to give and to take punishment has been the wonder of ring followers for the past thirteen years. In mental alertness and quickness to take advantage of openings he never had an equal in the ring."

However, O'Brien was said to be the cleverest matchmaker in the business. He knew that Fitz had gone back, and it was doubtful if he would have matched himself with Fitz unless he knew Bob's hands were weak. He saw Bob box Gardner, and felt convinced that he had a good chance with him. In fact, O'Brien had then said that Gardner allowed Bob to bluff and stall, using his foxiness to keep a comfortable pace, and that a faster pace would have worn out the elder Fitzsimmons. He noted that Bob was

---

[219] *New York Journal*, May 21, 1904.
[220] *Police Gazette*, June 25, 1904.
[221] *Police Gazette*, July 9, 1904.

slower, and no longer able to finish a man. "Poor old Bob. He fought a brainy fight, but he is not the man of old." Jack thought Bob should retire. O'Brien was something of a Corbett – a clever, quick-footed scientific boxer. Hence, he would have the advantage of youth and quickness, particularly against a boxer who had been sapped of some of his vigor by Father Time. Fitz had not fought since his late November 1903 victory over Gardner.[222]

Unfortunately, as often happened when it came to popular fighters, politics got in the way. Clergymen appealed to the mayor to stop the bout. Talk and advertisements used to hype the fight said that Fitz was going to attempt to knock out O'Brien, and that the bout was for the light-heavyweight championship. Arguments were propounded that it would not be a boxing exhibition but a brutal prizefight. Although the mayor initially declined to do anything, holding that 6-round exhibitions without a decision were legal, he eventually gave in and decided that the bout could not proceed.[223]

As of November 1903, it was reported that since 1758, only 124 pugilists had died from injuries sustained as a result of boxing. Yet, legal impediments and political and police interference continually hovered over the sport.[224]

The Fitzsimmons-O'Brien promoters took the matter to court. They eventually convinced a judge that the bout was to be a scientific affair, with no violence or brutality. The judge said the police could be present, and could stop the bout as soon as it developed into a prize fight. Hence, the bout was on again, though with a new date. All of this was a joke, of course, because there had been scores of brutal 6-round no-decision matches held in Philadelphia, but famous fighters and fights had a way of causing politics and the law to inject themselves into these bouts.

The promoters were criticized to a certain degree by hyping the bout too much, mentioning that Fitz was seeking a knockout. Giving it too much publicity, as well as the type of publicity they used, got the attention of the anti-boxing folks. "They killed the bout by the character of publicity which they gave it. … They wanted to thrill the public. With that end in view they caused to be printed statements which they admitted were only figments of a press agent's robust imagination." Softer talk got the bout to be rescheduled with legal approval, although under the watchful eye of the police.[225]

On the afternoon of July 23, 1904, eight months after he won the light-heavyweight championship, Bob Fitzsimmons fought Jack O'Brien in a 6-round no-decision bout. The ring was pitched over the home plate at

---

222 *Philadelphia Inquirer*, July 8, 1904; *San Francisco Bulletin*, November 26, 1903.
223 *Philadelphia Inquirer*, July 9, 1904;
224 *San Francisco Bulletin*, November 4, 1903.
225 *Philadelphia Inquirer*, July 16, 1904.

Philadelphia Ball Park, located at Broad and Huntingdon Streets. The bleachers were nearly filled, and some watched from the lower and upper decks of the cantilever. Some paid $5 for seats placed between the ring and the cantilever, and those were nearly filled. It was the first big affair in Philly held in the daylight. There were over 6,500 men and 83 women present. Another said there were over 7,000 men with 50 women present. 150 police officers were on the scene.

Fitz entered first. He wore a pair of sky blue tights held up by an American flag belt. O'Brien entered the ring at 5:18 p.m. He wore green tights and a light bath robe.

Fitz's hands were bandaged with white tape. Jack examined Bob's hand bandages and objected to them. Upon close inspection, O'Brien discovered something under the tape. Fitz declared that was merely soft plaster to keep the tape in position. O'Brien was not convinced, and maintained that they were hard as iron. He wanted Bob to remove the wrapping and to rewrap his hands. This Bob and his seconds tried to do, but the wraps had been put on to stay and would not yield. Finally, O'Brien offered to permit Fitz to keep the bandages on if he would cover them with more tape. O'Brien had no bandages, but tape, which he offered to lend to Fitzsimmons. Bob agreed to this.

Referee Ernest Crowhurst called the men to the ring center and instructed them that they were to box with no hitting on the breakaway. Technically, Philadelphia rules required the principals to box until ordered to break, and then to break clean. This fact was announced to the crowd. Fitz then said, "We can hit with one hand free." The announcer said, "Oh, yes." Fitz replied, "Then tell the people so." However, the announcer did not comply. Fitz wanted the crowd to understand that hitting in the clinches would be allowed, so that they would not turn against him if he did so, which in some instances, was considered foul.

Two sets of gloves were thrown into the ring – one pair green, and one yellow. O'Brien selected the yellow gloves. Fitz took the green, which went well with his red hair. One said O'Brien appeared to be the heavier man. Another estimated that Fitz weighed 174 pounds to O'Brien's 159. However, there was no public weigh-in, so no one knew for sure.

1 - O'Brien circled all around the ring, demonstrating his elusiveness. He landed his left jab flush on Fitz's mouth. Bob landed on Jack's body as the latter was retreating, and O'Brien slipped to the canvas floor. He was up in an instant and again landed the jab. Jack jabbed Fitzsimmons incessantly. Blood began flowing from Bob's lips, and his mouth bled freely. O'Brien landed his right and left to Bob's nose and a little stream of blood flowed from a cut on his nose. O'Brien's outside stick-and-move boxing left Bob's face smeared with blood, but he was not disconcerted. Bob knew that he was in front of a young, agile opponent and would have to take a few to land one. Fitz went to his corner with his nose and mouth bleeding. The round was all in O'Brien's favor.

2 - Fitz rushed but O'Brien jabbed his nose. Jack coolly stepped in and landed his right and left three times on Fitz's nose and mouth. Fitz tried, but could not land with leads or counters. O'Brien's footwork was nearly perfect. The crowd marveled at his side-stepping and circling. O'Brien's left jabs landed with monotonous regularity. Bloody Bob presented an unpleasant sight. Fitz did not seem to mind the jabbing, and in the clinches, he grinned over Jack's shoulder, just as he did with Corbett. In fact, the bout resembled Bob's championship bout with Jim. Finally, Fitz rushed hard and they pummeled each other viciously to the body with both hands when the gong sounded. This round was also decidedly in O'Brien's favor.

3 - An O'Brien right to the left cheek bone left a nasty cut, causing the blood to flow from it. Fitz rushed and landed his right hard over Jack's heart and shot his left to the face. Bob tried to follow up, but Jack danced around. When Jack skipped away from a swing he laughed tauntingly. Jack sent Bob back with three left jabs to the face.

The determined Fitz rushed and rallied. In some exchanges, Bob landed his famous hard left shift to the stomach that was loud enough to be heard a considerable distance from the ring. The blow landed under the local man's heart, and there was a look of distress on Jack's face. Fitz gave him no rest for the duration of the round. However, Jack fought back and landed his blows in return, almost at will. They mixed it up furiously. Fitz appeared bewildered by the storm of blows. Although Bob did much better work in this round than he had in the prior rounds, Jack still had the advantage. Fitz was again bleeding freely, while O'Brien did not have a mark. But Bob was making him fight more, and despite being hit a lot, was landing a few of his own at this point.

O'Brien lands on Fitz's body.

4 - The tide of battle turned Fitz's way. The effect of his body punches began to show on O'Brien's footwork, which was not quite as fast as it had been. Fitz came out of his corner with his left eye black and rapidly closing. He savagely rushed but Jack either moved away from or inside of his blows. O'Brien was forced to be evasive, and in that role was not dangerous. Fitz never permitted him to get set.

They spoke with each other in the clinches, repeatedly engaging in conversation. Bob landed both right and left to the body. He ignored O'Brien's jabs and continually pressed him. In the clinches, Bob landed his body blows, which, though not as flashy as Jack's jabs to the face, were "more far-reaching in their result." Fitzsimmons was about effectiveness, not showiness. O'Brien tried to block as many as he could, but many of his efforts were futile. Bob landed a left uppercut to the jaw and a hard left to the body. When O'Brien jumped away from a repeat dose, Bob laughed. Fitz landed a left jab that caused O'Brien's mouth to bleed a little.

The Philadelphia Press was the only local source that claimed (or reported) that Bob dropped O'Brien in this round. It said Fitz rushed again and landed a right squarely on the jaw, dropping O'Brien to the floor. When he rose, blood was coming from Jack's mouth and the bell rang.

5 - Fitzsimmons looked more revived after the minute's rest than did O'Brien. He walked right in and landed with both hands to the body. Bob received the usual jabs in return. Jack rushed and forced Bob to the ropes, but Bob shot a terrific right to the body and Jack broke ground in a hurry. Fitz missed a right but quickly landed his left to the nose, drawing blood. Bob landed several body shots.

O'Brien was unable to stall Fitz's rushes, and in one of the mixes, Fitzsimmons drove him across the ring and Jack was sent almost through the ropes, in part as the result of a slip. O'Brien rose and tried to fight back. Fitz, with blood streaming from his nose and mouth, would not be denied, and kept up the attack. The bell was a welcome sound to O'Brien, who retired to his corner with blood trickling from a cut over his left eye and with badly damaged lips. The round was decidedly in Fitz's favor and O'Brien's seconds worked on him furiously during the minute's rest.

6 - Fitzsimmons took the aggressive. He landed his left twice to the nose, drawing blood. A Fitz right over the eye sent the blood in a stream down Jack's face. O'Brien's footwork showed that he was rapidly tiring. Both fought hard, though. O'Brien landed a couple jabs to the mouth but Bob retaliated with a terrific right to the body. He repeated the blow. Fitz was quite willing to take one to give one, and he succeeded.

After 1 minute and 22 seconds of the round, when Jack was coming in and led, Fitz perfectly judged his distance and met and caught O'Brien with a well-timed hard left hook to the jaw. Jack tottered backwards and tried to hold his feet, but then sat down on the floor. He was up quickly, and Fitz went right after him. However, Police Captain James Hamm ordered that the bout be stopped, and the timekeeper rang the gong over a minute before the round had expired. Both were bleeding from cuts on their faces, as well as their bleeding mouths and noses. They were a sight when the bout was stopped.

Captain Hamm told the reporters, "I had orders to stop the contest if it became brutal. In the last round O'Brien was bleeding and pretty nearly done for. Then I jumped up and called to the referee to stop it." Politics had once again injected themselves into the sport of boxing.

The Philadelphia Inquirer opined that had the bout gone to a finish, Fitzsimmons would have won. It was fast from start to finish. O'Brien clearly had the better of the first 3 rounds, landing frequently, but Fitz had the better of the last 3 rounds. He was aggressive all through, and his punches had much greater effectiveness than O'Brien's did, particularly in the 5th and 6th rounds. It opined that a draw would not have been an unjust decision to either man, had a decision been allowed.

The Philadelphia Public Ledger said that Fitzsimmons, as old as he was, proved that he was Jack O'Brien's master. Captain Hamm's advancing to ringside and waving his hands for hostilities to cease was made necessary by Fitzsimmons' catching O'Brien with a straight left to the chin, sending O'Brien staggering back to the ropes and down to the floor. The captain wanted no rough work, and told referee Ernest Crowhurst to stop the bout to prevent O'Brien from being knocked out. 1 minute and 32 seconds remained in the round. "Analyzed, O'Brien had clearly the best of the first two rounds. The third was in favor of Fitzsimmons, while honors were even in the fourth. Fitzsimmons had all the best of the last two rounds." It felt that the police captain's stopping the bout when he did was further evidence that Bob had won, although the referee was reported as saying that he would have ruled the fight a draw if decisions were allowed.

Few spectators realized it had been cut short, unaware of the fact that the police had interfered. The women present enjoyed the bout. One said, "It was better than a football game."

The Philadelphia Press said it was a fast, clean, and bitterly contested bout. O'Brien with his speed and youth had the best of the first 3 rounds, frequently landing jabs, while Bob evened matters up in the last 3 with his powerful body and head blows. In the opinion of good ring judges, the no-decision bout was a draw. Many were surprised that O'Brien carried the battle to his opponent, though Bob was always eager to mix it up. Both were badly marked up with cuts. Bob left the ring with a black eye as well. O'Brien would be bruised for many days from the body blows.

O'Brien offered to fight Bob again for any number of rounds at catch weights.[226]

On August 26, 1904, James J. Jeffries stopped Jack Munroe in the 2nd round. Some wondered whether he would retire.

---

226 *Philadelphia Inquirer, Philadelphia Public Ledger, Philadelphia Press,* July 24, 1904.

CHAPTER 10

Crossing the Color Line for Top Contender Status

In late 1904, the contender being given the most press and considered the biggest threat to James J. Jeffries was Jack Johnson, the colored heavyweight champion. Johnson had established himself as the leading contender, having defeated the world's top black fighters, with two 20-round decisions (1903) and one 20th round knockout (1904) over big Sam McVey, a 12th round knockout (1902) and 6-round decision (1904) over the tough and experienced Frank Childs, and a 20-round decision (1903) and 2nd round knockout (1904) over the very tall "Denver" Ed Martin. Johnson had also won a 1902 20-round decision over George Gardner.

The Police Gazette promoted Johnson as the leading contender, having the size and skill to compete with Jeffries, even though it still felt that Jeff would emerge victorious. Jeffries, however, unequivocally drew the color line.

Marvin Hart also wanted consideration as a potential title challenger. Since his late May 1904 12-round draw with Ruhlin, for the rest of the year, Hart had not been able to find a match. He too had drawn the color line. However, it seemed that none of the top white boxers wanted to meet him. Hart could be outboxed to a certain degree, but he was a fierce, well-conditioned puncher who would not be denied. Fighters knew that a fight with Marvin Hart would be a tough ordeal.

A normally very active fighter, Hart was frustrated by his inability to make a match, and his lengthy inactivity. Time and diminishing funds can sometimes change minds. Given that Jack Johnson was garnering the most media attention as the top contender to Jeffries' throne, Hart was told that by defeating Johnson, he could quickly spring to the front as a Jeffries challenger. Hence, eventually, Hart reluctantly changed his mind about the color line in order to obtain a fight and to potentially put himself in the position as the top contender for the title.

Hart had traveled to San Francisco to try to get a fight, and to convince the locals of his merit as a title challenger. Jeffries' last four championship fights had been held in San Francisco, so it made sense to try to convince San Franciscans of his merit.

San Franciscans had seen Jack Johnson box several times. They were interested in seeing Johnson in with a man of Hart's reputation.

In December 1904, in San Francisco, Hart was sparring with the highly touted up and coming amateur heavyweight Al Kaufman. Kaufman was listed as 6'1" and 190 pounds. This gave the locals a chance to assess Marvin in person.[227]

The late December *Police Gazette* contained an article entitled, "Hart to Fight Jeffries For the Championship."

> It seems rather presumptuous on the part of Marvin Hart to imagine he has a chance to best Jim Jeffries, but the Louisville former middleweight has grown into a smashing big fellow, and being nothing loath to take a chance has gone to California with the ultimate purpose of fighting Jeffries for the championship, but says he intends to tackle Kid McCoy and Jack Johnson, the colored heavyweight, before fighting the big boilermaker. Hart…may even put it all over Johnson, but he hardly has a chance to beat Jeffries. Hart weighs about 180 pounds when fit, and would be meeting Jeffries at probably forty pounds the worst of the weight. He is slow, awkward and not a marvel in point of science, although he has a pile driving wallop that can do a heap of damage if it lands…. The Louisville fighter is game, ambitious and knows how to take care of himself, however, which is much in his favor.[228]

There was some uncertainty as to whether a Hart-Johnson match would take place, but a victory over Johnson would most certainly place Hart first in line for a title shot, or to fight for the vacant title should Jeffries retire.

> If Hart expects to succeed Jeffries as champion when the boilermaker retires, he can show his prowess in no better way than by tackling

---

227 *Police Gazette*, October 28, 1905.
228 *Police Gazette*, December 24, 1904.

Johnson. By whipping the black man he would at one bound take second place in the line, with no one ahead of him but the unbeatable champion. It is up to Hart to make good his challenge or class himself as a bluffer who wants easy game or none at all.[229]

By January 1905, the Hart-Johnson bout appeared to be on in San Francisco, although negotiations were continuing. Initial reports were that Johnson had agreed to knock out Hart as a condition for him to win. This was not mentioned in later reports regarding their fight, and the terms might have changed, but this is possibly insightful regarding the attitude or belief that Johnson was not going to win a decision and had to knock out Hart. However, this supposed condition might have just been a way to market the bout, owing to Johnson's predilection to coast and win boring decisions. Or, it could have been a way to stimulate Johnson to go for a more entertaining knockout and not hold back.

> The contestants will be Marvin Hart, the Louisville light heavyweight, and Jack Johnson, the king of colored scrappers, whom Jeffries has refused to fight. Johnson has agreed to stop the Southern man within twenty rounds, and Alex Greggains of the Yosemite Club has arranged everything. The two big men are to divide the proceeds on a sixty and forty per cent basis, and if Johnson does not put Hart away before the end of the bout he is to get the short end, regardless of what he shows as a clever boxer. In agreeing to knockout so tough a fellow as Marvin Hart Johnson has undertaken no easy task. Hart…is a big, tough boy, not overly clever, but with more than an ordinary amount of endurance. While he may not be able to reach Johnson with a knockout punch, it is certain that the colored champion will have to go some to put him away.[230]

Johnson had fought and defeated Hart's trainer/manager/sparring partner Jack McCormick. Against common opponents with Hart, Johnson had a 1901 LKOby3 Joe Choynski and D10 Billy Stift; 1902 W20 George Gardner; 1903 W10, ND6, and W20 Sandy Ferguson; and 1904 ND6 Ferguson. In comparison, Hart had a 1902 KO3 and W6 against Stift, 1903 6-round no-decision "draw" against Choynski, 1903 LKOby12 (broken hand) and 1904 D15 with Gardner (considered clear Hart victory), and 1904 W20 Ferguson (though most thought Ferguson at least deserved a draw).

Hart said he was 26 years old (although he was really 28) and his best weight 185 pounds. "You see, I'll be getting heavier all the time, and after three or four good fights I'm going right after that fellow Jeffries. I beat

---

229 *Police Gazette*, December 31, 1904.
230 *Police Gazette*, January 14, 1905.

Ruhlin, who is almost as big as Jeff, and I don't see why I wouldn't have a look-in with the big fellow."[231]

By March 1905, both Hart and Al Kaufman were sparring with 1904 Olympic heavyweight champion Sam Berger, who was preparing for his own pro fight scheduled for the 15th. Kaufman said he and Hart were sparring with Berger every day. Hart's bout with Johnson was scheduled for the end of the month.[232]

After Berger and Hart sparred on March 10, Berger complimented Marvin. "Hart is rounding into grand fix, and I declare myself right here that I think he'll beat Johnson. I've boxed enough with him to get a better line than most people, and, believe me, he's the goods."[233]

As of mid-March, the *San Francisco Bulletin* reported that for the past two weeks, the husky Hart and McCormick had been seen running every morning along park roads, wearing caps, sweaters, and heavy outer garments, at a pace that would be hard to follow. They would leave from Sheehan's, on Ocean Beach, where Hart was training, and cover no less than 8 miles. "The big Kentuckian seems to enjoy his work, and the more difficult the task the more he smiles."

In the afternoon, Hart was sparring with McCormick, Dave Barry (who in May 1905 would lose a 20-round decision to Tommy Burns), and world lightweight champion Jimmy Britt, 4 rounds with each. Britt's speed was great preparation for Johnson, whose speed was being compared with Corbett's. Hart handicapped himself in sparring, never turning loose with his full power, although he still packed power. "He is essentially an infighter, and such a vicious one that even pneumatic body protectors were of little service to his sparring partners. It is claimed for him by Jack McCormick that Johnson's extreme cleverness will avail him naught."

Jack Johnson was running 12 miles every morning at Joe Millett's, a training facility near Colma, California. In the afternoon, Johnson sparred Denver Ed Martin and New York heavyweight Jim Haywards, 6 rounds apiece. Johnson was in excellent condition.[234]

On March 17, Hart ran 10 miles on the road. "Nothing seems to tire the big man from Kentucky; He is a glutton for work, and is always reluctant to quit, whatever exercise he may be indulging in, when his trainer commands him to stop." Marvin wanted all the local talent to come spar with him, to show that he was the real deal, unlike Jack Munroe. Al Kaufman had joined his sparring crew.

McCormick wanted the soft surgical bandages to be put on in the ring. He said one of Hart's opponents had a plaster of Paris cast under his bandages, and he did not want to allow that to happen again. He wanted to

---

231 *Police Gazette*, January 21, 1905.
232 *San Francisco Bulletin*, March 10, 1905.
233 *San Francisco Bulletin*, March 11, 1905.
234 *San Francisco Bulletin*, March 17, 1905.

make sure that straight Queensberry rules would govern. Also, McCormick said that Johnson had been in the habit of wearing an elastic bandage which covered a portion of his abdomen, and he would object to it. He wanted Johnson to wear the regulation ring costume.[235]

Johnson was sparring the 6'5" 220-pound Denver Ed Martin. Jack instructed Ed to bore in all the time, as he expected Hart to do. Martin obeyed his instructions, continually coming after Johnson. Once in a while Johnson cut loose with a hard wallop that might put him to sleep, but the heavily padded gloves only made Martin stagger across the ring, and then he would come back for more.

> Johnson, realizing the importance of this mill and the possibility of the winner being matched with Jeffries, is working harder for this bout than for any of his previous ring affairs. Ten miles a day is the minimum of the road work, and he never boxes less than twelve rounds. After the gymnasium work in the afternoon Jack takes a six-mile walk; then he's ready to eat.

> Johnson said he ate well and tried to put on weight in the evening, given that he burned off pounds during the day. He was the picture of rugged health at 194 pounds.[236]

On March 18, wet roads kept the boxers indoors. Hart skipped rope for over an hour, an activity in which he was "in a class by himself, his skill and agility at the work being truly wonderful for a man of his size and weight." Marvin was described as a big, good-natured boy. He worked out for an hour and a half. Trainer Jack McCormick was pleased with Marvin's condition. "There is no difficulty in training as wiling a worker as Hart."

Jack Johnson had been devoting a considerable amount of time to developing his stomach muscles, reports having reached Millet's, where he was training, that Hart was a great body puncher. It was said that the possibility of being matched with Jeffries was probably the cause of the earnestness

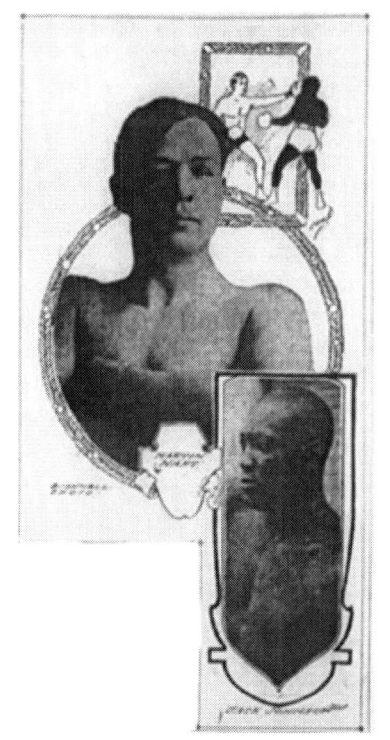

---

235 *San Francisco Bulletin*, March 18, 1905.
236 *San Francisco Evening Post*, March 18, 1905.

that both principals were showing in their daily work.[237]

Another writer opined that it was an evenly matched bout, and noted that both were training hard. The winner would be considered the logical opponent for the world championship. Hart was weighing 194 pounds, just 1.5 pounds more than Johnson. Hart was said to be stronger and more rugged than Johnson. However, Johnson's admirers claimed that he was the cleverest big man ever to don the mitts.[238]

On the 19th, Johnson spent 20 minutes at the punching bag, 20 more skipping rope, 10 minutes with the medicine ball, and then 6 rounds apiece sparring with Denver Ed Martin and Jim Gallagher, showing his delightful condition. "He was never idle for a moment, and even during the minute rest between rounds he gave as neat an exhibition of shadow boxing as any one would care to see. The spectators went away well satisfied with the shifty smoke's condition." Johnson's sparring bouts with Martin came as near to a real fight as anyone would care to see without paying admission. Jack was just as full of ginger at the end of the day as when he started. While being rubbed down, Johnson said, "I never felt better in my life. I've been working hard for nearly three weeks now, and I could fight tomorrow. They tell me that this Hart is a pretty tough proposition, but he ain't worrying me none. I'm looking right over his head at Mr. Jeffries."

That same day, Hart impressed spectators with his business-like approach to gym work at Sheehan's beach resort. Spectators gave him little outbursts of applause as they watched him train. He showed considerable speed in sparring 4 rounds with big Jack McCormick and 4 more with the shifty featherweight Dave Sullivan. Hart had a tendency to bore in continually. "In fact it is claimed for Hart that he has yet to break ground for an opponent." Hart delighted spectators with an exhibition of strength and endurance over 2 hours of work that would be hard to equal. Hart's wind seemed to be unaffected by his strenuous work.[239]

In spite of the rain and slush, on March 20, Hart took to the roads, running his usual 10 miles. Marvin was a glutton for road work, and kept a fast pace throughout, always finishing strong. He had no superfluous flesh on his body. Although practically a stranger in California, those who had seen Hart at work were impressed with his ever aggressive style and the ease with which he hustled about big men such as Jack McCormick and Al Kaufman. Hart boxed 20 rounds.

Likewise, Johnson was said to look better than ever, and the amount of work he was doing each day was proof of the fact that he would be in condition to go the distance on March 28, the night of the fight. "Johnson is well known in this city, where he has done his best work. He can take a wallop without flinching, and usually hands out as good as he receives."

---

237 *San Francisco Bulletin,* March 19, 1905.
238 *San Francisco Call,* March 19, 1905.
239 *San Francisco Bulletin, San Francisco Evening Post,* March 20, 1905.

Both men had trained earnestly and conscientiously. "Two more rugged, big athletes would be hard to locate."[240]

One paper said that Hart had been assured of a match with Jeffries if he was successful against Johnson. Hart's record was good enough to demonstrate that he was a high-class fighter. "He has met and defeated the best in the business, and his record shows that out of thirty-three battles he has received the short end of the purse but twice." When Hart hit someone solidly, they usually went to the mat. He had been a heavyweight for only about a year, but was strong enough to compete with anyone.

Jack Johnson had won all of his local San Francisco bouts, and had made himself conspicuous by challenging Jeffries at every opportunity. "Unlike most colored boxers, Johnson can take a beating if it comes his way, and has yet to show one trait of cowardice." At that time, Hart was weighing 194 pounds, while Johnson was weighing 192 ½ pounds.[241]

Johnson was described as tall, with a long reach, while Hart was "chunky and solid – a smaller edition of Tom Sharkey." Johnson heard that Hart would rely on infighting to win the battle. Jack responded to this by saying that he intended to show the public that he could change tactics and prove that he was just as much at home in the rough going as he was at long-range fighting. Johnson said,

> They tell me that Hart has yet to break ground for an opponent. Well, if that's the case, spectators will see something unusual, for I am going to make him back up some. I have been conditioning myself for close-range milling, and the Kentuckian cannot set too warm a pace for me. I am going to bet a little of my own money that Hart does not stay the limit.[242]

Johnson was in first-class condition, and expected to weigh in the neighborhood of 195 pounds on fight-night.

---

240 *San Francisco Call, Evening Post*, March 21, 1905.
241 *San Francisco Bulletin*, March 21, 1905.
242 *San Francisco Chronicle*, March 21, 1905.

Hart had originally come to California with the understanding that Kid McCoy was to be his opponent, but things didn't work out. He was eventually convinced to take on Johnson.

> He is a Kentuckian, born and bred, and has the Kentuckian's race prejudice. It took an even two months to convince him that it was to his best interests to meet a colored boxer, even though Johnson was colored heavyweight champion of the world. Nothing short of his desire to get at Jeffries by using Jack as a stepping stone brought about the change of sentiment. The fact that he does not care to be put on an equality with a negro will only add fuel to the flame next Tuesday night. A Kentuckian is going to take a world of beating before he will succumb to a man of Johnson's color.[243]

On March 21, Johnson did not spar. Instead, he spent 10 rounds punching the bag and 10 more shadow boxing. He finished the day with a 15-minute wrestling bout with Ed Martin. Johnson was looking faster, stronger, bigger and better than ever. Apparently, Johnson got lost during his roadwork, and wound up running an alleged 27 miles.

Hart was still sparring, but had cut the length of the rounds down to 2 minutes apiece. At 195 pounds, Marvin was looking as rugged and fit as any specimen of athletic manhood. "To say that Hart looks fit would be to put it mildly."[244]

W.W. Naughton said Hart had a world of confidence and feared no man. He had long ago established his reputation for grit. His punishing encounters with Kid Carter, another human bulldog, were sufficient to earn Marvin a name for courage. "He boxes in a free-handed, willing way with Kaufman and McCormick." The sound of the punching bag when he struck it gave ample evidence of his power.

> Johnson has been seen in action many times by the sports of San Francisco, and the opinion prevails here that he is the only fighter in the lists at present capable of making Jim Jeffries extend himself. Hart is a stranger in these parts. He has nothing to commend him but his record and the work he is doing at present. Truth to tell, the record is not an imposing one. He has never overlooked a chance to fight. He has hooked up with some of the hardest men among the second-rate heavies. He has won and he has lost, but, taken by and large, his past has been a bloody rather than a brilliant one. ... [A]ccording to Trainer Jack McCormick, he will enter the ring weighing 196 pounds. This is quite a gain for a fellow who fought at 170 a couple of years ago.

---

243 *San Francisco Bulletin*, March 22, 1905.
244 *San Francisco Evening Post*, March 22, 1905.

Hart knew that demonstrating his ability to perform well against a first-class heavyweight like Johnson could mean a heavyweight title shot. "I am a bigger man, or I might say, a bigger fighter, than I was. I feel that I have increased in strength as well as in weight. I am certainly big enough for Jeffries, and I know, of course, that my chances of getting a whack at the world's championship hinge upon what happens next Tuesday night."[245]

On the 22nd, Johnson played handball, an important part of his indoor exercise. He boxed 5 rounds with Martin, doing little leading, being careful not to injure his hands. Johnson ran a 100-yard dash and showed his remarkable speed. It was said that he might have been a 10-second man had he devoted himself to sprinting instead of pugilism. Jack was weighing 193 pounds, and claimed to be in finer fix than he had been in for the past two years.

Jack was overflowing with good nature and smiling all the time. He entertained no thoughts of defeat. Johnson told his camp members that Charles M. Schwab had the best private rail car in the world, for he had been in it as an invited guest. Likewise, Hart was also good natured and smiling at his quarters at Ocean Beach.

Both of the principals' respective managers wanted Alex Greggains to officiate the bout. However, initially, Greggains was reluctant to do so, feeling that as manager of the host San Francisco Athletic Club, he did not want to expose himself to criticism as the judge of the fight. He hoped that they would find someone else.[246]

Jack McCormick recognized that Johnson would be the odds favorite, likely at 10 to 7. In fact, Johnson was the heavy 1 to 2 odds favorite. McCormick felt that if more San Franciscans had seen Hart fight, he would

---
245 *San Francisco Examiner*, March 22, 1905.
246 *San Francisco Call, Evening Post, Chronicle*, March 23, 1905.

be the favorite. "If this fight was coming off in the East in any town where both Hart and Johnson have been seen in action, Marvin would be a one to two shot over the colored man." The confident McCormick was happy that Hart was the odds underdog, because he wanted to bet on him and make even more money. Johnson was clever, but Hart had fought clever men and beaten them. "I tell you these wise guys out here don't know how good a fighter Hart is. He is not a boxer, but he is a natural fighter, and when he lands one of his body wallops, it's curtains."

As McCormick was being interviewed, the building started to tremble, as if there was an earthquake. Someone asked, "What's that?" Mac replied, "That's Hart starting to punch the bag." The reporters went down the stairs to watch Marvin strike the bag with a vengeance until the rope holding it broke.

Hart's exhibition of endurance made the crowd of spectators open their mouths in amazement. He showed an immense capacity for work. "He is, beyond any question, the most earnest and the most nearly tireless of any fighter that has trained around San Francisco in the present generation." Marvin worked the pulley weights, wrist machine, and punching bag for 15 minutes each. He caused the entire building to shake from the tremendous power as the bag struck the platform. The heavy bag came next, and then shadow boxing with heavy dumbbells. Marvin hit the punching bag so hard that the rope broke twice. "At the same time he showed that he was shifty on his feet and that he has the speed of a lightweight." Skipping rope and work with Indian clubs were next brought into use. Finally, Hart bounced a tennis ball on the floor using his hands, moving about for 10 minutes. "He makes a neat piece of work out of the exercise, which keeps him constantly on the move and quickens his eye." Al Kaufman entered and the two big fellows tugged each other around until Kaufman was tired out. "Hart's breathing apparatus seemed absolutely unaffected by the hour and a half's work." Marvin then took a dip in the surf and got a rubdown. He weighed192 pounds after his work.[247]

When interviewed, Marvin said,

---

[247] *San Francisco Evening Post, Bulletin, Chronicle,* March 24, 1905.

> I don't see how I can lose. Mind you, I'll grant that Johnson is as clever as there is in the business, but his cleverness won't get him nothing with me. I broke up Joe Choynski's cleverness and did the same to Jack O'Brien, and Johnson cannot be any faster than these men. One punch is all I want to land on the nigger, and I'll do that before the fight is half over. I don't care how fast the man is, he'll go down for the count if I land on him, and I'm not afraid to take a few to get mine in.[248]

Another reporter quoted Hart as saying,

> I tell you right here that this coon will have to go some to beat me. He won't beat me. ... I realize that this coon Johnson is a clever fellow. I am not a clever fellow except in my own peculiar way, but I have got the wallop that will win. What has the coon ever done that should make him a favorite over me? I knocked out Billy Stift in three rounds. The coon was lucky to get a draw at the end of ten rounds. I fought Philadelphia Jack O'Brien six rounds in Philadelphia, and the papers agreed that if a decision had been rendered it would have gone to me by a mile. Has the coon done anything as good as that? I am a knockout fighter. He is a clever boxer. One punch will be all that's necessary for him.

That same day, the 23rd, Johnson boxed a few rounds with Denver Ed Martin, and did some light gymnasium exercise and roadwork.[249]

All the newsmen and experts were intrigued by the matchup, and analysis proliferated. Philadelphia's Frank Crowhurst, who had seen both men in action in their bouts, said,

> The fight should prove one of the most important fistic encounters of the year, as either of the principals may be, in the near future, the world's heavyweight champion. Both men are in line for this honor, and while neither is likely to defeat Jeffries for the championship, the mantle would assuredly fall upon the shoulder of one of them should Jeffries resign. Until a year ago Hart was practically classed as a middleweight. ... Nature has now supplied this want. ...
>
> No one will gainsay the fact that Hart is one of the cleverest, pluckiest and coolest ring generals over the middleweight limit, and the important question is, will his additional weight enable him to withstand the punishment which he is almost sure to get from his dusky opponent during the first few rounds. ...
>
> Fortunately for him, his increase in bulk and strength has come perfectly natural, whereas to some it might prove a handicap, to him

---

[248] *San Francisco Bulletin*, March 24, 1905.
[249] *San Francisco Chronicle*, March 24, 1905.

it is a decided advantage. He is as agile now as he ever was, while his endurance is nothing short of remarkable.

On the other hand, Johnson is a natural fighter, beautifully built for strength and agility, and a past master of the school of hit and get away. Unfortunately this dusky marvel has had few opportunities to show his real worth, and although such men as Frank Childs, Denver Ed Martin and Sam McVey have in the past fallen easy victims to his skill, he has never tackled such a tough proposition as he will face on Tuesday.

Judging of the past performances of the two men, Johnson appears to have a shade the best of it, but this may be more than offset by the additional weight and strength Hart will have at his command. ... Should both be fortunate enough to survive the earlier rounds the contest will be one of endurance. Therein Hart will have an advantage. If Johnson secures a victory it will be in the first few rounds, after which the betting should be strongly in favor of Hart.[250]

Crowhurst said the fight looked so even to him that he could not make a selection.

On the 24th, Hart did his usual 1.5 hours of work.[251]

---

[250] *San Francisco Bulletin*, March 25, 1905.
[251] *San Francisco Examiner*, March 25, 1905.

MARVIN HART, WHO FIGHTS "JACK" JOHNSON NEXT TUESDAY NIGHT.

    Promoter/matchmaker Alex Greggains, a former fighter himself, and manager of the San Francisco Athletic Club, the bout's host, had been refusing to be the referee, despite the fact that both sides wanted him. Hart would not agree on any referee other than Greggains. Johnson's manager, Zick/Zeke Abrams (papers use both spellings for his first name), was comfortable with Greggains as a fair man. Therefore, Alex eventually gave in and agreed to referee the bout.

    The newsmen were happy with Greggains' selection as the bout's arbiter. "Greggains has handed down the verdict in many important battles, and has yet to incur the disfavor of the fight fans. His name was the only one mentioned that was agreeable to both principals." Another paper said it was doubtful if the fighters could have made a better selection. "Greggains has always made good with the public when acting in the capacity of referee... [and] the local fight fans can depend on the ex-scrapper for an honest decision, based on a thorough knowledge of the game. Neither of the principals would stand for anybody but Greggains."

Still, the *San Francisco Evening Post* predicted that Greggains would have a tough job on his hands if the bout went the distance and he had to render a decision.

> If the fight is to be decided on cleverness, Johnson has a good chance, should the contest go twenty rounds. If aggressiveness will gain the verdict, Hart's chance looks to be the better.
>
> If the mill happens to go the limit the galleryites will no doubt be divided in their opinions, and will shout themselves hoarse for their favorite, so the referee's job will be no sinecure. Greggains, however...can be depended on to pick the best man, when all is said and done.
>
> Greggains will decide what looks to be the most nearly even heavyweight battle that has been contested in San Francisco in many a month.

Hart was 192 pounds of solid muscle and bone. "He is fit to go the distance at a terrific pace, and in shape to take every punch which comes his way without flinching. He has absolutely no fear of his opponent." Although a heavyweight, Marvin "moves around with the agility of a bantam." As he gradually increased his weight, his speed and shiftiness kept pace with his increase in bulk. He was as fast as he was when the newspapers first touted him as a "speed marvel" in the lower weight classes.

> His opponent, Jack Johnson, is conceded to be the fastest big man who ever stepped into the ring. Unlike most clever fighters, the colored boxer is also there with a punch. ... He depends mostly, however, on his ability to hit and get away, and in this respect compares favorably with James J. Corbett in his best days.
>
> Whether Hart can hit the black fighter or whether Johnson can elude the vicious onslaughts of the Louisville lad is a question that can only be decided after the two have settled their argument.[252]

Johnson was the public choice at 1 to 2 odds. He had been training for a month, and appeared to be in better condition than he had been for the past two years. "His workouts with 'Denver' Ed Martin have shown him shiftier than ever before and he is thoroughly satisfied with himself and confident of beating the Kentucky boy." Still, "In Marvin Hart Johnson will meet the toughest proposition of his career. ... Hart is continually after his man, willing to take any amount of punishment if he can only land his wallop once in a while."[253]

---

[252] *San Francisco Evening Post*, March 25, 1905.
[253] *San Francisco Call*, March 26, 1905.

MARVIN HART, WHO WILL MEET JACK JOHNSON TUESDAY NIGHT.

Most sporting experts felt that the odds should be even, and a slight majority actually thought of Hart a trifle more than Johnson. Harry Corbett said the contest was too close to wager. Jimmy Brittt said, "I can't see anybody but Hart. The coon might make him look cheap for the first few rounds, but Hart has the stamina and will finish strong." Tom Dillon said, "I like the coon to get the decision." San Berger said, "Nothing short of a death in the family could keep me from seeing that fight. It will be a case of a boxer against a fighter. I can't express a preference." Dave Barry said, "Hart for mine. Any man that puts Jack O'Brien to the floor six times in a six-round bout will have no trouble in reaching Johnson." Spider Kelly said, "I look to see the closest heavyweight fight of my life." Billy Wilson said Hart was "in grand shape and ought to win. He'll have a task on his hands with the clever smoke, but he's beaten fast fighters before." Tom Davis said he would bet on Johnson.[254]

The bout was a big deal. Hart was a "natural fighter of the slashing type." Johnson was a masterful boxer. "Although neither has yet proved the right to be considered in the class of the unapproachable Jeffries, the unquestioned fact that they are among the best of the other heavies makes the card attractive."[255]

There was some discussion and concern regarding Johnson's tendency to give dull performances, which could hurt ticket sales. The press raised this concern with Greggains. "It was suggested to him that the public should be assured that Johnson intends to fight from the first gong, and not to loaf along through the first twenty rounds to a decision." Greggains responded to this concern by saying,

> I have notified Johnson that he must fight all the time or the fight will be called 'no contest.' I don't expect any difficulty on that score. Johnson's manager, Zick Abrams, has also told him that he must win in a hurry. 'If you stay twenty rounds for a decision,' Abrams told him, 'we will run you out of town.'[256]

The following day, the *San Francisco Chronicle* said,

> Johnson's predilection for loafing during an engagement is well-known, but in meeting Hart he goes against a ripping, smashing fighter who will mix things from the first gong. Hart is not clever, except in a way that is peculiarly his own, but he has worlds of steam and willingness. His reputation is that of a short finisher, with a wallop that Jeff himself might well fear, and any hopes Johnson may have of easily getting away with something may be rudely shattered.

There was concern that Johnson would attempt to do what he did against Sam McVey in San Francisco the previous year, which was considered a clever but very boring sparring exhibition for 20 rounds, "with not enough vim and dash to it to keep the wildest enthusiast awake. In that battle he kept out of harm's way for nineteen draggy rounds, and in the twentieth dropped the Oxnard sugar squeezer with a punch that he could have delivered at any time during the fight."

The press wanted Referee Greggains to warn Johnson that if he attempted to loaf that he might decide against him or rule it a 'no contest.' San Francisco fight fans did not quickly forget a poor exhibition, and, "They will recall for some time, too, that sorry affair between Johnson and McVey." Fight followers were willing to give up their money only if they

---

[254] *San Francisco Bulletin*, March 26, 1905.
[255] *San Francisco Chronicle*, March 26, 1905.
[256] *San Francisco Chronicle*, March 25, 1905.

were assured that they would get their money's worth. They wanted the referee to ensure that they got it.

> Now if he will give 'Mistah' Johnson to understand that no money will be forthcoming if the big 'dinge' does not get busy, he will have the eternal gratitude of those who intend to occupy chairs.
>
> Of course, there may be no need for any suggestions of the sort. Johnson may have decided that the only way he can win back the regard he lost last year is to go in and make a brilliant fight of it. He realizes as well as anybody else that his stock has been below par ever since that affair. Nobody is questioning his ability to fight, but the jeers hurled at him through nineteen slow rounds were sufficient indication that no repetition of that sort of milling will be allowed. Hart will undoubtedly have something to say about this too. He will rush into the fray at the beginning, and will be plunging in from then until the finish.

The expectation was that Johnson would not be allowed to fight in that manner again. "If he attempts to loaf Tuesday night it is the duty of the referee to warn him, and then, if he still refuses to mingle with the gentleman from Kentucky, to stop the fight and declare it 'no contest.'" Thus, a prejudice existed against Johnson not simply because of race, but because of his less than entertaining style.[257]

Still, there was excitement surrounding the bout. Tickets had gone on sale at Greggains' café at 112 Ellis Street, and they were selling like wildfire.

W.W. Naughton said that Jeffries would need to be reminded on the day after the bout that he needed to return to the ring again. "Each individual admirer of the fistic game rebels at the notion of the big fellow retiring undefeated. A thing of that kind would leave an aching void. It is like being asked a conundrum and then told there is no answer." Naughton correctly identified the trouble and frustration with determining a new champion to a vacated title. "If Hart should down Johnson in fair fight the rest will be easy. Marvin will be the sensation of the hour." Jeffries would then be open to a match with him, because Jeff was out for the coin. "The champion has already said that he will not hesitate about giving Hart a match, if Hart disposes of the colored heavyweight."

But first, Hart needed an impressive and decisive victory in order to garner sufficient public and media clamor for a Jeffries-Hart bout, which was necessary for the fight to be sufficiently financially lucrative for Jeffries. Jeff was ready to retire, and was only willing to box again if the bout would yield a big payday. Jeff said that he hoped that Hart would win decisively so that he could draw fans and a big gate, "for I'm not going to be drawn into

---

257 *San Francisco Chronicle*, March 26, 1905.

another Jack Munroe farce. That affair did not yield me a penny. In fact, I lost money on it, and I don't like the idea of fighting for the love of it."

Jeffries was firm that he would not defend the title against Johnson if he won. Neither criticism nor cajolery had caused Jeffries to waver in his determination never to defend the title against a Negro. Jeff told a reporter, "I'm not going to discuss Johnson's abilities as a boxer. He may be a wonder and all that, but if any one is to take my title I want that man to be of my own color. If Hart wins I will cheerfully give him a fight." However, Naughton thought or hoped that Jeffries might eventually give in to the public pressure that might mount if Johnson won over Hart in a convincing fashion. Hence, there was pressure on both Johnson and Hart to either score a knockout or win clearly.[258]

On March 26, Hart proved conclusively to a packed crowd of spectators his ability to go 20 rounds at the fastest kind of pace. Marvin was absolutely tireless, and he entertained them with "as fast an exhibition of indoor work as they will ever see in their lives." Even Billy Jordan, who had seen thousands of fighters, said Hart was the hardest worker and hardest hitting fighter that he had ever seen.

Hart sparred 6 rounds with Jack McCormick, roughed it for a few minutes with Sammy Brooks, and boxed and wrestled with Al Kaufman for a half hour. He did his usual hour and a half of work. Marvin "proved beyond all doubt that he has an awful wallop." The way Marvin hustled each of them around "bodes no good for the dusky Mr. Johnson. Hart cannot box. He is essentially a fighter and even when trying to restrain himself his blows carry a sting." One local reporter said that had more of the public seen his secret boxing bouts the gold brick would have been discovered long before this fight. It would not take a good judge of fighting material long "to come to the conclusion that Marvin is there with the class." Veteran fight fans marveled at Hart's strength and speed. "He appears to be as fast as any lightweight, and the old-timers were unanimous in declaring him a wonder." Marvin finished the day with a plunge in the ocean.

Hart said that he was in perfect shape and had never before trained as hard as he had for this fight. He knew that it was his one chance to justify a match with Jeffries.

That same day, Johnson boxed with Ed Martin and Jim Haywards. Like Hart, Johnson was a perfectly trained athlete. "He is faster than ever and the amount of work he goes through without even breathing hard proves him to be stronger." Johnson said, "I'm stronger and heavier than ever before in my life, and if we were going to fight a hundred rounds I'd be prepared to go the distance." Johnson's gym work proved conclusively that his wind, speed, and endurance could scarcely be improved upon.

The Evening Post expected the bout to be a grand contest for several reasons. Neither had a weight advantage, both were in the best of form, victory meant a potential match with Jeffries, and, the fact that one was a white southerner and the other colored would mean that no friendly feeling existed between the two, so the bout was bound to be rough.

It was again noted that the selection of Greggains as referee was equally as pleasing to the fighters as to the fight fans. "Greggains has refereed important contests before. He decides a fight on his own judgment, and has never been influenced by the shouting of the gallery gods."[259]

---

258 *San Francisco Examiner*, March 26, 1905; *San Francisco Chronicle*, March 27, 1905.
259 *San Francisco Evening Post, Bulletin, Examiner*, March 27, 1905.

On the 27th, the day before the fight, Hart covered 4 miles by running and walking, mostly doing the latter. He spent 5 minutes on the wrist machine and 3 rounds on the punching bag. He then weighed himself and scaled 192 pounds.

Johnson only took a 6-mile walk. He was weighing about 191 pounds.[260]

A few days before the bout, Johnson had been a 10-7 favorite. The day of the fight, the odds were 2-1 for Johnson.[261] On the East Coast, it was reported that Johnson was the favorite at odds ranging from 6 or 8 to 10.[262]

MARVIN HART   JACK JOHNSON

---

[260] *San Francisco Bulletin*, March 28, 1905.
[261] *San Francisco Examiner*, March 27, 28, 1905.
[262] *Trenton Times*, March 28, 1905.

CHAPTER 11

Justifying The Shot

AS JOHNSON AND HART WILL LOOK IN THE RING TONIGHT.

On March 28, 1905, the day of the Hart-Johnson fight, each local newspaper offered its day-of-the-fight pre-fight analysis. *The San Francisco Examiner* said that in Hart, "Johnson meets the strongest opponent that has yet been matched against him."

> The Kentuckian has gone through a long and arduous training and has shown that he can go at a rattling fast pace and still breathe with ease. ... People who have seen him work think very highly of his chances with the cleverest colored pugilist in the world.
>
> Hart is a 'Battling' Nelson on an enlarged scale. He loves to root in and to carry the fight to his opponent. Nothing can daunt him. He will mix it as long and as furiously as the rules of the game permit.

Johnson's skills were recognized but his style was not appreciated.

> Johnson likes a different kind of game. The shifty big fellow prefers to hit and run away, winning his contests by the decision route. This sort of milling has made the dusky giant rather unpopular with the sports in this city and if Johnson wants to reinstate himself in popular favor he will have to try for a clean knockout.
>
> Tonight's fight looks to be the first good heavyweight match that has been carded for two years. Aside from this, general interest is being manifested because of the probability of a match with Jeffries, should Hart be returned the winner. Jeffries has, of course, persistently declared his determination to draw the color line. If Johnson, however, would give incontestable proof that he is a knockout fighter as well as a boxer there is no telling what popular clamor might do to disabuse the world's champion of his prejudices.[263]

The San Francisco Chronicle reported that it was again confirmed that Johnson would be required to fight rather than just defend, if he wanted to win. It also assessed the bout.

> Greggains stated last night that he will allow no loafing from Johnson, and that both men must fight all the time they are on their feet. With this assurance the public will be inclined to give the show liberal patronage.
>
> Both men have trained hard and faithfully for the battle, and the outlook is that it will be one of the best between heavy-weights that has taken place for a long time. Hart is a slashing fighter, with wonderful powers of endurance, and if he follows the plan of campaign which has been his in other battles he will give the colored man plenty to do. He isn't clever, as cleverness is judged in fighters, but he has plenty of speed and will be mixing things all the time.
>
> As a matter of cold fact, Hart's ability as a fighter is being underestimated here in San Francisco. The fact that he gave 'Philadelphia' Jack O'Brien the hardest fight that careful Quaker ever had, knocking him down five times during six rounds, is overlooked

---

263 *San Francisco Examiner*, March 28, 1905.

by the local dopesters. Johnson's pronounced cleverness is the only thing which many are taking account of, not realizing that a fighter of Hart's style may connect from the cleverest man in the world and win with a punch. That is what Hart is liable to do to-night. He has a terrific wallop, and if he succeeds in reaching a vulnerable part of the colored man's anatomy it will be 'curtains.'

As a special inducement to the two men to go in and make a rattling fight of it, Greggains has practically promised a match with Jeffries to the winner – in case the winner should be Hart. If Johnson wins, matters will not be altered so far as an opponent for Jeff is concerned, since the Hairy One has not withdrawn the color line and has no intention of doing so. If Hart wins, however, and brings about his victory in a way that looks good to the sporting public, he will be next in line for the champion of champions.[264]

Some on the East Coast wondered whether the fight or its decision would be on the level. *The Trenton Times* wrote,

The bout has a peculiar looking angle to it, for the reason that Hart has repeatedly declared that he would not enter the ring with a negro. He once announced in Boston after winning a bout from Kid Carter that he was a Southerner and would not insult his friends by fighting a colored man. For this reason sporting men are somewhat skeptical about the genuineness of the fight, some hinting that Johnson is certain to lose in order that Hart may force Jeffries to a meeting, the latter having refused many times to fight Johnson.

The negro on physical points, is Hart's superior. He has longer arms, is taller and stronger than the Louisville man and has shown himself to be very scientific. Hart affects the rushing style and is considered a slugger pure and simple. Many good judges say that Johnson would give Jeffries the hardest fight of his life.[265]

However, just before the bout, Hart explained that he was fighting Johnson because no other fighter was willing to fight him. Hence, out of frustration and inability to obtain a fight during the second half of 1904 and the first part of 1905, he was forced to withdraw the color line. He had not fought in ten months, since late May 1904.

This is the first colored man I ever fought and it will be the last, win or lose. Fighting is my business, and I am just forced to fight Johnson, as he is the only man that will fight me. I have been idle for the past year and have tried to get Gardner, Root, McCoy, O'Brien,

---

264 *San Francisco Chronicle*, March 28, 1905.
265 *Trenton Times*, March 28, 1905.

Willie and others to fight me, but they all passed me up. I have been out here four months trying to get on a fight.[266]

Oddly enough, though, back in Louisville, it was said that "Johnson must knock Hart out to win." *The Louisville Times* quoted Hart as saying, "Johnson has to knock me out in twenty rounds to get the big end of the money, and this fact will work to my advantage, as it will cause him to attempt to carry the fight to me."[267] Was there an agreement that Johnson had to knock him out? Was it understood that Johnson could not win a decision? No one said so after the bout, including Hart and Johnson.

The San Francisco Evening Post prophetically discussed how the bout might be scored, based on the time's understood scoring style for closely contested bouts.

> Johnson, although having won most of his success by his extreme cleverness, has declared his intention of roughing matters with Mr. Hart. … In fact, Johnson realizes that he will have to equalize the aggressiveness of this match if he expects the verdict to come his way. It will be necessary for him to exchange blow for blow with the southerner, for by merely showing his ability to avoid a punch he would not be much of a drawing card if matched with Jeffries. The public much prefers seeing a man take a punch and making an attempt to return it than sidestep it cleverly without striking a blow.
>
> Hart…is one of those never-say-die scrappers, willing to mix from the first tap of the gong, never stopping until something drops. He is never beaten until counted out.[268]

The two men scaled within a pound of each other. Hart was a stranger in San Francisco, while Johnson had won all of his San Francisco bouts, so Jack was a 2 to 1 favorite. However, the *Evening Post* said, "Hart's record appears to be even a little better than Johnson's, and why the black man should be installed favorite is hard to guess."

When interviewed on the day of the fight, Hart said, "I'll not give Johnson a chance to use his cleverness. I'll not give him a minute's rest, and if he lasts more than ten rounds I'll be surprised. The betting looked exceptionally tempting to me, and I bet every cent I possess that I win."

Johnson said, "I don't see how I can lose. My condition was never better, and I think I am stronger than ever. Hart may be a big strong boy, but I've met and defeated his kind before. It's up to 'Jeff' to cut out that color line for I'm the man he will have to meet."[269]

---

266 *Louisville Courier-Journal*, March 30, 1905.
267 *Louisville Times*, March 28, 1905.
268 *San Francisco Evening Post*, March 28, 1905.
269 *San Francisco Evening Post*, March 28, 1905.

The San Francisco Call said that the night before the fight, the odds were 10 to 4 in Johnson's favor owing to the fact that Hart had never fought before in San Francisco. Both men were highly motivated to do well and show their stuff in order to justify a title shot.

> Johnson will in all probability use his cleverness and ring generalship on his husky opponent. Johnson is one of the cleverest big men who ever pulled on a mitt, and he can hold an opponent at bay in grand style. ...
>
> If Hart wins the battle and makes any kind of a showing it is about settled he will be matched with Jeffries. ... He is anxious to get after the big fellow and for that reason he will probably put up the fight of his life when he steps into the ring to-night.
>
> Johnson is also after the champ, and should he beat Hart quickly and decisively there is a possible chance that Jeff may take him on, though he vows and declares he will not. Johnson figures on winning quickly and showing beyond a doubt that he is Hart's master.[270]

The San Francisco Bulletin said the time-honored custom of shaking hands would be eliminated from the proceedings, owing to race. "A natural hatred seems to exist between the two, and every blow struck, besides bringing the smiter that much nearer the long end of the purse, will carry more than the ordinary sting on account of the clashing of the two ever warring races." As both were the same size, the loser would not have the usual excuse used in heavyweight bouts, that the opponent was too big. Both were in the best possible condition, so that could not be an excuse either.

> Johnson realizes that he will have to stand his ground and mix with his husky opponent, for by depending entirely upon his cleverness the decision would certainly go to Hart for his aggressiveness. He will have to prove that he is a fighter as well as a boxer, if he expects to meet Jeffries in the future. On the other hand, Hart can be depended on to mix matters from the start. He knows no other style, but to bore in and fight from gong to gong. This characteristic explains his having so many knockouts in his record. He is game to the core, and if he is beaten, his seconds will have to pack him out of the ring.[271]

On March 28, 1905 at Woodward's Pavilion in San Francisco, 28-year-old Marvin Hart fought 26-year-old (just days short of 27) Jack Johnson. As it was a heavyweight bout, no official weigh-in was required, but it was generally estimated that the two fighters weighed anywhere from 193-198 pounds.[272]

---

270 *San Francisco Call*, March 28, 1905.
271 *San Francisco Bulletin*, March 28, 1905.
272 *Louisville Times, Trenton Times*, March 28, 1905; *Louisville Courier-Journal*, March 30, 1905.

Both men appeared to be in superb physical condition. Present in the crowd were Jabez White and Charley Mitchell, the famous English boxers, and Battling Nelson.

Johnson examined Hart's hand bandages carefully, and initially objected to their thickness, but finally retired to his corner and had some light bandages fixed on his own hands.

The local *Examiner*, *Chronicle*, and *Call* each gave round by round accountings of the fight, in addition to global summaries, while the other local papers simply offered overall analysis.

1 - Hart crouched low and jumped at Johnson with his left. They clinched and tried for blows while holding on. It seemed that it would be a rough and tumble fight. Both worked the body and head. Johnson particularly worked his right at the body. They exchanged blows and clinches. Johnson liked to block and hold between punches, and laughed at Hart's efforts to land. Hart was much busier. *The Chronicle* said, "Hart led time and time again before Johnson woke up to the fact that he was there to fight. When he did mix it he had the better of the argument." Johnson landed a vicious right to the cheek at the bell. *The Examiner's* W.W. Naughton said it was Johnson's round. *The Call* said there was very light fighting in this round and no damage was done. Johnson was apparently the much cleverer man.

2 - Johnson clinched, landed rights to the kidney and jaw, and smothered Hart on the inside. Hart landed his right to the heart a couple times when he rushed in. When Marvin was trying to get close, Jack landed a left hook to the stomach that hurt, and also landed some right uppercuts, getting the better of the mix-up. Hart liked to focus his right on the body. Jack cleverly blocked some rights and lefts to the jaw, and blocked body shots with his elbows. In the breakaway, Jack landed heavily on the jaw. Hart landed a stiff left to the head but Johnson retaliated with a right and left hook to the nose that drew blood. At the bell, Hart landed a corker to the ribs and an overhand right to the neck that sent Jack back. *The Call* said the honors of the round were in Johnson's favor. Hart bled from the nostrils as he took his seat.

3 - Johnson feinted rapidly. He mostly made Marvin miss, but Hart exhibited some good defense as well. They sparred and clinched. In the infighting, Hart tried uppercuts and swings, but Johnson was too shifty. Jack sent in his right hook to Hart's face and drove his left to the stomach. Hart landed a right to the jaw. Johnson hit the body but Marvin landed two telling blows to the "bread basket." Hart followed with a left lead, "and the coon swung a left uppercut that raised Hart to his tiptoes." Hart landed a right to the ribs. Both were inclined to rough it. Johnson sent in a right uppercut. Hart landed a right to the body and received a right to the head in return. For a time near the end of the round, both seemed afraid to lead, content to feint at long range. They were clinched at the gong. *The Call* said, "Practically it was an even round."

4 - Johnson forced Hart to the ropes with lefts and rights which did not land cleanly. Hart hit the ribs with both hands. "It hurt, and the negro grew vicious for a minute." To the surprise of the spectators, Johnson swung like an amateur, while Hart eluded the blows. Hart landed a left to the face and right to the wind. Johnson retaliated with his uppercut. There was a good deal of clinching and their leads were smothered. The spectators jeered Johnson for some rough work on the ropes. A lively mix-up followed, with Hart landing overhand punches and Johnson landing rights to the ribs.

Near the end of the round, each landed a right uppercut. They were clinching at the bell. *The Call* said Hart had a slight advantage in the round.

5 - Johnson jabbed repeatedly, but "there was not an ounce of strength in his blows." As Hart would step in, Johnson would land straight lefts and then clinch. Hart landed a right before a clinch. Jack landed right uppercuts. Johnson eluded and blocked some blows to the body and head. They sparred for a bit and then both exhibited some clever blocking. Hart landed a right to the body and they clinched. They fought at close quarters again, both missing several body shots. Hart swung his hard right on Johnson's ear but then Johnson uppercut him with his right to the jaw. *The Chronicle* said Hart forced the fighting, but

> [T]he coon was intent on being clever, and sparred lightly. It was not until Marvin reached his jaw with a corking half right swing and doubled him up with a left to the digestive organ that Black Jack really began to fight. He threw right and left into the Louisville man's bleeding face almost without a return. Hart came back just at the end with strong wallops to the coon's kidneys.

The Call said Hart landed a vicious left to the head as the gong rang. It said Hart had a shade the better of the round.

6 - Johnson kept up his jabbing tactics, paying particular attention to Hart's left eye, which was troubling him. A Johnson left jarred Hart's head back. Johnson shot in another straight left, "the most telling punch of the fight." Jack threw a left hook to the stomach before a clinch. Both used rights to the body and head on the inside, mixing it viciously. Jack wrestled Marvin to the ropes. Johnson landed a right to the jaw and a right to the body, but they had no effect on Hart, who seemed possessed of remarkable vitality. After the referee separated them from the usual clinch, they went right back to a clinch. Johnson hooked his right to the jaw and also landed a right uppercut. They clinched, and as they broke, Hart hooked a vicious right to the jaw. After breaking, as Hart was trying to get close and his lead fell short, Johnson struck him with a hard right. Jack followed up with a shower of blows, but Hart kept coming and landed a right on Jack's jaw. Marvin blocked several Johnson right uppercuts with a crossed forearm. Hart landed the customary right swing to the head at the bell. *The Call* said that overall, it was a tame round, and most of the blows that landed lacked force. It was an even round.

7 - They clinched constantly and fought at close quarters, neither landing much. Johnson hooked and jabbed several times, and used the occasional straight right to the jaw, but there was a great deal of clinching in between. As they broke out of a clinch, Hart landed a hard left to the head. He followed with a left to the body and received a right in return. Hart swung a

right to the ribs but Johnson twice hit him on the jaw with his right. Hart went at him, but Johnson caught him with a left hook to the body.

However, they did more clinching than actual fighting and the crowd constantly yelled for them to fight. Hart tried several rights, but Johnson blocked them. At close quarters, Johnson hooked a left to the body. According to the *Chronicle*, after Jack jabbed, a wild swing from Hart jolted Johnson. "With this prodding Johnson set to work and rushed his man all around the ring." However, Hart was inside several of Johnson's hardest punches. Marvin then landed a left to the ribs that hurt.

Still, the *Chronicle* said, "At the end of the round Hart was bleeding badly and weakening. His left eye was beginning to show signs of distress." However, the *Call* said the fighting this round was very tame and the fight dragged on in a monotonous manner. It said there was no advantage in the round.

8 - Johnson landed with straight lefts and left hooks, and blocked Hart's swings. Hart landed a chopping left to the face and right to the heart. They fought at a brisk pace at close quarters, but the blows were ineffectual as they mostly smothered each other's punches in the clinches. Johnson landed a right to the stomach, and on the break, a right uppercut. Hart landed a good right to the neck that caused several of his sympathizers to jump to their feet and yell. Johnson laughed and landed his right to the temple. Hart landed a right to the body and left to the jaw. Johnson landed a straight left to the face. Hart shot in a vicious left to the stomach and Johnson winced.

Hart was strong. He landed a left uppercut and followed with a right to the head. He also scored with a left to the body, but received a right uppercut in return. Johnson resorted to jabbing tactics, hitting the nose and bad eye. Hart got inside and rocked Johnson's head with right and left hooks before being held. Marvin roughed it with Johnson, forcing him around the ring. Hart walked into a right to the body which shook him up. Still, near the end of the round, Johnson was holding on to escape punishment. Hart landed a right to the body that made Johnson wince, and followed with a right to the head. Johnson landed a heavy right cross at the bell. *The Call* said that they fought at a faster clip in this round, stimulated by the numerous calls from the spectators. If anything, Hart had a shade the better of the round.

9 - According to the *Examiner*,

> Johnson loosened up in this round and did some fast two-handed punching, reaching Hart's face repeatedly. Hart stood to his guns. He drove Johnson back with swinging blows, but Jack came at him again. Johnson reached the face repeatedly with both gloves and Hart bled freely. Johnson's straight lefts were particularly punishing. It was very

evident by his exhibition in this round that he was either ultra careful or else was holding himself in reserve in the previous rounds.

The Chronicle said of the round that Hart went right at him, landing right and left to the stomach, "satisfied to take a wallop on the jaw in return. The fighting was terrific. Hart was beaten here had the negro followed up his advantage. He was bleeding badly and his eye was all but closed. Johnson let up, however, and Hart's trouble was over."

The Call said Johnson sent in a right and left to Hart's head that did not stop his onrush in the slightest degree. Hart's long range right connected with Johnson's jaw. Hart landed a left jab, but Johnson chopped him with rights to the jaw. As Johnson backed him against the ropes, Hart drove his right to the face and swung his right to the kidneys. Jack retaliated with a vicious right over the eye.

Near the end of the round, they mixed it in the center of the ring and Johnson landed right and left to the face, bringing the blood in a stream from Hart's nostrils. Johnson punished Hart severely, making him bleed profusely from the nose and mouth. Johnson hooked his right to the stomach. Hart bore in to escape punishment. Marvin bled freely as he went to his corner. It was "Mistah Johnson's round by a wide margin."

10 - Hart rushed all the time but Johnson administered punishment all the time. Johnson jarred Hart with jabs, and in the clinches, pressed Marvin to the ropes. Jack went after Marvin's sore eye. Johnson also struck him with a number of left hooks and right uppercuts. However, there was no finishing power in his blows. Hart kept rushing, trying all the time. Marvin kept sending in rights and lefts, some of which landed and had the effect of making Johnson still more cautious. Hart had Johnson in a corner at the end of the round. *The Call* said the very cool Johnson again had the advantage in this round and at this stage appeared to hold a safe lead.

11 - It was give and take for most of the round, and they engaged in slugging. Johnson landed a staggering right, but Hart landed a left to the body. Hart started to improve. When Hart landed overhand wallops, Johnson rolled his head with the blows. Johnson landed a right uppercut and a number of rights, puffing Hart's left eye.

Hart landed a right to the stomach and short-arm rights to the head, but Johnson retaliated with two forceful pokes to the ribs. Hart was forced to cover up quickly to avoid the onslaughts. Leaning against the ropes, Hart drove his right to the head and then shot two lefts to the stomach. Johnson countered with a left hook to the jaw and fast infighting followed.

They swung rights simultaneously. Hart was the first to land to the jaw and Jack reeled back. Hart drove his right stiffly to the body and the bell rang. It was a good rally for Hart and gave him the honors of the round by a margin.

12 - *The Chronicle* said there were fast and furious exchanges. Hart hit the stomach and Johnson hit the face.

The Examiner said the round was a series of clinches, and in between, Hart's face was battered. Hart continued pressing and landed lefts and rights, but did little damage. He finished the round by landing a right to Johnson's jaw.

The Call said Hart continued on the aggressive, the most effective blow being his right to the body followed by a right to the head. Marvin rushed in, attempting to land, but was met with a right hook to the jaw that shook him up a bit. In some infighting, Hart worked his right to the stomach. He blocked Johnson's attempts to dislodge him. They each cleverly blocked some blows. Several clinches followed, and finally, Hart planted his hard right on Johnson's jaw. Jack fought back, but Hart kept his head and sent Jack's head back with a straight right to the jaw. Johnson did some stalling, but never appeared to be in distress. It was Hart's round by a slight margin.

13 - *The Call* said Johnson devoted most of his energies to uppercutting, but he could not keep the aggressive Hart off. Johnson had the better of the round.

The Chronicle said Johnson grew cautious and tried to evade Hart's left to the stomach. Johnson only liked to punch hard and show some aggression when Hart landed a good one. Marvin was constantly after him, "and it was not until the coon was riled that he got to fighting hard. He landed time and time again on Hart's bad face, but the Louisville gent seemed satisfied to take all that was coming."

According to the *Examiner*, Johnson looked serious.

> There was a deal of clinching and scuffling and Johnson in every breakaway managed to shoot right uppercuts in on Hart's chin. Hart did not clinch. He was continually trying to free an arm and get in a punch while they were grappling. Johnson set himself repeatedly and drove in right crosses. Hart's face swelled up, but he did not stagger nor fall.

14 - Hart landed a right to the ribs and a hard overhand right that knocked off Johnson's broad grin. Johnson landed jabs. Hart swung a left and right to the face but Johnson landed a crushing left to the mouth and nose. Hart led wildly and was met with a right and left. Hart landed his right a couple times and smothered Johnson's uppercuts. Near the end of the round, Jack ripped his left into the body hard.

There was a divergence of opinion. *The Call* said the round closed with honors even and both apparently strong. *The Examiner* said Johnson was slower in this round than in preceding ones. *The Chronicle* said, "The coon had all the better of the infighting, landing short arm hooks on Marvin's face at will. Hart kept plowing into the stomach, but with very little effect."

15 - Hart was the aggressor throughout the round and landed some hard right swings to the head. He charged and rushed Johnson to the ropes. Johnson landed left jabs, while Hart relied on the right. Marvin landed a few times to the neck and sent Jack's head back with a left.

On the inside, Johnson repeatedly landed uppercuts. Although the blows had to hurt, they did not slow Hart down. They fought at close quarters and Hart put his right to the body twice, but received a right to the jaw that partially turned him around. Nothing daunted, Hart waded in and hooked his left to the jaw. After a clinch and break, Hart landed his right to the ear. Johnson landed a vicious left uppercut on the jaw and Hart clinched. Johnson again landed his left uppercut on the jaw. A hooking right hook found Hart's face as well.

The Chronicle said Johnson got Hart on the ropes and hit him at will, but Marvin came back with right and left swings that "caused the coon to show a little of the yellow. Hart landed low and Johnson looked appealingly at the referee. When no notice was taken, he went at Hart hammer and tongs and the bell saved the man from the Whisky State." Hart was bleeding from the nose.

Despite Marvin's aggression, the *Call* said Hart took considerable punishment in this round and Johnson had the honors.

16 - They exchanged lefts. Hart began using a straight left and "tilted Johnson's head a couple of times." Both landed lefts to the face. Marvin landed a hard one before they came together in a clinch. Hart landed rights to the ribs and Johnson landed lefts to the side of the head. A wallop to Johnson's ribs made him grunt.

Johnson landed a wicked left uppercut to the jaw, and repeated it. Jack rushed in but failed to connect. He missed a left jab and Hart sent his head back with a straight left to the jaw. They clinched repeatedly and fought at close quarters without result. Johnson did some clever blocking. No damage done. Hart stepped back and drove his left straight to the jaw and Jack's head went back. The bell rang with Hart having somewhat the better of the round, which, on the whole, was tame.

17 - *The Chronicle* said, "Johnson put it all over his adversary from the very beginning. He jabbed his left into Marvin's bleeding nose and swung over his right on Hart's eye time and time again, but Hart was there asking for more at the end."

The Examiner said Hart jarred Johnson's head with a straight left. Johnson pressed him to the ropes and landed a right uppercut. Hart forced him back and landed a right to the body. Johnson landed another right uppercut. After Hart landed a left and right to the face, the crowd cheered. However, Johnson backed Marvin to the ropes and smashed his face with punishing lefts and rights. Hart rushed and rammed in a right to the ribs. Marvin was "well hammered in this round and appeared to be tired."

The Call said that early in the round, Johnson rushed in, missed a right to the body but landed his left to the head. Johnson fought Hart to the ropes and landed right and left to the head as Hart tripped over the ropes. For a moment, Marvin's head and shoulders were outside the upper rope. Johnson landed a hard right and left to the body but received a hard right to the body that hurt. Hart came inside quickly and sent in a stiff right to the jaw. Hart landed a vicious left hook that made Johnson wince. Hart landed a straight left, but Johnson sent him against the ropes with right and left hooks to the jaw and face. Hart fought back with great gameness and drove a straight right to the jaw. The fighting was desperate, both administering and receiving severe punishment. Hart showed the effects, the blood starting again from his lacerated nostrils. The round was about even.

18 - *The Examiner* said Hart landed a right to the heart and rushed and landed a right to the jaw. Johnson loosened up and landed lefts and rights to the face. Hart hit the kidneys with rights. They exchanged rights and mixed it up, but Johnson landed the greater number of blows. Hart did not falter though, and drove a right to the ribs and was pressing Johnson into a corner at the bell.

The Chronicle said Hart was stronger than ever and rushed Johnson, receiving some lefts and rights as he was "endeavoring to cave in the coon's ribs. When Hart would stop rushing Johnson would let up also."

The Call said Hart was the aggressor all through the round. Hart missed a right to the body and Johnson smashed him with a right to the face. They roughed it and Johnson hooked a wicked left to the stomach that caused Marvin to clinch. Hart fought back but ran into a jab. Hart landed his right to the body. Hart jabbed to the face and Johnson retaliated with left and right swings to the jaw, forcing Hart to the ropes. Hart got in a straight right to the face and then left to the head. Johnson then put a left to the stomach and missed some swings to the head. It said the honors were even.

19 - According to the *Examiner*, Hart landed a left to the mouth, and in a clinch, a right to the ribs. Johnson landed two jabs and Hart again landed a right to the ribs. Hart continually hit the ribs, while Johnson countered to the face. Johnson appeared tired, but met a Hart rush with lefts and rights. Hart landed a right on the jaw to the cheers of the crowd. Johnson's cornerman shouted to Jack, "Will you please hit." Hart was outworking him. The crowd chanted Hart's name.

The Chronicle said Hart rocked Johnson with vicious jabs, and followed with left hooks to the ribs. Johnson looked weak. It was Hart's round.

The Call said Hart was again the aggressor throughout the round. He waded in with blows, but Johnson eluded or blocked them and hit Marvin with jabs. Hart swung his right to the body and then made another series of failed attempts. Johnson drove a jab to the jaw that sent Marvin's head back. Johnson was very cool. However, Hart did most of the leading. Near the end of the round, Johnson landed a right and left that rocked Hart's head. Hart came back fighting and landed a hard right swing to the jaw, which took a lot of fight out of Johnson. The bell rang, with honors even.

20 - This was a vicious round, with Hart on top of Johnson all the time. After shaking hands, they rushed to a clinch, fighting desperately at close quarters. They grappled and punched, with the referee separating them several times in between exchanges of blows. Johnson landed several short-arm rights over the kidneys. They continued fighting hard at close range. Hart landed a stiff right to the jaw. Johnson uppercut with his right to the jaw and they again clinched. Johnson held on. Hart hooked his left to the jaw, but in a clinch, Johnson planted his left to the stomach. Hart landed a clean, straight left. Johnson used some footwork to evade Hart when he could.

They fought all over the ring, but Johnson would not take a chance with the nervy Kentuckian. He hung on for a time and the house was in a wild uproar, the spectators on their feet cheering for Hart and yelling for him to knock Johnson out. Hart seemed as fresh as when he started, and although he was no beauty to look at, he kept up a fusillade on any part of Johnson's anatomy within reach.

Just before time was up, a sudden flash of light from a photographer in the balcony made them think the round had ended. The referee told them to continue, and Hart quickly rushed at Johnson, who had stopped, and landed a right to the jaw. The bell then rang. *The Call* said the round was all in favor of Hart.

Referee Greggains at once pointed to Hart and declared him the winner of the 20-round decision. The applause which greeted the decision lasted for several minutes. The crowd overwhelmingly agreed with the decision.

In explaining his decision, the various local newspapers quoted Referee Alex Greggains as saying,

> I gave the decision to Hart because he was the aggressor throughout and carried the fighting all the way. The damage done to Hart's face was done by a few jabs. Hart blocked the majority of the colored man's blows. I always give the gamest and most aggressive man the decision. Johnson, in my opinion, dogged it. He held at all times in the clinches.

> Before the men entered the ring I warned them that if the fight went the limit the aggressor would get the decision. This was in order to make Johnson fight. Hart forced the fighting every step of the way, and, in view of my warning to them, no other decision was possible. I believe Hart won and I believe that he won all the way. It was a good fight to look at, but Hart did the work, and he properly received the decision. Under the same circumstances I would give the same decision at any time.

Of the contest, Hart said,

> Johnson is a big, clever nigger with a long left arm, and that is why I wear this battered face. Outside of his straight left jabs he had no punch. I nearly broke his ribs with the blows I sent in with both hands. If I hadn't injured my right in the second round I could have knocked Johnson out.

Marvin was also quoted as saying,

> The coon is big and clever and has a good left hand, and I think that lets him out. I nearly broke his ribs with right and left punches. I hurt my right in the second on the coon's hip. It was the hand I broke in my fight with Gardner and it was of little use to me in the balance of the fight. I did all the leading and wasn't blowing a bit at the finish. He didn't hurt me any, although, of course his jabs bothered me. He has eight inches longer reach and that counted. Now I want a chance at the big fellow, but I want to wait long enough for my hand to heal.

Conversely, Johnson denounced the decision. "Hart is a big, tough fellow, very awkward and hard to hit. I will leave the verdict to those who saw the mill, and let them form their own opinions. All I can say is that I was robbed. After fighting until I reached the top, I have been thrown down by an unfair ruling." He was also quoted as saying,

> I was robbed. That is all there is to it. I fought a good fight and am satisfied with the showing I made. I got the worst of it. Had I had my way I would never have stood for Greggains at any stage, but it was all Abrams' say and I have to suffer.... I put up the best fight I knew how and was satisfied that I was a winner at every stage.

Hart was the marked one, but his proponents noted that the wounds were all superficial and external. "Hart showed no distress after the fight, in spite of the fact that his face was very much warped on the left side. His left cheek and the left side of his lips were badly puffed."

The decision from this bout garnered a great deal of subsequent discussion and debate. In explaining the verdict, the local *San Francisco Examiner*'s W.W. Naughton entitled his article, "PLUCK AND AWKWARDNESS BETTER THAN MIXTURE OF CLEVERNESS AND COWARDICE."

> [Hart won the decision by being] persistently aggressive and steadfastly game. Though his face was prodded into a condition of puffiness by Johnson's straight lefts he never faltered for an instant. Except when carried back by the force of blows he was constantly pressing towards his opponent.
>
> Johnson simply fought when he felt like it. He gave an admirable imitation of his Colma affair with Sandy Ferguson. He held himself

in reserve until the ninth round was reached and then he cut loose as though bent on finishing his man in double quick time.

He kept up his lick for a couple of rounds and then slowed up. With nothing else to guide him but the yells of disgust from Johnson's corner a tyro would have no difficulty in determining that Johnson's confidence had deserted him. The indifference to punishment and great pluck displayed by the white man seemed to discourage the negro. Johnson beyond a doubt showed that he lacks that essential fighting qualification – grit.

It would be ridiculous to say that Hart is a better ringster than Johnson. If Johnson were only as stout-hearted as the man from Louisville the chances are the negro would dispose of his opponent of last night in ten rounds.

Johnson did his best work with a straight left. He also bruised the side of Hart's face with right crosses. Hart, although anything but a neat boxer, had an awkwardly clever way of stopping Johnson's uppercuts.

Hart scored his biggest successes with a heart punch. He reached Johnson's ribs with this blow a number of times in every round. He also clouted Johnson on the temple and jaw with right swings.

There was a sameness between the rounds from the tenth onward. Johnson spurted occasionally and hammered Hart to the ropes. Then Marvin would pull himself together and force the big negro back across the ring. Johnson's seconds seemed to be in despair. They leaned in through the ropes and railed at the weak-hearted colored champion.

Johnson's second, Tim McGrath, several times cried to him, "Please hit him. You can't win unless you hit him." Jack's manager Zick/Zeke Abrams was also perturbed, saying, "For goodness sake go after him." However, "All this time the man from Louisville kept up a fast and even gait, hurling himself against the negro and bringing yelps of satisfaction from the watchers every time he planted what appeared to be a telling blow." The 20th round saw Johnson, as usual, "inclined to clinch," and Hart the usual aggressor.

Still, Naughton said the decision was possibly in doubt for Hart. "From the manner in which the Louisville heavyweight skipped around it almost seemed as if he had not expected more than a draw." However, another *Examiner* writer said, "Hart was the aggressor all the way and the referee could do nothing but give him all the glory."[273]

---

273 *San Francisco Examiner*, March 29, 1905.

The San Francisco Chronicle said that both men were strong when the final gong sounded. Johnson was strong on points, but not as active as Hart, and that cost him. One of its headlines announced, "Colored Man Not Aggressive, Hence He Lost the Fight, as the Contestants Had Been So Forewarned." It explained, "Greggains had warned the men in advance that the fighter who forced the battle, who rushed in and gave the crowd something to see, would be accorded the decision." Hart was aggressive at all times. Johnson was "clever but unwilling."

The decision was "immensely popular." During the fight, the crowd yelled Hart's name, cheering when he landed, but remained silent when Johnson did so.

> In all this enthusiasm there was doubtless a great deal of racial prejudice. There was also admiration for the under dog in the fight – for the short-ender. Throughout the entire battle the spirit was manifest. Johnson's clean hitting, his cleverness at blocking and his work all through was allowed to pass with scarcely a murmur, while every blow landed by the white man was cheered to the echo. This blinded the judgment of many, beyond a doubt. But, even then, casting aside all favoritism, a big majority of the people present felt that Hart had won and was justly entitled to the decision. The minority cursed their luck and said under their breaths: "Robbery."

> Few decisions have been given in the history of pugilism that have not had their dissenters. Those who did not agree with Greggains last night based their argument on the assertion that Johnson had shown pronounced superiority over Hart at all stages: that, if there was nothing else, his clean hitting should have entitled him to the verdict. The Hart faction answered this with the statement that Hart had forced the fighting all the way, and that if he had not done this there would have been no fighting to speak of.

> While admitting that Johnson was far the cleverer of the two, it still seems that there is a deal of justice in this view. Johnson did more actual fighting last night than he has done in all his other fights in San Francisco put together. When he went against Sandy Ferguson, he did not fight – would not fight. When he met Sam McVey here a year ago, the jeers of the crowd could not taunt him into making a fight of it. Last night, Marvin Hart rushed him all the time, kept lunging at him, kept on top of him all the time, and Johnson was forced to retaliate. When he did retaliate it was much to Hart's discomfort, for the black man had everything in the way of cleverness, and the white man had little or nothing beyond his indomitable grit and his infinite willingness.

> To put the thing briefly the way it appeared to a man who had no interest one way or the other – only a desire to see fair play and to

have the better fighter win – on the score of aggressiveness Hart was entitled to the verdict. On any other score Johnson should have been the favored one. This is a thing that will be argued on the street corners for days.[274]

The San Francisco Call said that although Johnson's muscles showed to better physical advantage, Hart was stronger and the harder worker. "Hart was ready for a severe contest, as the farther it went the better he seemed to get. He began to show a slight lead when half the route had been traversed, and did much the best work in the last ten rounds."

The Call said the spectators had a chance to cheer throughout, as Hart outgamed his clever opponent in a hard battle. Both were busy throughout, but Hart was the busier. Johnson had the superior cleverness, but he did not take any chances. Hart matched his gameness with Johnson's cleverness.

> Referee Alex Greggains gave an entirely just decision in favor of Hart. He was the aggressor throughout, and there was never an instant that he was not trying in an awkward style to land on the elusive negro.
>
> When the men shaped up for the first round, Hart's position seemed only a caricature of the way a fighter should shape up, while Johnson was the beau ideal of the boxer. It seemed the fight would last but a few rounds but Johnson showed his usual lack of aggressiveness and would not take advantage of the many openings his less skilled opponent left for him. At the beginning of each round Hart would make a dash at Johnson and invariably landed. Johnson would then get into action with right and left, but he was then satisfied to let well enough alone and would not follow up his man.
>
> While Johnson is fairly sheathed with muscle, the majority of his blows did not seem to have an ounce of strength behind them. It was astonishing the little damage done by the two powerful men, considering the apparent effort they put forth. Had Johnson a small part of the aggressiveness shown by Hart there would have been nothing to the fight.[275]

British lightweight champion Jabez White said,

> The only difference I saw between fighting here and in England is the holding that seems to be indulged in a great deal in San Francisco. … I have not been accustomed to the tugging and holding that I saw to-night. … I enjoyed the evening's entertainment very much and

---

274 *San Francisco Chronicle*, March 29, 1905.
275 *San Francisco Call*, March 29, 1905.

> Hart was certainly entitled to the decision. We were somewhat disappointed in Johnson.

White was also quoted as saying, "Hart was the aggressor all the way and the referee could do nothing but give him all the glory. The big fellows clinch too much, something you very seldom see across the pond."

The San Francisco Evening Post said Hart put up a gritty fight against Johnson, who lost "because he would not fight." Still, it also said that Hart's only redeeming point as a fighter was that he was a glutton for punishment, coming on for more no matter how hard he was walloped. Hart fought hard all the time, whereas Johnson only opened up in spots, showing flashes of offensive brilliance, followed by long periods of defensiveness, cautiousness, and clinching.

> Johnson had the fight well in hand all the time, but failed to carry home the victory just because he would not fight. At times when Hart did land and it stirred up the black fellow the latter would open up and make things so lively that it was thought that the white man would not last, but these were only flashes, and Johnson would settle back in his old jabbing tactics and clinching.
>
> As a fight on ability, the fight belonged to Johnson, but when it is taken into consideration that Alex Greggains warned both men that they must keep fighting and aggressiveness would decide the fight it can be seen how the verdict could be given to Hart.
>
> One point in favor of such a proposition is that it will keep men fighting all the time they are in the ring.

The ticket sales yielded $6,200, of which the club retained 40%, or $2,480, with $3,720 to be divided equally between Hart and Johnson, or $1,860 each. "Few that saw the mill would go through the same mill for ten times $1,860."[276]

The San Francisco Bulletin, disagreed with the decision, feeling that Johnson should have at least received a draw, if not a victory. It said that Johnson had a decided lead on points and cleverness. In the first two or three rounds, it looked like Johnson would win easily. However, Hart's remarkable recuperative powers made the battle interesting.

> He was so aggressive and bored in with such determination that Johnson could never set himself for a punch, and the colored man's shifty left couldn't be brought into action with such telling effect as in his former local battles. At that he landed so often on the face of the Blue Grass State's aspirant for championship honors that the right side wouldn't recognize the left side if they should perchance gaze upon each other in a looking glass. Hart's left eye was put very

---

[276] *San Francisco Evening Post*, March 29, 1905.

> much to the bad in the early stage of the contest, and his face began to puff out like a toy balloon. ... However, this was the only damage suffered by either man, both being strong on their feet when the final gong sounded. ...
>
> Naturally, the house was with Hart, not only because he was the short-ender, but also owing to racial prejudices. Whenever the Kentuckian landed a blow, no matter whether it was a love tap or a hard body punch, the gallery would howl with delight, and long before the final rounds cries of "Hart! Hart! Hart!" rang through the pavilion. So, when Referee Greggains pointed to Hart as the winner at the end of the contest, pandemonium reigned supreme throughout the auditorium, but if a person looked at the contest from an unbiased standpoint and carefully weighed everything in the balance, he would be compelled to acknowledge that the worst Johnson should have received was a draw. Looking at it from a scientific angle, the colored man should have been declared the victor. It is true that Hart did all the forcing and was ever on the aggressive, but his blows rarely landed on a vulnerable spot, and he never had his opponent in distress. On the other hand, Johnson outpointed and outboxed him from start to finish, and on several occasions forced the white man to break ground with such alacrity that the ropes alone saved him from going into the audience. ...

It compared the decision to the Battling Nelson – Jimmy Britt fight, which was similar to this one. There, although Nelson was clearly the aggressor like Hart and Britt was content to block and retaliate with jabs and uppercuts like Johnson, Britt won the decision, although with a different referee – Billy Roche.

> Of course, Greggains took the stand that he told both men that he would give the fight to the man who did the fighting, and on this score gave the decision to Hart. But this was not justice to the betting public who wagered their money on the merits of the two men as fighters and not simply on a man's bulldog tenacity and ability to assimilate punishment. What Johnson should have done was to have waded in and forced his adversary, as he was sufficiently clever and had such a decided advantage in reach to enable him to beat Hart to the punch, but like all clever men, he deemed discretion was the better part of valor and laid back with the expectation of getting the decision. This proved to be a fatal mistake. ... The general public was extremely pleased over the decision, but if Johnson was a few shades lighter and had no trace of negro blood in his veins there would have been a different story to tell.[277]

---

[277] *San Francisco Bulletin*, March 29, 1905.

Regardless, the *Bulletin* also said that there had been 20 rounds of mediocre fighting in which neither man had particularly distinguished himself.

The Los Angeles Daily Times, via direct wire dispatch, reported, "From appearances, Hart was the beaten man from a physical point of view." Hart's face was swollen and his left eye closed, while Johnson did not have a mark. Interestingly, the report stated that Johnson "did not even appear to be tired, and yet he had fought as nobody had ever seen him fight before in California."

> Hart's gameness was what won the fight. He appeared to be awkward, and to know little of the art of boxing, but he carried the fight to his opponent all the time, and did his share of the leading. It was his forcing and fighting at all times throughout the fight upon which Greggains based his verdict. In point of cleverness and point of blows landed, Johnson led all the way. At times, he placed as many as a half a dozen short-arm uppercuts upon his opponent without return. In the mixing, he also landed oftenest; but Referee Greggains made up his mind that the Kentuckian's work was most effective. From the ninth round on, Hart was bleeding from the nose continuously, and it seemed at many times during the rough infighting that he could not see his opponent at all. But he lasted out, and fought and tugged like a demon all the time. Often during the twenty rounds he was borne to the ropes and received full-arm uppercuts. Throughout the last five rounds he had the crowd shouting wildly for him. The Kentuckian's gameness won nearly every man in the house. Color certainly figured to some extent in this support of a practical stranger.
>
> Johnson was a badly disappointed man. He considered he had landed two blows to every one that his opponent gave him, and he believed that he had led fully as often as the Kentuckian. Referee Greggains, however, figured that Hart's work was the best, and his decision went.[278]

The Associated Press report in that same newspaper had a similar version.

> Hart was as badly punished a man as has been seen in the ring for a long time, but he was game to the core, and kept boring into the big colored man all through the fight.
>
> Johnson's much-vaunted cleverness did not count for much. While he was able to hit Hart frequently, his blows did not seem to damage the white man.... The sympathies of the large crowd present were

---

[278] *Los Angeles Daily Times*, March 29, 1905.

> openly with Hart…and every lead he made at Johnson, whether he landed or not, was greeted with yells of joy. Hart did manage to deal the only effective blow in the eleventh round, when he landed a right swing on Johnson's jaw that staggered the black man and nearly knocked him over.
>
> Referee Greggains stated that he gave the decision to Hart because, all through the fight, Hart did all the forcing and leading. According to Greggains, if Hart had not pursued his tactics, there would have been no fight, as Johnson merely contented himself with countering.
>
> Hart's face was battered to a pulp, but Johnson's blows did not seem to have much sting to them. Johnson did a great deal of uppercutting, but Hart covered up, and the blows did not seem to hurt him.

The A.P.'s round by round description gave the impression that it was a fairly close and competitive fight. Certainly, it did not mention Johnson as tiring and the impression it gave from its round by round description is different from other versions, highlighting the difficulties in describing a bout that does not exist on film. Essentially, the impression gathered from the report's description is that it saw the 1st round as dull, the 2nd for Johnson, the 3rd even, 4th and 5th slightly for Hart, 6th and 7th as dull with clinching, 8th for Hart, 9th and 10th for Johnson, 11th for Hart, 12th - 14th as even, 15th for Johnson, 16th for Hart, and 17th - 20th as even.[279]

On the East coast, the *Newark Evening News* and the *Trenton Times* presented exactly the same reports. They gave a fairly detailed, balanced and neutral account of the fight, but were equally critical of both fighters, saying that "neither pugilist showed any championship form."

> Hart was the worst punished of the two, and had the negro fought a fight which he showed himself at times capable of he would have won handily. Referee Greggains gave the decision to Hart because of his gameness and aggressiveness. The spectators were wholly of the opinion that Johnson was suffering from a streak of bright yellow. Whenever he did fight, he made Hart look like an amateur. The Louisville man's aggressiveness seemed to rattle Johnson and his courage would ooze….
>
> The last ten rounds resembled each other. Johnson pegged away with straight lefts and rights, which cut Hart's face, while the Kentucky colonel walloped away with right swings to the body and head.

Overall, this account has Johnson doing very well when he was active, particularly through the first half of the bout, landing solid blows, cutting Hart and outboxing him. However, Johnson chose to be active only in spots, often in retaliatory fashion after he was hit, or when forced to fight.

---

279 *Los Angeles Daily Times*, March 29, 1905.

He took every opportunity to clinch. Greggains explained that Hart was aggressive throughout and wanted to fight continually, while Johnson "dogged it."

Johnson landed well to the head and body in the 1st and 2nd rounds. Hart was aggressive in the 3rd but unable to land effectively as Johnson kept away and did not do much. After the first few rounds, Johnson let Hart do most of the leading. There were several clinches in the 4th and no damage done. Hart tried to work in close during the 5th, but Johnson blocked his leads. In the 6th, Hart rushed but Johnson sent him back with a straight left that was the hardest blow of the fight. The 7th was Johnson's, as he repeatedly hooked his left to the jaw. The 8th and 9th were fast and Johnson's superiority and strength were evident. His quick two-handed punching had Hart bleeding. Hart was still aggressive though. Johnson punished him with lefts and rights in the 9th. In the 10th, Johnson jammed him into a corner. There were good exchanges in the 11th round, and Hart was still eager and game. Johnson visibly slowed for the next three rounds and "seemed perturbed at the way Hart was assimilating punishment." Hart kept wading in, driving Johnson around the ring with vicious blows to the body and head in the 15th and 16th rounds. Johnson showed better form in the 17th round and hammered Hart hard and often.

> Hart was the aggressor in the last three rounds and kept piling in with hard rights to the body. Johnson acted as though he was tired and his seconds kept calling him to hit it up. Hart made a target of the negro's ribs. The fight closed with little doing and the referee, because of Hart's aggressiveness, gave him the decision.[280]

The Police Gazette, which had generally been a Johnson advocate, said that the referee gave the decision to Hart because he had been the aggressor, trying to fight all the time, while Johnson had been guilty of holding.

It noted that Hart was badly puffed and bruised, while Johnson was unmarked. Johnson "believed himself entitled to the decision by reason of his clean-cut and terrific punching." In fairness though, it recognized that Johnson held considerably and did not have as much power. "His blows, though, did not have as much steam behind them as did Hart's. The Southerner, when he landed, hurt his man."

Johnson was superior in the first 10 rounds, but after that, Hart made a better showing. Hart "showed far more gameness than Johnson, who fought cautiously after Hart began to force things. In the closing rounds Hart carried the fighting to Johnson so frequently that the black repeatedly clinched and held." Still, the *Gazette* questioned the legitimacy of Hart's victory. "He did not have the better of the going and a draw would have

---

280 *Newark Evening News*, March 29, 1905; *Trenton Times*, March 29, 1905.

been a present to him. Johnson undoubtedly prejudiced the referee by holding until he was ready to break." Johnson had the edge in cleverness and blows landed, but Hart "fought doggedly and like a man who would not be beaten." The crowd liked Hart, and the incessant shouts of support for him at least had a subconscious influence. "There is no doubt that Greggains' opinion was affected by the tremendous shouting of the crowd for Hart."

Johnson had a distinct advantage in the first 3 rounds. Hart took several hard jolts while rushing in. Johnson kept him at bay with his long arms. Johnson held so often in the 4th and 5th rounds that Hart could not do anything. Johnson cut loose in the 9th and did clever punching with both hands.

Hart's gameness began to tell in the 11th round. "He had the negro fighting hard then, and landed several blows that staggered him." In the 15th round, "Johnson slowed perceptibly, and after that it was Hart's fight." Both were tired after the 17th. In the 19th, "Johnson swung wildly, while Hart's blows all told. The final round brought a flash of speed in both men, Hart landing more effectively."[281]

The Louisville Times reported that early on, Johnson's science was so much superior that Hart appeared overmatched, but this did not daunt him. Johnson landed several more to every one of Hart's, but Marvin's blows were much harder. Hart kept forcing no matter what. He won on his courage and stamina. Johnson's early advantage "was more than offset in the closing rounds, and the decision was well earned by Hart, who forced the fight throughout and was more than holding his own at the finish."[282]

The excellent conditioning, hard-punching, ferocious, busy aggressiveness that Marvin Hart had exhibited throughout his career came through for him in this one. This was a take-what-you-like fight. Johnson landed more clean blows, which were less powerful, but did more damage as far as appearances go. However, Johnson also did more clinching and less leading, something which cost him in the scoring because at that time aggressiveness and fighting spirit counted in decisions. A draw might have been more appropriate. This was one of those fights that probably should have been scheduled to a finish in order to truly determine who the better man was. But that would have required the bout to have been held in the less populated state of Nevada.

Quite frankly, watching Johnson on film years later against Jim Flynn, a fighter whose aggressive style was similar to Hart's, it is understandable why an official might decide against Johnson. He was very skilled defensively, and carefully chose when to punch, but clinched often, kept the pace slow, and did not punch very hard. He was not what one would call an exciting

---

281 *Police Gazette*, April 15, 1905.
282 *Louisville Times*, March 29, 1905.

fighter. This style was not one which would ingratiate Johnson with the fans or officials, even putting racial prejudice aside. Being boring and black didn't help. Conversely, Marvin Hart's exciting style had won for him several close bouts (and/or gained him draws in bouts in which he was behind on number of blows landed), even prior to Johnson, even against white fighters. So, his style was one which could give him an edge in close fights.

A day after the bout, Alex Greggains put forth an additional explanation for his decision.

> When the men met to discuss the rules under which they were to fight I warned them both... They decided on straight Queensberry. I know, of course, that Johnson was unpopular with the sports over the way he held off in his fights with Ferguson and McVey, and I was determined that he should extend himself this time, if it was possible to make him. I said: 'Now, you fellows have agreed to straight Queensberry rules, and you know what that means. If there is no knockout I will decide this fight on aggressiveness; so you know what to expect.' Well, any man with half an eye could tell who was the aggressor. Hart wanted to fight all the time. Johnson just loosened up in spots, especially after he got a stomach punch in the tenth. He kept holding in the clinches and asking me to come and break them. I told him to fight himself loose, as the other man was trying to do. I think that if every referee would let it be known that aggressiveness would weigh the most when there was no knockout, he would have better contests.[283]

Many believed, and rightfully so, that clinching should count against a fighter in a points match. In early 1900, the *Louisville Courier-Journal* had an article entitled "Clincher Should Be Disqualified." Billy Madden, manager of Denver Ed Martin, noted that the Marquis of Queensberry rules "forbid clinching or putting your hands on a man except to hit." He felt that clinchers should be disqualified. Barring that, referees should not be too quick to break when a fighter had a hand free and was able to punch while the other was holding.

> If you make a rule that a boxer can't hit a man when he gets close to an opponent, with both hands free and the other man hugging, then you may as well put a rope across the stage and let them use blackened gloves for long-range points. Then there would be more fighters, as they would not be afraid of getting punched. ... The clincher should be disqualified, as it is very hard for a fair boxer. He

---

[283] *San Francisco Examiner*, March 30, 1905.

has to be a wonder, like McGovern, to defeat his man, when the other man is holding him.[284]

Clearly, Johnson's clinching style also cost him with Greggains.

A couple days after the bout, Jack Johnson left for Philadelphia, while Hart returned to Kentucky. Johnson was broken up over the decision, and disputed Greggains' claim that he told the boxers before the fight that he would give the decision to the most aggressive fighter. "I want to say that he never did any such thing. All that he said before the gong sounded was, 'You fellows know the rules, don't you?' We said we did, and went at it. I did not want Alec to referee, but Hart would not take Welch or Graney, whom I mentioned. Hart said it was Greggains or nobody." Johnson said he hurt his hands in the 6th round, which prevented him from carrying out his intention of a knockout within 10 rounds.[285]

---

[284] *Louisville Courier-Journal*, February 11, 1900.
[285] *San Francisco Bulletin*, March 31, 1905.

CHAPTER 12

The Unfulfilled Match

After Marvin Hart won a 20-round decision over Jack Johnson, heavyweight champion James J. Jeffries said that he was happy the white man won.

> I am glad Marvin Hart won over Johnson last night. Not that it means a prospective candidate for my title, but it places the negro out of the running. If Johnson had won he would never have fought me. My decision never to meet a negro while I am champion would have been faithfully kept.... I will retire from the ring this year, and when I do retire it will be forever.[286]

Jeff also said that he would sign to fight Hart only if the public demanded a meeting between them.

Jeffries' manager Bill Delaney said,

> In June 1905 Jeffries will arrive in California, and if by that time there is no white man ready to make a match with him Jeff will forever retire from the ring. I understand Jeff thoroughly, and know that in order to fight well he must fight often. I do not propose to have Jeff make the mistake that all former champions have made – that is, of fighting once too often.[287]

Hart wanted to fight Jeffries. "I am the only man in the world who would have a chance to beat him. I have beaten Jack Johnson, a man Jeffries has been side-stepping for months, and I can put it on the boilermaker, too."

> Hart and his friends are so jubilant over the way he polished off the colored man.... They say that to outfight Johnson as he did, giving the negro many pounds and a beating, shows that Hart is the best heavyweight in the world, outside of Jeffries.... Every man who saw the fight gave Hart credit for the battle he put up, and there were many who said the Kentucky man would make Jeff extend himself to the limit to win.[288]

However, there was a mix of opinion regarding Marvin's relative merits, and whether Hart was a viable contender to challenge Jeffries. Many who

---

[286] *Trenton Times*, March 29, 1905.
[287] *Louisville Times*, March 29, 1905.
[288] *Trenton Times*, March 30, 1905; *Newark Evening News*, March 30, 1905.

saw the Johnson fight said, "I tell you this fellow Hart is a tough customer and likely to give Jeffries a whole lot of trouble." That was "a common remark among fellows usually credited with judgment and discrimination in matters pertaining to pugilism." However, W.W. Naughton said Hart "would be candy for Jeff," that it would be inhuman to put him in the ring with the champion.

> Just at present, Hart's principal fighting qualifications – pluck and endurance – are the very things that would place him in a serious predicament were he left alone in a Queensberry enclosure with the modern pine-bender, big Jim Jeffries.
>
> Jeffries has all that Hart has in the matter of strength and ruggedness. He is heavier, more forceful and more durable than Hart. He is as fast as a feather weight and he would have little difficulty in landing on Hart. The Kentuckian's grit and powers of assimilation would only serve to prolong the agony. … For Hart and Jeffries the time is not yet. Hart may develop into a suitable adversary for Jeffries some day, but for a year at least he should devote his time to improving his knowledge of glove work.[289]

Regardless of whether Hart should have won against Johnson, or a draw would have been more appropriate, or even a decision victory for Johnson, all of the local writers who had seen the bout immediately afterwards in their next-day post-fight reports said that Jeffries would easily defeat either Johnson or Hart.

The San Francisco Call said, "It was the consensus of opinion that if either of them ever decides to fight Jeffries there will be another death in the ring." However, it agreed with the decision for Hart.

The San Francisco Evening Post said, "From what was seen last night in the ring, what a joke either fighter would be before Champion Jeffries. They would go down about as fast as Munroe passed away."

The San Francisco Bulletin said that it was the unanimous opinion of the spectators that neither man would have a chance with Jeffries. "There is no doubt that Jeffries could take the two men on the same evening fighting each man alternate rounds and put them both away inside of ten rounds." Hart was criticized as not possessing the terrible punch he had been credited with, and was in Jack Munroe's class in terms of cleverness. "The only redeeming qualities he possesses is rare gameness and a willingness to force matters. But if he should run into one of Jeffries' pile-driving solar plexus punches with the frequency that he displayed last evening in stopping Johnson's wallops it would be 'curtains' for the Kentuckian in short order." The hope that either man would be matched with Jeffries was

---

[289] *San Francisco Examiner*, March 30, 1905.

eliminated when "they demonstrated that the necessary qualification for a champion was lacking, namely – a knockout wallop."

Both men had incentives to fight hard due to the fact that they wanted to legitimize their challenges to Jeffries. However, "Johnson was not willing to mix matters with a vengeance, while Hart lacked the necessary cleverness and punch to decisively defeat the negro."

Of course, in Hart's defense, it is not always easy to appear like a big puncher when you go up against a cautious, defensive specialist with height and reach, who knows how to duck, block, move and clinch. In Johnson's defense, anyone who closely followed Hart's career was fully cognizant of the fact that he was one tough dude, who had only been stopped once on a fluke when he was caught cold. Two good fighters meeting each other often have a way of offsetting their strengths and weaknesses.

Still, the Associated Press reported, "Hart was far from demonstrating that he is qualified to meet Jim Jeffries." It also said, "The general opinion of those who witnessed the fight was that neither man would stand any chance with Jeffries."

The Police Gazette was also tough on Hart, saying that "the critical public was not favorably impressed by the manner in which Hart won from Jack Johnson." Of a bout with Jeffries, it said that "there will hardly be any crying demand for such an unequal match."

> Hart did not prove himself a first-class pugilist. The only thing that he showed in the scrap was that he was capable of taking a lot of punishment. Johnson's defeat was as big a surprise to Hart as it was to the negro, and although the crowd as a body upheld Referee Greggains, he could only find one favorable thing to say in Hart's favor, and that was that he forced the fighting. [290]

A week later, the *Police Gazette* said,

> Marvin Hart has not exhibited any frantic eagerness to force Jim Jeffries into a match.... Hart has a Chinaman's chance. He will be the softest proposition that ever crossed the path of the Herculean Californian.... Had Jack Johnson fought up to his standard he would have beaten Hart.... When he did mix it up, Hart looked like a handful of nondescript change, which only goes to show that the Southerner was lucky in getting away with what he did.[291]

Bob Fitzsimmons said of Hart, "It looks like Johnson received a bad deal, but I'm willing to fight him if he wants to make the match. I do not know much about him, but from what I've heard I guess he is a comer."[292]

---

[290] *Police Gazette*, April 15, 1905.
[291] *Police Gazette*, April 22, 1905.
[292] *Police Gazette*, April 22, 1905.

Yet, another week later, another reporter from the same newspaper was giving Hart more of a chance against Jeffries, or at least to make a good showing.

> It is true that Hart's victory over Johnson was not a decisive one.... But he won, just the same, and a win by a close margin is as good as a win by mile. Hart...scales over 190 pounds, and at this weight he is quick and agile in his movements.... Hart is a fighter who keeps coming all the time, and these tactics enabled him to predispose Referee Greggains in his favor.... As to Hart's gameness there is not the shadow of doubt. He took all that any man of his physique could stand in his mill with Johnson and never faltered. It is true that Johnson is not one-third the hitter that Jeffries is, but it must be admitted that the champion is not as clever as Johnson. The deduction is, it seems at this stage, that Hart has a fair chance of making a good fight.[293]

However, another reporter said, "Marvin Hart is now considered the next best man to Jeffries, but to borrow an expression from another game, there is a broad streak of daylight between Jeffries and Hart."[294]

The Philadelphia Record suspected something more nefarious at work behind the decision in the Hart-Johnson bout, saying,

> The heavy-weights are not apt to figure in pugilistic history in the near future. The match between Jack Johnson and Marvin Hart, as well as the result of the same, seems to have been cleverly planned, but, according to the old Scotch saying, 'the best-laid plans of mice and men aft gang aglee,' the public appears to have gotten wise, and there is little demand for a fight between Hart and Jeffries, for which all the fine work was done. It may be easy to fool some of the people, but you can't fool them all the time.[295]

Hence, although there were those who felt that Hart would put up a competitive showing against Jeffries, the overall reception to a Hart-Jeffries bout was lukewarm at best.

Just over a month after the Johnson bout, on May 8, 1905, Hart was back in the ring again in Philadelphia in a rematch with Chicago's John Willie. It was a scheduled 6-round no-decision bout at Philly's Washington Sporting Club. Since his 1904 6-round draw with Hart, Willie's results included: 1904 D6 Jack Root, D6 George Gardner, WND6 Jack O'Brien,[296]

---

293 *Police Gazette*, April 29, 1905.
294 *Police Gazette*, April 29, 1905.
295 *Philadelphia Record*, May 7, 1905.
296 *Police Gazette*, October 22, 1904, November 26, 1904.

LDQby5 Root;[297] and a February 1905 LND6 O'Brien.[298] John Willie could trouble the best in the business.

Hart had advantages in height and reach, and was about 15 pounds heavier. However, the *Philadelphia Record* said Hart looked fat and not in the best of condition, having a vomiting spell before the bout began. Willie appeared to be in good shape. They agreed to break when ordered, and generally boxed cleanly, although they occasionally forgot the rules.

1 - Hart stood with his left arm extended and his jaw well covered up by raising his shoulder. He landed a hard right to the body. Willie landed some light punches in quick succession, but Hart followed with a savage smash on the heart. Willie ducked another vicious swing and landed a left to the body. Both landed some light punches. A clinch followed, and Hart hit the body. Both mostly devoted their blows to the body in this round, though Hart also occasionally landed a left jab to the face. Just before the bell rang, Willie landed a nasty left swing that rocked Hart's head. *The Philadelphia Press* said Hart landed the majority of the punches.

2 - Willie rushed Marvin to the ropes and landed a couple light lefts to the head. Hart landed a telling punch on the body, but Willie slipped under the head shot. Willie walked into a body shot, but came back with a smash on the ribs. Marvin again got to the heart with his terrific right. John landed to the side of the head. *The Philadelphia Press* said this round was also in Hart's favor, with his right smashes to the body being the hardest blows in the round.

3 - This was one of the hottest rounds. They tried hard, but most of their efforts ended in clinches. Referee Schlichter had trouble getting them to break without hitting. Willie was reluctant to break when told. Willie landed a right to the ear, but Marvin at once rushed and sent in a right uppercut to the mouth. Willie then grabbed Hart and pushed him across the ring. This enraged Hart and he sailed in and furiously pounded Willie hard about the body. Willie clinched. The eager Hart missed many swings for the face. Hart got in some good body blows, one of which seemed to sting Willie, and he held on for a while. Willie hurt Hart with two rights to the body, but Marvin came back with two right uppercuts, one of which raised a small lump on Willie's forehead. Before the bell rang, Hart landed a hard right under the heart and left swing on the face. This was another Hart round.

4 - This was not as strenuous a round, for the hard work began to tell. It was mostly in Hart's favor, although Willie was there all the time, and landed one very stiff punch on Marvin's ribs. Hart occasionally landed his left to the face, but it was the body blows that had Willie in such distress

---

297 *Police Gazette*, December 24, 1904. Willie had the best of Root, twice dropping him with body shots in the 5th, but was disqualified that same round for a subsequent low blow.
298 *Police Gazette*, February 18, 1905.

that he hung on as much as possible. Referee Schlichter was kept busy separating them. This was Hart's round as well.

5 - Willie landed a couple stiff blows, but had to take some pretty hard body punishment, which caused him to keep clinching. Hart again won the round.

6 - Hart was very aggressive and followed Willie all over the ring throughout the round, trying to force matters to a conclusion. John escaped many furious swings. The crowd cheered Willie when he landed left and rights swings on Hart's face. Marvin came back hard and kept both hands working on Willie's body.

Near the end of the round, Hart dropped Willie with a hard right uppercut to the body. The Chicago man was up in an instant and fought back gamely, but the blow had hurt him. Hart won this round as well.

According to the local reporters, Marvin Hart unofficially "won" the 6-round no-decision. *The Philadelphia Press* said Hart's showing was "none too good, but it didn't have to be with Willie in the ring." Willie fought as if his one goal was to last the 6 rounds. Hart did practically all of the work, devoting most of his blows to the body, but missing many swings for the face. When Willie was in distress, his strength and clinching abilities enabled him to recover. Willie clinched often to save himself from punishment. He hardly landed three good blows per round, devoting most of the time to escaping swings. Neither was marked at the end, though Willie's body had to be sore. Hart was the only man in the fight.

According to the *Philadelphia Public Ledger*, "It was Hart's fight, but by an extremely narrow margin." Hart focused on the body, for Willie had good defense.

The Philadelphia Inquirer was much harder on Willie, saying that he was a "dub" who would not box, and tried to wrestle. It was a poor bout, but it was not Hart's fault. Marvin deserved what honors there were.

The Philadelphia Record said Hart had the best of the bout, although he did not do any great damage to the Chicago boxer. Taken as a whole, the bout was a disappointment.[299]

With Jack Johnson's image tarnished by the Hart bout, in his attempt to get Hart back into the ring, "Johnson has been saying some sassy things about the Louisville idol." However, Hart was reported to have said that he would never again fight a colored man. "The referee of the Hart-Johnson fight may have given a strictly fair decision, but it must have been very close when it took a column to explain it." There would be no Hart-Johnson rematch.[300]

---

299 *Philadelphia Press, Philadelphia Public Ledger, Philadelphia Inquirer, Philadelphia Record*, May 9, 1905.
300 *Police Gazette*, May 13, 1905.

No Hart-Jeffries bout would occur either. Just over a month after Hart defeated Johnson, and five days after Marvin fought Willie, on May 13, 1905, James J. Jeffries officially retired. He said that there was no one in sight to give the public a run for its money against him. Apparently, there was not sufficient public clamor and excitement for Jeffries to fight Marvin Hart, and seeing that there would not be a sufficient financial incentive to fight him, Jeff decided to retire.

Initially, when asked if he would turn over his title to Bob Fitzsimmons, Jeff said that there was nothing to turn over. He then said that although Fitz was one of the best men that ever boxed, he was getting on in years, and if he won the title, age would force Bob into retirement. However, he also said, "The younger crop of champion aspirants do not appear formidable." This left open the question regarding who would be champion in Jeff's absence.[301]

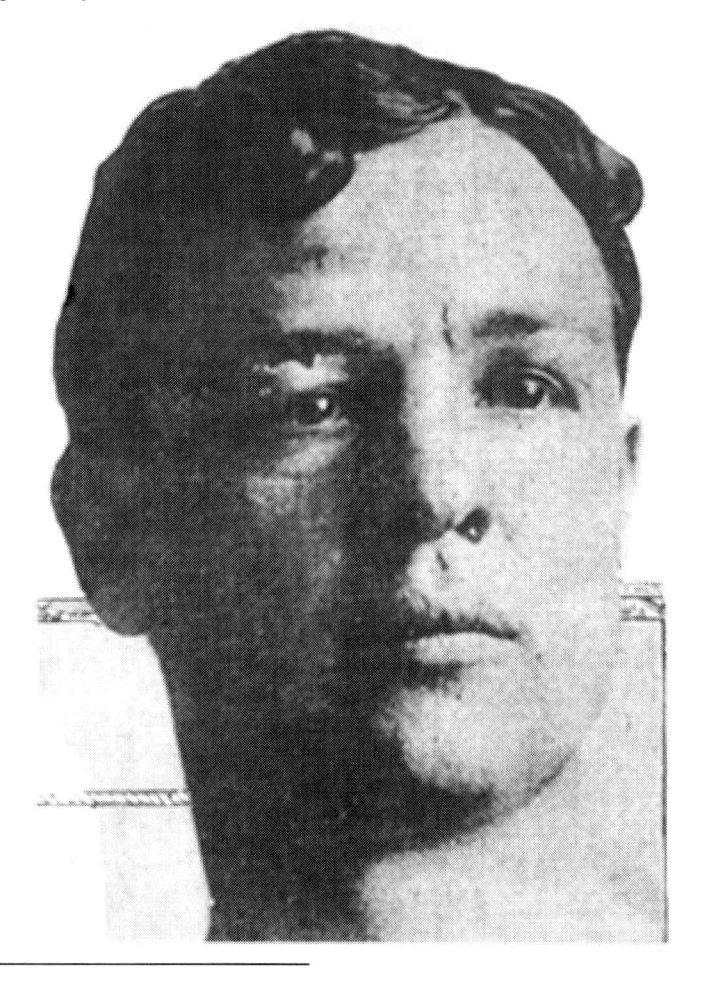

---

301 *Chicago Tribune*, May 14, 1905.

CHAPTER 13

Filling the Vacancy

After James Jeffries retired, the question was, 'Who was the most deserving to fight for the vacant title?' In truth, Marvin Hart and Jack Johnson probably should have fought a rematch for the title, but the color line was not going to allow that. Racial separation was the social norm in America, and would continue as such for several decades. It was especially so for boxing's top prize, the heavyweight championship. In fact, no black man was allowed the opportunity to first win the heavyweight crown from a white man in America until 1937. Baseball's Jackie Robinson did not break the color line in team sports in America until 1947.[302]

According to the *Police Gazette*, Fitzsimmons, Hart, and Mike Schreck of Cincinnati were the most prominent men eligible to be considered as successors. "Hart looms up as the most eligible because of his victory over Jack Johnson, a win that has been questioned in many quarters." Hart was number one, but if Johnson was not going to be number 2, the question was who should be. This requires a discussion of what the various contenders were doing at the time.[303]

Bob Fitzsimmons

Bob Fitzsimmons was highly regarded because he was the last champion before Jeffries and had given Jeff his most recent toughest battle, although it was a 1902 LKOby8, three years earlier. Fitz had a KO5 over Choynski, who had fought Hart to a D6. Fitz had a KO6 over Ruhlin, who had a L6 and D12 against Hart.

In 1903, Fitzsimmons had won a 20-round decision over George Gardner to win the world light-heavyweight title, but he had not done much since then, and those who saw him against Gardner felt that Bob was on the down swing even then. Bob's only 1904 bout, albeit an exciting one, was a 6-round no-decision against Jack O'Brien. Bob had not fought at all in 1905. Fitz was an inactive 42-year-old whose best days were behind him.

---

[302] The eventual Johnson-Burns championship bout took place in Australia, and therefore, Johnson was already the champion when he fought white challengers in America. Johnson's reign was actually more of an anomaly than anything, and might not have ever existed had he not been given the opportunity to fight for the title in a foreign country, by Burns, who was a Canadian.
[303] *Police Gazette*, June 10, 1905.

Mike Schreck

Southpaw Mike Schreck's career included: 1902 D6 Jack "Twin" Sullivan, D6 Hugo Kelly and W6 Kelly (twice); 1903 W10 Tommy Burns, L15 and D20 Kelly, L6 Stift, and L6 O'Brien;[304] 1904 LND6 Sullivan,[305] D6 Burns (Burns considered superior),[306] L15 O'Brien, L10 Sullivan, and D10 Kelly;[307] and 1905 LND6 George Cole[308] and KO20 George Gardner.[309]

Schreck was called "clever, besides being extremely strong. He whipped George Gardner by knocking him out in the final round of a grueling contest."[310] Schreck's April 1905 20th round knockout victory over Gardner was impressive, but Schreck had recently lost a 15-round decision to Jack O'Brien, who was still competing as a middleweight, and Mike had sketchy results and losses in several other bouts.

Fitzsimmons and Schreck were matched to fight each other, but the promoters could not come up with the finances, and the bout never took place.[311]

George Gardner

Gardner had a 1902 LDQby7 and WKO17 against Jack Root, but a L20 to Jack Johnson.

In 1903, Gardner scored a KO12 over Hart when Marvin retired owing to a broken hand. Gardner then scored a KO12 over Root to win the world light-heavyweight crown, but lost it in a 20-round decision to Fitzsimmons.

In 1904, Gardner was considered to have been given a gift even by his local fans and newspapers when he received a 15-round draw against Hart. That year, he also had results such as: D6[312] and L6 Root, D6 Willie, and D10 Jim Flynn. In April 1905, he suffered the LKOby20 to Schreck. He had no recent victories that would legitimize him as a title challenger.

---

304 Against O'Brien, although Schreck went down from a right in the 2nd round, the decision was hissed, as the fight appeared even. *Police Gazette*, December 26, 1903.
305 "Sullivan had all the better of the milling and clearly proved he was Schreck's master." *Police Gazette*, January 23, 1904.
306 *Milwaukee Daily News*, February 29, 1904.
307 Kelly had Schreck at his mercy but failed to take advantage of his opportunity and allowed Schreck to stay the limit. *Police Gazette*, November 12, 1904.
308 Cole had twice before bested Schreck and was far superior to him this time. *Police Gazette*, March 18, 1905.
309 Schreck-Gardner was a bloody test of endurance as they slashed away at each other throughout, until an overhand right swing to the neck dropped Gardner. He rose but was so weak that the referee stopped it. *Police Gazette*, May 6, 1905.
310 *Police Gazette*, June 10, 1905.
311 *Police Gazette*, July 1, 1905.
312 *Police Gazette*, March 12, 1904; *Chicago Chronicle*, February 27, 1904: It was considered a fair decision. Root "had a fair shade the better of the clean hitting and long range work, while Gardner did the more effective punching, most of his work being confined to the short ribs."

"Philadelphia" Jack O'Brien

Jack O'Brien fought Hart to two 6-round no-decisions, one in 1902 and another in 1903. However, both times, the larger and stronger Hart dropped O'Brien towards the end of the contests. O'Brien had tasted Hart's power, and given their size disparity, he was not overly eager to fight Hart in a lengthy bout.

In 1903, O'Brien won a 6-round decision over Mike Schreck (who had won a 10-round decision over future champion Tommy Burns).

On January 27, 1904, Philadelphia Jack O'Brien fought world middleweight champion Tommy Ryan in a 6-round no-decision bout. O'Brien had a slight advantage. Jack outfought Tommy in the first 4 rounds and dropped Ryan in the 5th with a punch to the jaw. However, Ryan rose and clinched, and soon thereafter landed a left to the stomach that dropped O'Brien during the same round. Ryan continued landing wicked body shots, and Jack was saved by the bell. The 6th round was even.[313]

O'Brien again decisioned Mike Schreck, in 15 rounds.[314] This was important because Schreck then knocked out George Gardner in the 20th round, after Hart defeated Johnson. O'Brien also fought Bob Fitzsimmons to a 6-round no-decision in July 1904, but was decked by Fitzsimmons in the final round. O'Brien won an October 1904 6-round decision over Tommy Burns.

In April 1905, O'Brien lost a 10-round decision to Hugo Kelly.[315] Coming off a loss when Jeffries retired did not help O'Brien's chances to be considered as a vacant title challenger, especially given that he really was a middleweight.[316]

John "Sandy" Ferguson

Sandy Ferguson was another fighter who could have been, but was not considered. He had a number of decision losses to Jack Johnson, some of which were very dull, and a 1903 D15 with Ruhlin. He lost a 20-round decision to Hart which many thought Ferguson had won or at least earned a draw. However, he followed that with a May 1904 10-round draw with the vastly smaller Joe Walcott, a fight which Walcott would have won had there

---

[313] *Detroit Free Press*, January 28, 1904.
[314] With the exception of the 2nd round when O'Brien was badly dazed, the fight was all O'Brien's. *Police Gazette*, March 26, 1904, April 2, 1904.
[315] *Philadelphia Public Ledger*, May 7, 1905; *Police Gazette*, May 20, 1905.
[316] Tommy Burns would later defeat Kelly in a 20-round bout in July 1905. Actually, it was officially ruled a 20-round draw. Burns had indeed defeated Kelly on the merits, but had made an agreement that if no one was knocked out that it would be declared a draw.

been no agreement that the decision would be a draw if there was no knockout.[317] He had only fought a couple times since then, with a November KO1 Charlie Haghey and January 1905 WDQ5 Jack McCormick, both of whom were the lower class of fighter. Bat Masterson said of him,

> I saw Ferguson in his fight against Marvin Hart, and thought he was the making of a champion, and, with Jeffries eliminated from the running, looked to have more than an even chance to defeat any of the heavyweights now before the public. There must surely be something wrong with this big bruiser or he would be commanding the attention of the fight promoters of this country.
>
> Ferguson can fight if he will. He knows the game, and besides being one of the cleverest big men I ever saw perform in the ring, he carries a knockout punch in either hand. He is over six feet, and weighs about 220 pounds in condition. Ferguson is red-headed, which is good grounds for believing that he is a cur, and as he has failed to get to the front in the fighting game it must be due to a yellow streak.[318]

For whatever, reason, writers and promoters didn't get behind a Ferguson title shot.

Jack Root

Jack Root's career merits some discussion because he wound up fighting Hart for the vacated heavyweight championship.

Root's results included: 1900 D6 Tommy Ryan, KO1 Creedon, and KO9 Byers; 1902 WDQ7 Gardner, KO2 Stift, LKOby17 Gardner, W6 Carter (who earlier that year held a KO1 over Choynski), W6 Hart; 1903 W10 Kid McCoy (world light heavyweight championship),[319] LKOby12 Gardner (loses title), and KO8 Jim Flynn; and 1904 D6 Willie, D6[320] and W6[321] Gardner, NC4 Ryan (referee alleged the bout to be a fake when Root dropped Ryan with an apparently light punch),[322] and WDQ5 Willie.[323] He had not fought in 1905.

---

317 Ferguson-Walcott was an official draw per agreement if there was no knockout, but the referee said the decision would have gone to Walcott if one was allowed. *Police Gazette*, June 11, 1904.
318 *Seattle Post-Intelligencer*, January 29, 1905.
319 Root won easily. *Police Gazette*, May 9, 1903.
320 Root had a "fair shade the better of the clean hitting and long range work, while Gardner did the more effective punching, most of his work being confined to the short ribs." *Chicago Chronicle*, February 27, 1904.
321 Root dropped Gardner in the 2nd and 5th rounds and had the better of it. *Police Gazette*, May 21, 1904.
322 A November 1904 bout with Tommy Ryan was declared a no-contest when Root and Ryan only exchanged light blows through 4 rounds and then Ryan was knocked out from a very light punch in the 4th and everyone thought it was a fake. *Police Gazette*, December 10, 1904, December 24, 1904.

Root had KO'd Stift, who fought Johnson to a draw. Root had won a decision over Hart, who had defeated Johnson, though Root lost to Gardner, whom Johnson had defeated. However, Root was coming off a 6-round decision victory over Gardner in a bout in which Root had dropped Gardner in two of the 6 rounds and clearly had the better of the bout.

Root was probably no more deserving of a title shot than some other contenders were. However, Root had a win over Hart, having dropped Hart in their short rounds bout. His skill and style were well respected, having won about 46 fights, and having lost only twice, both times to Gardner, whom he had recently defeated in an impressive performance. He was a skilled boxer and a hard puncher whom the fans appreciated. Hence, promoters arranged a championship battle between Hart and Root.

Marvin Hart

Jack Root

---

323 John Willie had the best of Root in a December 1904 bout, twice dropping him with body shots in the 5th, but was disqualified that same round for a subsequent low blow. *Police Gazette*, December 24, 1904.

CHAPTER 14

Road to the Championship

In truth, no matter who fought for the vacant world heavyweight championship, the public was still going to consider James Jeffries to be the best fighter alive. None of the top contenders had particularly distinguished themselves anywhere near the extent that Jeffries had, although Hart and Johnson came the closest.

The Hart-Root championship fight was scheduled for July 3, 1905 in Reno, Nevada, a state which allowed fights to the finish. Scheduling the bout as a fight to the finish was important because it lent championship credibility to the bout. Fights to the finish had more of a special and true championship aura. It was the first heavyweight championship fight to the finish since Corbett-Fitzsimmons in March 1897. Hence, there was great interest in the fight.

Hart was in Reno on June 9, 1905 seeking suitable training quarters for the fight. He eventually chose Wheelman's training quarters. "The fighter was closely followed by a large crowd of enthusiastic and admiring people, all eager to obtain a close view of the man who hoped to wear the belt which has been discarded by Jeffries."

Hart was a hot topic in Reno, and the local *Nevada State Journal* had almost daily reports on his activities.

Marvin planned to take off flesh and get down to 193-195 pounds, which he considered to be his best fighting weight. He would train for two hours in the morning and two hours in the afternoon.

Hart was a hard worker, training diligently at Wheelman's. On June 12, first Hart ran, played handball, and jumped rope. His bag punching proved to the satisfaction of those in attendance that he had a wallop with enough steam behind it to put most men into dreamland.

Despite being 225-230 pounds, Jack McCormick had enough of Marvin after sparring 2 rounds, so "Deafy" Thompson, Maurice Thompson's middleweight brother, stepped in and sparred 2 more rounds. An old-time sport follower who saw Hart train that day said, "Marvin Hart is one of the greatest fighters of recent years. The only man, in my opinion, who is capable of giving him any kind of a hard battle in a finish fight is Jeffries."[324]

On June 13, Hart ran 8 miles in the morning. In the afternoon, he did his usual gym work before sparring. Hart boxed 2 rounds with McCormick

---

324 *Nevada State Journal*, June 13, 1905.

at a lively pace, then "Butch" Welfit attempted to last 2 rounds, but was taken out in 1 round. Deafy Thompson went 2 more with Marvin.

JACK ROOT

MARVIN HART

On the 14th, Marvin boxed 4 rounds with McCormick, then wrestled with him and Thompson. Hart looked as sturdy as an oak.

When Hart stepped on the scales after a hard day of training on the 15th, he weighed 195 pounds.

It was anticipated that the betting would be about even. Root was fast on his feet, cleverer and quicker than Hart, with a good deal the best of the argument from a scientific point of view. However, Hart was stronger and more aggressive, with an unlimted amount of strength and staying power, and a punch to back him up.

A man who saw Root work out on the 16th in Ogden, Utah said that Root appeared to weigh at least 190 pounds, and wore out three sparring partners. He looked as hard as a rock and as quick as a cat.

Sports writers were anticipating the greatest battle of recent years. "Throughout the country the sporting fraternity is looking to Nevada for a new champion of the heavyweight division." Jeffries was out of the fighting business. "The championship must fall to some one. The promoters of the Reno fight looked about for the best men among the big ones and selected Hart and Root. Jeffries, the retiring champion, regards Hart as the logical champion." It was anticipated that "Jeffries will be here to hand the title over to the winner."

On June 19, during their sparring, in the 2nd round, Hart let himself out a bit too much and dropped McCormick with a punch on the ear, knocking him out. Marvin sparred 3 rounds with Thompson as well.

Afterwards, McCormick said, "Hart is a whirlwind fighter and he scarcely knows his own strength. ... It is a difficult matter for him to hit light, even in a casual bout in the gymnasium. What he considers a 'light one' is a sledge hammer blow." McCormick had been in boxing for many years, so his perspective carried some weight. "I can say without any desire to unduly boost Hart up that he is one of the hardest hitters and roughest fighters in the business. ... If Hart is not the coming champion I am very much mistaken."

Speaking of the Hart - Johnson fight, those who saw the bout said that Hart never gave Johnson a moment's rest, forcing the fighting all the time, despite the fact that Johnson was clever and fast. "Hart is willing to take two blows if he can land one. He goes in and makes a fight that from the spectators' point of view is in every way a satisfactory contest."

Reno, Nevada, July 3d, 2 P. M.

Finish Fight for the Heavyweight Championship of the World

HART ~vs~ ROOT

JAMES J. JEFFERIES

Expected at the Ringside to Confer Championship Upon the Winner

PURSE $5,000

Newly Constructed Arena

SEATING 6,500 PERSONS

Box Seats $10.00, Reserved Seats $7.50 and $5.00
General Admission $2.00

For Reserved Seats See Local Agent or Address

J. P. EGAN, Secretary   A. LIVINGSTON, President

Orders Unaccompanied by Check or Money Order Will Not be Held Later Than 12 O'clock Noon July 24

Promoter and host club manager Joe P. "Kid" Egan gave the $5,000 purse to neutral stakeholder Harry Corbett. Both Hart and Root each posted their $1,000 forfeit money guaranteeing their performance.

Hart and Root's managers, Jack McCormick and Lou Houseman, agreed to James Jeffries as the referee, if he would consent.

On June 21, Hart ran 12 miles, in addition to his usual work.

300 women (only allowed in with male escorts) were allowed to watch Hart train on June 22. A lady writer reported that wearing pink tights, Hart was "as graceful as an Apollo and as playful as a puppy dog or a three weeks old kitten." The women hoped that Marvin would win the world's heavyweight championship, "for he is so gentlemanly and graceful in his movements. We don't see how it will be possible for him to lose." After an hour of exercises, which included 15 minutes of punching a football tied to a string, Marvin sparred lightly with McCormick. Next up to spar was Thompson, who "attacked his huge antagonist with trip hammer blows, but Mr. Hart made no attempt to avoid the young man's fists, appearing to enjoy the terrible beating he received."

It was anticipated that a huge crowd from San Francisco would be on hand to see the championship fight. A special train would be arranged. Seats would be $2, $5, $7.50, and $10. "The sporting writers have acknowledged the Hart-Root fight as a championship battle and both its principals as logical candidates for the toga which fell from the shoulders of Jeffries when he relnquished the championship."

Root had remained in Ogden, Utah for so long because of the quality sparring partners that were there. He was boxing with Mike Schreck and George Gardner, both of whom were top fighters in their own right. Those who saw Root train said he was never faster nor stronger in his life.

The Nevada State Journal reported on June 27 that Jeffries had agreed to referee the bout and would confer the championship on the fight's winner.

On June 29, after completing his gym work, Hart sparred 8 rounds, 4 rounds each with McCormick and Thomspon. During their last round, Hart twice dropped McCormick. Marvin had skipped rope, wrestled, exercised with weights, and sparred, and did not lose his breath even during the most strenuous of work.[325]

As the fight approached, the *San Francisco Call* said the championship battle was the one subject of discussion among sporting men, and that the intermountain region was aflame with excitement. The bout was considered to be an exciting match-up between two top fighters.

Jim Jeffries was paid a hefty $1,000 fee to referee the bout. This was obviously done for two reasons – 1. Jeffries was hoped to be an additional gate attraction, and 2. His refereeing the bout gave it increased credibility as a championship bout. A multitude of sports gathered in Reno from all portions of the country to witness the fight.

Lou Houseman, Root's manager, and Jack McCormick, Hart's manager, met and agreed to a divide the $5,000 purse with 65% going to the winner

---

[325] *Nevada State Journal*, June 10 - 30, 1905.

and 35% to the loser, or $3,250/$1,750. They were to box on the afternoon of July 3 at about 2 p.m., before the Reno Athletic Club, which guaranteed the $5,000 purse. An article that was inserted into the agreement said, "This contest shall be recognized as a championship battle and the winner is to be declared the heavyweight champion of the world."

Although Hart was acclimating himself to the altitude and heat of Reno, Root remained in Ogden Canyon, Utah, sparring with Mike Schreck. Root later said of his sparring partner, "Schreck is a splendid fellow to work with. He is strong and fast and I got in many spells of good work while with him."

Some wondered why Root had remained in Utah for so long rather than coming to the fight site. They felt that this hurt the promotion. However, Houseman responded that Root remained in Utah because there were several Chicago fighters training in Utah who could provide valuable sparring, and also because he heard the heat was above average in Reno, and he did not want it sapping Root's vitality and interfering with his training.

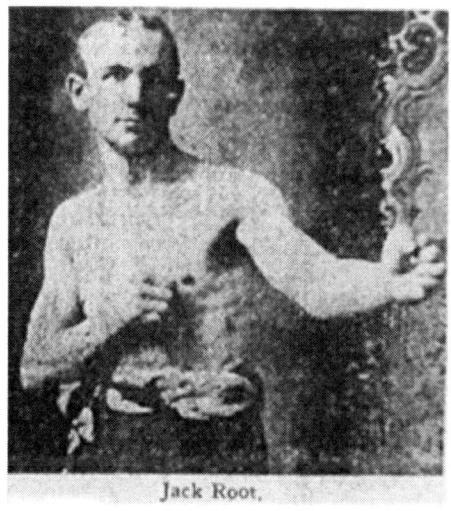

Jack Root.

As of June 30, Root was weighing 175 pounds. Houseman said Jack was prepared to put up the fight of his life. "Root realizes that Hart is no baby to handle, and that only hard and fast fighting will win the money and championship honors which James J. Jeffries will bestow on the victorious man." He acknowledged that Hart was a persistent and game foeman.

Root said that never before during the eight years that he had been in the fighting game had he felt better than he did at present. He had been training consistently and well. "To see him today and compare him with the Jack Root of a year ago would be to picture two different men. ... Today he is strong as an ox and as speedy as a streak of greased lightning. It is wonderful to see how he has increased his speed." Root said that Hart was a good man and one who would be willing to stand a beating.

> I will keep jabbing for eight or ten rounds, then go to it good and strong. If I feel as good the afternoon of the fight as I do this minute I will beat Hart as sure as the sun comes up on July 3. My trips up the mountains and down the rough roads and the climbing of trees have

improved me wonderfully, and I can see nothing but victory ahead of me.[326]

Hart, who trained in Reno, intended to go right after Root and set a fast pace. All accounts said that he had been training hard and was getting faster every day. Trainer McCormick said Marvin was confident and ready to receive many hard jabs, punches, and unlimited punishment as long as he could finally land the championship.

> I am not arguing for a minute that Hart is as clever as some of the men who have boxed for the championship, but I think he is the equal of any one at present on the list so far as general fighting qualities go. He is game, he is aggressive, and is entirely on the level. I might add that he is improving all the time in ringmanship. He is ambitious to become champion and he is willing to box any man living. I feel certain he will win his way into the hearts of the sporting public.

W.W. Naughton said Hart had the appearance of a man who had been training faithfully. He had rid his frame of surplus weight and was brown skinned and active looking.[327]

Interestingly enough, it was not entirely clear that Jeffries had designated Hart and Root to fight for the championship, or that the winner would be recognized as champion, despite reports to the contrary. On one hand, it was reported that they were to fight to the finish for the championship in the first finish fight since Corbett vs. Fitzsimmons, in Nevada, the only state in the nation that had legalized finish fights. That gave the fight the flavor of a championship bout. Newsmen generally referred to the fight as being for the vacant championship.

However, when asked whether he recognized the fight as being for the championship, Jeff replied, "I do not." When told that the club was advertising that he would be on hand to bestow the title on the winner, Jeff said, "I know it, but they have no right to. The title is something I can't give

---
[326] *San Francisco Evening Post*, July 1, 1905. The San Francisco papers are reliable sources because they had reporters on scene.
[327] *San Francisco Call, San Francisco Examiner*, July 1, 1905.

to whomever I please. ... No, the title is something they must all fight for, and it is for the press and public to decide who is the champion."[328]

The next day, another paper reported,

> Jeff...stated positively a couple of nights ago that he will not confer the heavy-weight title upon the winner, because he does not consider this in his power.
>
> "The public confers the title," said the big fellow. "I won it by fighting for it, by going over the route twice with every candidate. Let whoever wants it now get it in the same way. The public will declare a man champion if he is entitled to the honor. It is not in my power to do so.

Of course, Hart was willing to fight Jeffries, but Jeff had retired, so it was unclear regarding exactly what Hart had to do in order to become champion if Jeffries was not willing to fight him. Regardless of Jeff's statement, the same article said that Root and Hart were to struggle for the championship.[329]

Jeff's manager and trainer, Billy Delaney said,

> It makes me smile to read about Jeff giving the championship to this man or that one, for, although Jeffries was the undisputed champion, he has no right to give the title to another. It's absurd to think that because a man is champion he is vested with the power to give it to any one. And so, let me tell you right here, there is at present no champion heavyweight.

However, Root's manager said,

> The fight is for, practically, the heavyweight championship of the world. There may be some cloud on this assertion, yet the title will, tentatively at least, go to the winner of this engagement.
>
> Jeffries having retired, with Fitzsimmons admittedly out of the game and Corbett assuming the same stand taken by Jeffries, there is, as a matter of fact, no one now before the public to dispute the claim of the winner to the title.

He supported Root's right to fight for the championship based upon the fact that the only one to defeat him was Gardner, whom Root had recently defeated, and for his clean-cut and decisive victory over Hart. He said Root would enter the ring at about 175 pounds.[330]

Others reported that next to Jeffries, Root and Hart had the best claims to heavyweight honors because Marvin defeated Jeff's most logical opponent in Johnson, and Root had a victory over Hart. That said, even

---

[328] *San Francisco Bulletin,* July 1, 1905.
[329] *San Francisco Chronicle,* July 2, 1905.
[330] *Louisville Courier-Journal,* July 2, 1905.

Hart's own hometown paper said, "Jeffries is and will be the heavyweight champion of the world until somebody has fought him for the title and whipped him decisively. If he never fights again, he will carry this coveted honor to the grave with him." This statement was ridiculous, but it definitely showed that it was not going to be easy to obtain the status of champion as long as James Jeffries was alive, even if Jeff was not fighting.[331]

As referee, Jeffries said that he would insist on clean breaks upon his orders. Regarding knockdowns, he felt that it was wrong for a referee to count over a man, owing to the fact that the referee might be too fast or too slow in his count. He thought that only the timekeeper should conduct the count, by standing up and calling out the seconds.

l to r, Jack Roberts, Marvin Hart, Jack McCormick, "Deafy" Thompson

Root remarked that finish fights were unique in that a man did not have to worry about being outpointed or losing a close or controversial decision. Both knew that they had to go on until there was a decisive finish. Hence, there was purity and clarity to finish fights. They left no doubt about who was the better fighter.

Both Hart and Root did their training on July 1 at Reno's Wheelman's Club, although at different times. Root, who was being seen in Reno for the first time, punched the bag in snappy fashion and did some shadow boxing, exhibiting his quick footwork. He seemed to be in excellent shape. Although the Reno sports on the whole had been Hart men, at that point, after seeing Root, some impressed spectators wondered whether Root was the safer bet, with his athletic shape and quicker movements. Houseman put $1,000 on Root at even money.[332]

---

331 *Louisville Courier-Journal*, July 3, 1905.
332 *San Francisco Examiner*, July 2, 1905.

Root expressed confidence.

> In my six round fight with Hart in Chicago I had both of his eyes closed at the end of the sixth round and had the fight gone two more rounds, Hart would certainly have been put to sleep. Although we both have improved considerably since then, I look for Monday's battle to be fought along the same lines.

Root said his cleverness would overcome Hart's 20-pound weight advantage. "My twenty-one days training with Mike Schreck, one of the toughest nuts in the country, has done me a world of good." He had boxed 3 to 10 rounds a day for three weeks and climbed mountains. "I can say in all candor that I was never faster or better in my life." He was certain of victory.[333]

W.W. Naughton reported that Root was not happy about the thought of fighting outdoors in the sun. He wanted a canopy erected over the ring, but the club refused to do this, because it would interfere with some of the spectators' views from the elevated seats. Joe Egan told Root, "What is fair for one is fair for another," meaning that Hart would have to endure the broiling hot sun too. However, Hart had been in Reno working out in the blistering sun and had become accustomed to it.

Root was still confident, saying that he had defeated Hart before and could do so again. His condition was perfect, and together with his superior cleverness, he would win.

---

333 *San Francisco Bulletin, Nevada State Journal*, July 2, 1905.

Root allowed for the fact that Hart was a tough, rugged fellow and thoroughly game, but saw no reason why he could not do to him what he did in their first fight, for he had the superior class, knowledge of boxing, and the punch to put Hart into dreamland. Root said his punching power had improved, which was saying a lot, because in their first bout he had cut up Hart's face a good deal and knocked him down, while Hart did not place a scratch on him. Root's only concern was the broiling sun, which could do as much harm to a man as punches.

Wise sports felt that Root's superior cleverness would enable him to punish Hart in the early rounds, but if he did not stop Marvin within 10 rounds, most felt that Hart had the better chance to win after that. The wagering was actually at even money.

HART LOOKS FIT AND SAYS HE'S READY TO BATTLE WITH ANY MAN ON EARTH

W. W. NAUGHTON, RECOGNIZED THE WORLD OVER AS THE ONLY AUTHORITY ON THE QUEENSBERRY GAME, WITH A STAFF OF ASSISTANT WRITERS AND ARTISTS, IS AT RENO TO TELL THE STORY OF THE HART-ROOT FIGHT. MR. NAUGHTON'S INITIAL ARTICLE AND THE FIRST OF THE MANY PHOTOGRAPHS WHICH WILL COME FROM THE BATTLE GROUND ARE PRESENTED TO THE READERS OF "THE EXAMINER" THIS MORNING.

W. W. NAUGHTON.

MARVIN HART BUSY WITH JACK M'CORMICK, WHO IS THE KENTUCKIAN'S MANAGER AND TRAINER

Hart said that Root had made a great deal of capital out of the fact that he had once obtained a 6-round decision over him. Marvin disagreed with the decision, and noted that his boxing had improved a lot since then. He said that his ruggedness, weight and strength would ensure certain victory and prevent defeat. He knew it was the most important battle of his career, and therefore he was in perfect condition. Hart said he would go after Root all the time and not let up for a minute until the job was done. He was ready for a hard fight and would be able to go any distance until he had won the title. "I will bring home the championship."[334]

Hart was reported to be in even better shape than he was against Jack Johnson. He was happy that there would be no debate about the verdict. The confident Hart said, "Well, there won't be any decision in this fight. This is going to be a knockout and he can't hurt me, let alone knock me out." Marvin spoke of his victory as if it were certain.

George Siler had a good pre-fight analysis, saying that while Root was cleverer and the rule calling for clean breaks would favor him, Hart was the larger and more powerful with both hands, and could take an immense amount of punishment in order to win. Prophetically, he said that Hart's "best blow is a right-hand upper cut to the body, which is apt to land low, and a smashing good round arm swing to the kidneys…. Hart, it is said, has been cultivating a new kidney punch with which he hopes to win." Such blows would feature prominently in the bout.[335]

Hart was seen as the favorite in a finish fight, because he had the qualities necessary to win such a bout – endurance, power, and the ability to

---

[334] *San Francisco Examiner, San Francisco Chronicle*, July 3, 1905.
[335] *Louisville Courier-Journal*, July 3, 1905.

absorb punishment. "He has the qualities which will prove most effective in a battle of any distance. Root is a far better boxer…but…he will not have a punch sufficient to hurt the stronger man. … Hart will outlast his opponent and will win on sheer endurance and brute strength." Marvin said he would weigh about 195 pounds.[336]

The night before the fight, at 9 p.m., Jeffries met with the boxers. Jeff said that many recent crooked fights had hurt the fight game by shaking the confidence of the sporting public. Jeff insisted that everything would be on the level.

Jeffries told the men that they had to break clean when ordered to do so, and they must not hit in the clinch or in breaking away after being ordered to break. However, prior to that, if one man held, the other was permitted to hit.

JEFF WHIRLS INTO RENO.

For those of you who incorrectly think that a boxer was entitled to stand over his fallen foe, Jeff informed them, "If either man is knocked down the other must walk to his corner and remain there until his opponent regains his feet."

When a man was down, the timekeeper would call off ten seconds and Jeff would repeat them in the fallen fighter's ear.

Jeffries and the boxers went through in pantomime the various moves that would likely develop during the fight. Root and Hart were satisfied with Jeff as the referee, as well as his interpretation of the rules.[337]

---

336 *San Francisco Chronicle*, July 2, 1905.
337 *San Francisco Bulletin, San Francisco Chronicle, San Francisco Call*, July 3, 1905.

CHAPTER 15

To Be a Heavyweight Champion

On July 3, 1905 in Reno, Nevada, 28-year-old Marvin Hart took on 29-year-old Jack Root for the vacant world's heavyweight championship. *The San Francisco Bulletin* reported that Jeffries would referee the battle and at the conclusion acclaim the winner to be the heavyweight champion. *The San Francisco Chronicle* said the winner would claim the heavyweight championship of the world. *The San Francisco Evening Post* said Hart and Root would fight for the title relinquished by Jeffries. *The San Francisco Examiner's* W.W. Naughton agreed that the winner would be proclaimed the champion and world's best fighter.

Nevada had an odd state law that required a physical examination to take place ten hours before the battle. Hence, the boxers had to wake up at 4 a.m. to be examined.[338]

---

[338] *San Francisco Evening Post*, July 3, 1905.

The local *Reno Evening Gazette* reported that Hart weighed 190 pounds to Root's 170 pounds. Others listed Root at 168-170 pounds, while Hart was about 192 ½ -195 pounds. Hart was listed as standing 6 feet tall to Root's 5'10 ½".

The Call said Hart's greater weight could mean greater strength and vitality, but Root being the more finished boxer with the ability to make every blow count could offset this. "It is expected Hart will rush the fight from the start in an effort to keep Root from getting set, thus impairing the efficiency of his blows. It is conceded his chances of victory are slim if he stands off and boxes, as he is far from being a master of the art."

Host club manager Joe Egan expected a $15,000 gate, for $11,000 in tickets had already been sold in advance. The streets were decked in carnival colors, and were full of strangers who were coming in on special trains. The $5,000 purse was allegedly going to be split 65% to the winner and 35% to the loser.

The great outdoor arena was located within a mile of Reno, on the sagebrush-dotted plain. It was a big square amphitheater structure of glistening yellow pine, 125 feet by 175 feet, erected especially for the fight and designed to accommodate 6,530 spectators. The ring was 24-square-feet, with stakeless ropes. Outside the platform in each man's corner was a special shelf for the accommodation of buckets and bottles. Close to the ring were desks and reserved areas for newsmen. Several sections of boxes were filled with chairs, and beyond those were rows of benches. The outermost divisions of seats rose in tiers to the top walls, which were 12-feet in height. A high fence enclosed the arena. The ring floor was padded and covered with canvas.

The day proved to be the hottest of the season, as the thermometer registered in the neighborhood of 100 degrees. Both the fighters and spectators would suffer from the heat.

The spectators gathered at the arena long before the contest. Every available vehicle was pressed into service, while many arrived on foot. The seats filled rapidly. The spectators paid anywhere from $2 to $10 per seat.

Three-fourths of the stadium space was filled with over 3,000 people, perhaps close to 4,000. Umbrellas and fans, together with cold drinks, were the creature comforts.

Nevada was represented by Lieutenant Governor Snow and acting Governor Lem Allen. State and U.S. senators were present, as well as many state officials and dignitaries. Some 15 or 16 women were also present.

Hart arrived at the arena at 1:30 p.m., looking jolly and chewing gum. He said, "It's going to be mighty hot fighting here today."

There were no preliminaries. The finish fight constituted the entire card. The biggest reason why there were not more fights in Nevada at that time and there was only one bout on the card was that the $1,000 license was for only one fight. That was the amount a promoter had to pay for *each* fight. Hence, for financial reasons, Hart-Root would be the only bout on the card. There was talk of lobbying the legislators to make the license fee applicable to the entire card, regardless of the number of bouts.

Hart's manager won the toss for corners, which was significant given the heat. McCormick chose the corner which put the sun at Hart's back.

Shortly before the men entered the ring, the band played "My Old Kentucky Home" as a compliment to Hart. There was applause. The majority had a kindly feeling for Hart, for he had trained in Reno for nearly a month, and they had become acquainted with him.

The boxers were allowed to wear soft bandages. Their hands were bandaged with tape before they entered the ring.

Before entering the ring, Root told a *Bulletin* reporter, "I don't expect to win in a round, but I ought to in less than twenty. I don't intend to run away entirely, but I want to make Hart fight and fight hard. If I can get him to fight himself out then it will be so much easier to drop him with a punch. All that I want to do is to keep myself fresh so that I can hit him hard when he is weak."

Root entered the ring at 2:54 p.m., carrying an umbrella to shade him from the sun. He wore a black sweater over his fighting clothes. In Root's corner were Battling Nelson, Teddy Alexander, Paddy MacKay, and Clan McKenzie.

Hart followed immediately to a big ovation. He was attired in a flaming red bath robe/dressing gown with the emblem of the Reno Wheelmen's Club on the back, and also a small tweed cap. Hart's seconds were Jack McCormick, Jack Roberts, "Deafy" Thompson, and Hal and Lee Updike. Marvin was the popular idol of the crowd.

Seeing the men together, the weight difference was not as apparent as expected. Root was well developed, and the muscle definition was apparent. Hart's powerful frame was well muscled as well, but it was not as apparent to the eye as Root's muscles, which stood out more.

One source said Root's gloves were tan, while Hart's were a deep red. Another said Root's gloves were yellow and Hart's tan colored. Go figure.

The sheriff inspected the gloves and pronounced them satisfactory. The gloves were required to weigh 5 ounces.

Their seconds held umbrellas over their

heads in order to protect them from the sun's rays. Root seemed a bit nervous, while Hart appeared as cool as a cucumber.

It was announced via a telegram that Jack Johnson challenged the winner, but the spectators greeted his name with jeers.

James J. Jeffries was more warmly greeted than any other person. There was a great commotion over him. He wore a straw hat, blue trousers, a pair of suspenders, and a blue shirt.

Jeffries was paid a hefty $1,000 to referee the bout, which likely influenced his decision to announce before the fight that the winner would be the new heavyweight champion of the world, changing his earlier position that he could not confer his title. As a result, this bout was eventually recognized as being for the vacant championship, particularly when Jeffries did not come back. The reporters did not make the argument, but it is quite likely that the real reason he was paid so much was as an inducement to announce that the winner would indeed be champion.

Officials also included Frank Shortell, the official timekeeper, Albert Updike (known as Hal), Hart's timekeeper, and William Nolan, Root's timekeeper. The same bell used for Corbett-Fitzsimmons was brought over to be used for the bout.

The spectators broiled under the hot sun that practically blistered them. By fight time, a thermometer at ringside registered 120 degrees. At 3:07 p.m., Jeffries gave the order to clear the ring and the men shook hands and readied themselves for the start of the fight.

1 - At the bell, they rushed into a clinch. Root landed punches to the body and head with both right and left, displaying his full arsenal of punches. Hart landed a couple rights to the head. The fancy touches of feinting and flirting were dispensed with, and the thuds of solid blows rang out. Root sent in lefts that tilted Hart's head and brought trickling streams of blood from his nostrils. Hart, "whose greatest fighting qualification is his indomitable grit," braced himself against the punishment. Many thought it would be Root in a walk, as he scored neatly and drew away, allowing Hart's lunges to hit the air.

While clinching, Hart punched Root in the ribs. Hart used his right on the break and Root complained to Jeffries. Root met him with a hard left jab on the nose. Hart got Root on the ropes and swung a hard left and right to his the face. Root landed a right on the ribs, a swift left to the face, and rapped Hart in the stomach with a right while going into a clinch. The thud of Root's left on Marvin's nose and mouth could be heard up on the bleachers. Marvin struck out wildly. He rushed and got in a right on the neck. Root scored a punishing right cross. Most scored the round even.

2 - Root was confident. He danced away and then came back with a left on the mouth. He repeated, drew out of range of a punch and countered with a snappy right cross that bruised Hart's eye. Root drew the Hart left and then crossed Hart heavily with the right. Root liked to get Hart to lead and then he would step in briskly with counter right crosses, which made Hart's face take on a patchy, swollen look. It looked as if one of those shots would put Marvin on Queer Street. However, Hart was as steady as a rock. He raised and used his shoulder as a barricade and intercepted some of those blows, defending himself better. In a clinch, Marvin jolted Root in the neck with a right. He also began swinging for the kidneys.

Root landed a couple hard lefts to the jaw and they clinched. Jack landed body shots. They exchanged lefts and clinched. Root landed a left and right to the head hard, and then went after the body and they clinched. Root kept poking his left to Hart's body. Hart landed a hard left to the body. It was Root's round.

3 - Root seemed to feel that his best chances of success lay in making a fast fight. He jabbed Hart's face and discolored his left temple and brow with right crosses. It was a scuffling fight and Jeff told them several times to step back. Root was doing the greater execution.

They rushed to a clinch. Root landed a left hard to the jaw and Hart returned with his hard right to the body. Before the round was half over there were red splotches above Root's left hip, where Hart had been landing his rights to the body.

They clinched and indulged in rough infighting. Both were fighting hard. From the outside, Root's keen left kept landing on Hart's jaw. Hart landed a right hard under the heart. He was fighting desperately. Root landed a left to his jaw. Hart landed hard to the stomach. Root landed a hard right to the jaw and they clinched. They hung together and Jeff warned them. Root landed a left to the body. They exchanged lefts to the jaw. Root struck Hart a foul body blow. Hart drew attention to it and then fought on. Each landed a right to the head.

The pace seemed to tell on Root, and when Jeffries chided them for continuing to clinch after he had told them to break, he embellished his words with special rebuke to Root, who was holding more than Hart. Honors of the round were about even.

4 - Both seemed comparatively fresh. They exchanged lefts to the jaw. Hart landed a hard right to the kidneys. Root uppercut him and put a hard left to the jaw. Root landed a hard right. Root also landed left and right. They clinched, and on the break, Root landed a left to the jaw. Desperate infighting followed. There was blood on the lips of both men, but Hart's mouth bled more.

Jeff kept calling them to break from clinches. It became clear that the men would not break when ordered to do so. Jeff kept threatening them with what he would do if they did not mind him better.

During the round, a bottle of ammonia exploded and a quantity of the liquid flew into Hal Updike's eyes, one of Hart's seconds, temporarily blinding him.

Root sidestepped and hooked Hart with lefts and rights. Hart covered his face with his arms and threw his right to the body hard. Root kept ducking Hart's swings and countering with rights and lefts at the head. A swift left tilted Marvin's head. Hart put in a telling body blow with the right and they clinched. This was another even round.

5 - Root feinted and shot in a left to the mouth that made it bleed. Hart ducked the next one and when breaking from a clinch, caught Root a right uppercut on the chin. They exchanged lefts to the body and clinched. Root landed a right over the heart but took a right in return. Hart landed a right to the jaw and they clinched. Root landed left and right. Hart hit the body hard with his right and they clinched.

During this round, the clinching between exchanges continued. Jeffries angrily ordered them to break. Eventually, Jeff was compelled to do what he did not want to do, which was to push and pull the men apart, because they were not heeding his orders to break.

Hart landed right and left swings to the head and Root uppercut the body. Root landed a right to the jaw and hard left to the body. Hart landed two stiff body punches with the right and Root uppercut him on the mouth with the left. One version said Hart cut Root on the mouth and under the right eye slightly. However, the sources agreed that his was Root's round.

6 - Root landed a right to the body and they clinched. Root rammed in a left to the body. After the usual clinching and breaking, Root scored a left jolt on the jaw. Hart landed his right to the kidneys. Root retaliated with a left to body. Marvin crowded him to the ropes and landed two heavy lefts on the neck. Root dodged away and met Marvin with a stiff right on the stomach. Hart landed right swing to body and Root swung his left to jaw, repeated it, and then sent his right to the body. Hart landed a left hook to the chin. They clinched and both held on hard. Jeff had to pull them apart more than once. They continued exchanging right and left to the body and head.

Hart ripped his right into the body a couple times. There was plenty of covering up on both sides and plenty of scuffling. Jeff had to break them.

Hart placed his swinging right on the kidneys. Root seemed a little tired as he went to his corner. It was an even round.

7 – Between rounds, McCormick attempted to give Hart a drink of whiskey, but Hart refused the drink, instead content with the shower of water his seconds spilled over him.

They fought viciously this round. Root had been prodding Hart's face into a puffy condition. Marvin was placing rasping blows on Jack's left side. Root landed a snappy left to the mouth. Hart crowded him to the ropes but could not land squarely. Root scored with an uppercut. Hart clubbed him over the kidneys with his right. Root landed a stinging right cross on the ear, and in the holding match that followed, jammed his left into the stomach several times. Hart's right uppercut brought blood from Root's lips. Hart scored again in the same fashion and then drove a right to the heart. Both were fighting hard.

Near the close of the round, they were mixing it up near the ropes. Just as the bell rang, Root whipped a terrific right cross to Hart's chin and Marvin went down on his knees. Regarding this sequence, Jeffries later said that both men swung their rights simultaneously just as the timekeeper hit the gong, but Root's landed.

Another version of the knockdown said that the blow did not take immediate effect. Hart stood holding the upper rope for an instant, with his knees wobbling. His face looked blank and before his seconds could reach him he sank slowly to the ring floor onto his knees and then over on his side.

McCormick made a feeble attempt to claim a foul, but the blow had been thrown prior to the bell, even though it might have landed at or after the bell rang. Hart was lucky that he was saved by the bell, because he rose in a dazed condition and his seconds splashed him with water. His seconds half dragged and half carried him to the corner. This was a big round for Root.

8 - Despite the knockdown, Marvin recovered quickly and went right back to work at the start of the round, looking fresh, showing steam, and boxing his way into the inside, where Root clinched. Root showed very clever footwork. Jack landed a jab but Hart blocked a right with his shoulder. They fought while holding. Both hit the body. Root said to Hart, "I have got you now." Hart responded, "Not now, old man. I haven't commenced to fight yet." Hart landed a heavy right on the ribs and left on the cheek. Root used his left jab after the break and Marvin's nose bled freely. They indulged in rough infighting. They exchanged left hooks to the jaw.

Left jolts on the jaw administered at close quarters rattled Root, who held on like grim death. After breaking, Hart's seconds yelled, "Go to him, you've got him." Root got through his temporary distress and used jerky left and rights to the face. They rushed into another clinch. Jeff broke them and Root scored a damaging right uppercut. Root landed a hard right to the body and they clinched again. Hart landed a hard right to the jaw. Jeffries broke them. Root landed hard to the body. Root landed a left and right to the jaw, and Hart hung on. Root sent rights and lefts to the head. He landed a terrific right just as the gong sounded. It was Root's round.

9 - A stinging left smash on the mouth caused Hart to spit out a mouthful of blood. However, the stout-hearted Kentuckian stood his ground, then rushed at Root and smashed him on the ribs with the right. Jack jabbed him fiercely. In the scuffling and short-arm work that followed, Root twice sank to the floor. One source said that Hart had grabbed Root around his waist and wrestled him down. Jeff told him to get up. Hart kept up these wrestling tactics until Jeffries warned him. However, at one point, Root went down without being hit. He appeared to be weakening. Jeffries had difficulty separating them. They continued exchanging blows to the body and head between clinches. Root went to one knee in a mix-up. Toward the close of the round, Hart caught him with a punishing right uppercut to the chin which did not improve Root's condition. They were hanging onto each other at the bell. Hart's spurt gave him a slight lead in the round.

10 - Between rounds, Hart's seconds gave him a little brandy. In Root's corner, liquor was taboo, but they held a chunk of ice on his head and another at the base of his neck. At the bell, there were more jabs, kidney thumps, clinching and shuffling, and louder cries from Jeffries that further holding would result in disqualification. Root jabbed and countered with his right. Hart swung for the body and hooked for the head. Amongst the exchanges and clinches, Hart landed a solid right to the ear or neck that rocked Root, who held on as though badly hurt. Root ducked and clasped around the hips. Hart tried to shake him off, but it took Jeffries to separate them. Jack recovered though, and his left jabs brought fresh damage to Hart's bruised face. Honors were about even.

11 - This was a much slower round. Root jabbed Hart's nose. They exchanged, clinched and scuffled. Jeff blamed Root for holding unnecessarily. They slugged between clinches. Root landed right and left to the head and a left to the stomach. Root pounded the stomach with both hands. Hart landed a hard right swing to the kidneys. Root put a left to the chin and right to the body. Root drove a left to the stomach but received a left to his body. Hart forced him to the ropes with body blows. Root's best work was done with his left to the face. Root pecked Marvin's face with the left and Hart reddened his ribs with the right. Jack landed a snappy right to the head. Some thought the end was near for Marvin, but they did not know Marvin Hart. Hart was in distress, but landed a hard kidney punch, his most effective blow. Root missed a head blow but landed a couple hard body shots. Root had the round.

12 - Hart rushed, Root ducked and clinched. Marvin landed a left on the face and a right on the ribs. He scored another left on the jaw and

smothered a left uppercut. Hart blocked a right with his shoulder. Hart landed a left to the body. Root ducked a swing and countered with a right to the ear. Root scored his left to the head.

They fought into a clinch and roughed it. Jeffries broke them, but they again fought into a clinch. Jeff cautioned Marvin for punching after being ordered to break. They fought up close, each trying to land an uppercut.

Root stepped in with a left hook for the jaw that missed. Hart quickly stepped in close and ripped in a terrific right uppercut that landed under and a little to the left of Root's heart, near the short ribs, possibly in the solar plexus. The sound of the punch could be heard in every part of the arena. Root dropped to the ground and began writhing. His face wore an expression of extreme pain. He was a "quivering mass of humanity." Jack rolled over and grasped the lower rope. He tried to pull himself up, but was too feeble. He sank back to the floor and was counted out. "A new world's championship was proclaimed."

The crowd swarmed into the ring. Everyone was bent on congratulating the new champion. Root sat in his corner, gasping for breath. Afterwards, a red welt could be seen on his body. Hart had a badly cut lip and a blackened eye. Both fighters had sunburned backs with necks wreathed in perspiration.

Another report said that after the fight, when many spectators entered the ring, one actually had the audacity to throw a punch at Hart, who responded by beating him out of the ropes. The sheriff entered, brandishing a revolver, and the disturbance was quelled.

The end was eerily similar to its 1897 heavyweight finish-fight predecessor, Corbett-Fitzsimmons. Corbett too was dropped by a body shot (although Jim was decked by a left) and was unable to reach and use the ropes to pull himself up.

It had been a good bout, with neither man afraid to remain in range and mix it up to the body and head. They thumped each other from corner to corner without apparent advantage, until Hart landed the knockout body blow.

Referee Jeffries claimed it was a punch on the jaw that ended Root, but all of the reporters agreed that it was a body blow. W.W. Naughton said the fact that Jeffries erringly thought it was a punch to the chin showed that he was human after all. "We were amazed because most of us had seen or had thought we had seen Hart's right fist plowing its way in to the soft flesh near Root's short ribs." Another newspaper said the fact that Jeff thought it was a punch to the jaw "serves to show that sometimes the hands move faster than the eyes, and this explains why few people see a fight alike." Root and Hart both said it was a body shot, and this was confirmed by "practically everybody close enough to the ring to see the blow delivered."

Root told the reporters that he was beaten by a lucky punch. "He gave me a sickening punch in the stomach and I remembered no more." Regarding the knockout, Jack said, "I led for the head with my left and as I missed Hart caught me with a heavy blow in the pit of the stomach.... At the time I was leading with my left and throwing my weight forward. This position intensified Hart's right-hand smash." Root told another paper that the sun was in his eyes at the time, so he did not see the punch coming. "The first I knew my seconds were taking me to my corner." He felt that it was his fight up to that time.

Root thought he had Marvin beaten and would have won in a few more rounds but for the chance blow. He wanted a rematch. "Hart is a big, strong fellow and fought a good fight and I don't want to detract from his glory, but still I firmly believe I am his master. ... I was strong and fast till the end came." Root called it a chance blow, but throughout his career, Hart had a way of landing those chance blows.

Some thought that Root was tiring from the grueling pace, clinching to obtain rests. However, a disappointed Root said he was not as tired as people thought. He claimed to be stalling along. He knew that he could reach Hart with his left when he wanted, but was banking upon being able to nail him for a knockout with his right. He claimed to be strong when hit with the knockout right to the body.

Root's second, Battling Nelson, a top lightweight, said Root was fighting a better fight than Hart until the last blow. Still, Nelson called Hart a great fighter. Root's manager also felt that Jack that had the best of it until the knockout. "Hart put up a surprisingly fast fight, and showed his ability to take severe punishment."

Hart said that it was a good fight, and that Root was a good, fast, game man.

I was never in doubt as to the result. I went into the ring expecting to have my face mussed up. Well, it turned out that way. Root has a clever left hand and I wasn't much of a success at stopping his straight lefts. I figured that I was stronger in the right-hand department than he was, and now I am sure of it. The blow I settled him with, a right-hand body punch, was the one I depended on.

Hart also said, "I knew I'd get him with that body smash." Some quoted Hart as saying that it was a clean blow in the kidneys.

Regarding being knocked down in the 7th round, Hart claimed that the gong had rung so he ceased fighting, dropped his guard, and got hit. "Several years ago Root beat me. I knew then I was a better man than he, and I proved that I was right. I am satisfied. I will try to wear with honor the belt that Jeffries has taken off."

Hart would openly draw the color line as champion. Regarding his future, Marvin said, "I am now ready to meet anybody in the world, except a negro. I fought Johnson because he was said to be the next best man to Jeffries. I will not fight another negro." He also said, "When I fought

Johnson it was very much against my will, but as I had defeated all the big ones outside of Jeffries I was obliged to take on Johnson." Jack Johnson and George Gardner had both issued challenges to the winner of the bout.

James J. Jeffries said that had Root put up a good fight, but went down from a punch that would put any man out of business. "Hart is a great fighter and is deserving of every bit of the credit for his victory, for he beat a good man." He seemed weak at times, but Marvin was good for many more rounds.

> Two better matched men never faced each other in the ring. It was a splendid exhibition of the manly art.... Hart won fairly and squarely. At times it was difficult to keep the men from hitting in the clinches but neither offended more in this respect than the other. The winner of this fight, I hope, will fight his way to a point where none can dispute his claim to the championship.

Regarding the title, Jeffries was also quoted as saying,

> I have no power to confer the title of world's championship upon any man. If I had I would give it to my brother Jack. Hart is capable of fighting for the title and in my opinion will be able to defend it.

> The championship, however, rests with the people. They and the press alone can confer the title of world champion upon the victor and they will name the heavyweight champion. ... I hope the victor will fight his way to that point where no one can dispute his title.

Thus, even though Jeff announced before the fight that the winner would be the new champion, his language after the fight was more equivocal, similar to what he said in the days leading up to the fight. The sense was that Hart was the new champion, but to truly gain firm recognition, at least in the general public's mind, he would need to solidify it with in-the-ring performances.

W.W. Naughton was impressed. "Judging from his work today, he has little to fear from any of the heavyweights at present in commission, so long as he decides to confine himself to finish fights." The point was that Hart could be outpointed, but in a finish fight, with his ability to absorb punishment, his condition, and powerful punch, he would be tough to beat.

The San Francisco Call said Hart looked like a loser until he whipped in a terrific solar plexus punch. Up until then, Root had met many wild rushes with great skill and cleverness. Hart showed no class and was outboxed by the vanquished man from the start. Rushes and clinches marked the fight.

Hart showed that he certainly was not a brilliant boxer, swinging wildly time after time, and absorbing punishment while being outboxed. The clean break clause hurt him, because it eliminated a lot of the infighting, the only branch of the game in which he was able to inflict punishment. This allowed Root to clinch and neutralize him. Both men infringed on the rule regarding hitting in the clinches, and seemed loath to break at Referee Jeffries' order. After a time, Jeff had to go between them frequently to separate them.

Root showed all his old-time cleverness, jabbing away and sending in his right with unerring accuracy throughout the fight. He practically landed at will. Before many rounds had elapsed, many were willing to wager all they had that Root would wear him down and win.

Hart had been badly punished and knocked down at the end of the 7th round. However, two minutes into the 12th round, Hart sent his right to the solar plexus. "The blow sounded to the spectators almost like the pop of a pistol, and its effect on Root was instantaneous. He dropped to his knees, and with his face distorted with pain he clutched at his body with one hand, while with the other he held the lower rope of the ring and made vain endeavors to regain his feet." Root tried to rise, but could not. He was still down when the fateful ten seconds was called off. The victory was sudden and sensational. Some called it a lucky punch, but those who had followed Hart's career knew otherwise.

The Call recognized Hart as the new champion. "Marvin Hart became the champion heavy-weight boxer for the world this afternoon by landing a knockout punch on Jack Root's solar plexus in the twelfth round of a vicious fight."

According to the *San Francisco Evening Post*, up to the 11th round, Root was holding his own and seemed to have the situation well in hand. Root made a fast fight of it, and before 2 rounds had elapsed he had Hart's face bleeding and chopped up. Hart did not discourage, however, and at the end of the 4th round there was blood on the lips of both. Root's grueling pace told on him early, and in the clinches, he seemed to want to hold on longer than Hart did.

In the 7th round, Root had a good lead and it looked like curtains for Hart. It was a vicious round and they mixed it all over the ring. Just as the bell sounded, Root sent Hart to the floor. The gong saved him.

Root went all to pieces in the 8th round when Hart showed up strong and full of fight, none the worse for his experience in the previous round. Still, Jack fought in as lively a fashion as he could.

In the 12th round, Hart left his corner full of ginger and rushed immediately. Root ducked and clinched. Hart got in a left to he face and right to the ribs. Hart was at his best and repeated with blows to Root's head and body, at the same time blocking cleverly. Each tried to deliver a knockout punch. Suddenly like a thunderbolt came a punch that dropped Root, doubled up in a heap. He grasped for the ropes and tried to regain his feet, but was too weak. He sank to the floor and was counted out.

The San Francisco Bulletin felt that up until the knockout, the fight was "as even as honors could be. One round would look like Root and the next like Hart." Root was the better boxer and ring general, but Hart was stronger and more aggressive. Marvin had the 20-pound weight advantage and a longer reach. Root made it a scientific fight because he could not afford to swap blow for blow. "Root had to side-step, back away, clinch, duck, and feign grogginess to offset Hart's superior strength and weight." That said, Hart had shown defensive skill. "Root missed more yesterday than he was ever known to do before." Jack was usually an accurate puncher and fine judge of distance, but many of his blows were wild. "As to Hart, he fought better than he did when he met Jack Johnson. He was less slovenly, less awkward, and used fewer wild swings. His style of fighting was the same. He relied on his strength and ability to absorb punishment to carry the day, and he carried the fighting to Root right from the start.

Pursuant to his pre-fight plan, Root stalled a lot and feigned weakness to get Hart to put forth his best endeavors so that he would wear himself out. As a result of forcing the milling more, Hart fatigued himself at times, and he had more tired spells than Root did. Still, with his mouth and nose bleeding, and ear cut, he was game all through.

Regarding his championship status, the *San Francisco Bulletin* said, "The new champion. Marvin Hart has been heralded as such, and doubtless he will lay claim to the title which Jim Jeffries voluntarily surrendered, but the public at large will not recognize him as the real thing in heavyweight circles until he has won other battles." It wanted Hart to prove himself further.

McCormick said that Hart was not claiming the championship of the world just yet. He said Hart was willing to meet Mike Schreck, who had just knocked out Dave Barry in the 20th round the previous day. McCormick said Hart was improving, and he expected him to be the real champion before he was through fighting.

The San Francisco Chronicle provided its overall analysis. The fight started slowly for the first 2 rounds. "Each man was feeling the other out, and, since it was to be a finish, there was really no hurry any way. This apparent unwillingness to do anything but clinch provoked this remark from a village wit: 'You fellows must be rooming together.'" This brought laughter.

However, the fight heated up in the 3rd round. Both were trying hard and fighting at a good pace. "They were trying too willingly for their own good. Slow, careful fighting is to be expected in a finish battle, but these two men went after each other after the manner of the Philadelphia six-round boys, who try to finish things up in a hurry." Hart began using his kidney punch. Root was clever at ducking head shots.

Jeffries had to force the breaks and step between them, despite his previous statement that he would disqualify them if they refused to break. The articles called for clean breaks, but neither wanted to take a chance of having the other sneak in something on the break, so they waited for Jeff to get between them.

Hart began bleeding a little at the mouth in the 4th round. In the 5th, Root sustained a slight cut below the left eye and began bleeding at the mouth as well. Root's second, Battling Nelson, gave him smelling salts between these rounds.

There was no advantage until the 7th round, when, "Right at the gong, some thought it was after, Root caught Hart on the jaw with a right. The Kentuckian sank to the mat and had to be helped to his corner, while his manager, Jack McCormack, made a protest about the round being over. Jeff waved him away and ordered the battle to proceed." Root tried to finish him in the 8th, but could not. "Whatever else you may say about Marvin, he is game." Blood was smeared all over Hart's face.

In the 9th, the blood streamed from Hart's nose and mouth, and he was cut slightly behind the ear. Hart lost his temper and wrestled Root to the ground, but Jeff overlooked it because Jack was refusing to break. The 10th and 11th rounds saw "whirlwind" fighting.

The 12th round knockout blow was unexpected. At that point, neither man had an advantage. Hart shot out his right in a semicircle. Root sank to the canvas in agony, "his whole body writhing and quivering with pain. He reached his arm up for the ropes like a blind man reaching out into the darkness for he knows not what. His fingers clinched the ropes and then gave way from sheer weakness and he rolled over on the canvas."

Hart looked much better than he did than when he fought Jack Johnson. He was in even better condition and had better judgment of distance.

The Reno Evening Gazette's post-fight analysis said that neither fighter seemed to have an advantage. Root was bleeding at the mouth and Hart from the nose. The hot sun sapped their strength. Root was fast and shifty, jabbing away, but Hart's thunderous body punch won him the fight.

Reno's *Nevada State Journal* said Root was unlucky, because he got the corner with the sun in his eyes, and also because he dropped Hart at the *end* of the 7th round, so the bell saved Marvin. Root was aggressive in most of the rounds, and fought with the cool deliberation of a veteran. He took good care to watch Hart's right.

Both men fought a hard fight. They went at it and mixed matters. Hart relied more on his right. Hart on several occasions made use of the famous haymaker overhand swing. Root was a two-handed fighter, though the left was quicker than the right. He landed effective lefts to the body which distressed Marvin. Root landed his remarkable left almost at will, "although Hart did better work getting away and blocking in yesterday's fight than many of his friends give him credit for."

Those reporters present who had seen Hart against Johnson said Marvin had improved wonderfully.

> The oft-repeated declaration that Hart lacked science was thrown to the winds in yesterday's fight. His opponent carried the fight to him in many of the rounds and that he fared so well was due to the fact

that he got away from many strong leads and was truly clever and shifty.

Root did most of the holding in the last few rounds. In some of the hottest rounds, Hart complained to Jeffries that Root was holding and not breaking clean. Marvin would hold up his hands and show Jeffries that he was not holding on, but trying to break clean.

Afterwards, Root had a slight discoloration about the solar plexus and a bruised cheek. Hart had a slight cut on his lip.[339]

Apparently, despite previous representations, the purse was evenly split, so that each received $2,375 after Joe "Kid" Eagan had been paid $250 for making the match. Jack McCormick said Root refused to fight unless the purse was split 50/50.

The Nevada State Journal said the club made a nice profit, the proceeds of the fight being between $14,000 and $15,000.

Naughton later said the club paid $5,000 to the fighters, $1,000 to Jeffries, and $1,000 for the license. The arena cost $2,000 to build. The expenses all told were about $11,000, so the promoters made some good money, but not a great deal. It was said that Root staying away from Reno until the last moment had hurt the gate.[340]

The San Francisco Evening Post criticized Hart for drawing the color line, given that he had obtained a questionable decision over Johnson.

> While Marvin Hart proved that he had endurance and that he was there with the knockout punch, his victory over Root does not necessarily entitle him to serious consideration as the probable heavyweight champion. Those who journeyed to Reno say that there is no question but that Hart has improved considerably since he fought Jack Johnson in this city early in the year.

Regardless of Hart's improvement, the paper felt that Johnson was the better man.

> At the end of the twenty rounds, with rings boxed all around him, the referee practically made him a present of the contest. A draw would not have been giving Johnson the best of it.

> With Root's scalp hanging to his belt the first statement uttered by Hart was to the effect that he was ready to fight any man in the world, barring a colored man (meaning, of course, Johnson). In other words, Hart is not particularly anxious for Arthur's game, and the only way to side step it is to draw the color line.[341]

---

339 *San Francisco Call, San Francisco Examiner, San Francisco Evening Post, San Francisco Bulletin, Nevada State Journal,* July 4, 1905; *San Francisco Chronicle,* July 4, 5, 1905; *Reno Evening Gazette,* July 3, 1905.
340 *San Francisco Examiner,* July 5, 6, 1905.
341 *San Francisco Evening Post,* July 5, 1905.

However, in the South, the *Louisville Courier-Journal* said that Hart, "having defeated Jack Johnson, the black boxer picked to defeat the champion, stands, in the estimation of the majority of sporting men, as a bona fide defender of the title." Before the fight, Jeffries had gone to the center of the ring and announced that he had retired for good and that the winner of the fight would be entitled to the name of heavyweight champion of the world. Jeffries could not change his mind afterwards.[342]

A few days after the fight, Root claimed that he had been injured as a result of his sparring with Schreck, and that doctors had advised him not to go forward with the Hart bout. It is interesting how fighters often claim that they are in the best shape of their lives before the fight, but after they are defeated, they have an excuse that contradicts their pre-fight statements. However, Root also said that Hart "landed a punch that easily would have toppled Jeff over, and is entitled to all the honors of war."[343]

The Police Gazette said Hart had the worst of it in the earlier stages, just as Fitzsimmons did against Corbett, but he wore Root down with body shots. "Hart today is a big, tough, fairly clever, game fighter, who has business now with any man in sight." It said that 4,000 spectators, including women, had witnessed the bout.[344]

The Police Gazette did not necessarily recognize Hart as champion. It argued that just because Jeff was champion, that did not vest him with the power to give the championship to someone. It said there was at present no champion.[345]

The San Francisco Chronicle said,

> Tentatively the championship of the world went to Hart, but his claim to it will not be taken seriously until he has proved his right to the title – not in one battle, but in a number. He is not a champion yet. His hard work is all ahead of him. And yet, looking over the field of heavy-weights, who is there who has a better right to the title? Fitzsimmons and Corbett, the two men who held it before Jeffries, are out of the game.

It again noted Jeffries' earlier statement that he could not bestow his title but that it had to be earned by beating all other claimants. This paper granted, "However, for the time being, in order to have a champion, Hart may be considered as holding the honor until he is beaten." So, Hart was at least the tentative champion in the absence of another.

It was even unclear as to whether Hart was claiming the championship. Marvin had said after the fight that he was the new champion. However, his manager, Jack McCormick "states that Hart is ready to meet any

---

342 *The Louisville Courier-Journal*, July 4, 1905.
343 *San Francisco Examiner*, July 7, 1905.
344 *Police Gazette*, July 22, 1905.
345 *Police Gazette*, July 8, 1905.

heavyweight in the world. He is not claiming the heavyweight championship yet, but he hopes to win it by defeating all comers."

Jeffries was quoted shortly after the fight as saying,

> Marvin Hart is a great fighter. He is not a fancy boxer, by any means, but he is a game, willing, aggressive and hard-hitting fighter. I believe he should be able to hold his own with any of the present-day heavyweights. At least, I know of none who has anything on Marvin....
>
> I have maintained for several years that a man to win and hold the heavyweight title in the present day must be a real heavyweight, a man weighing 200 pounds or more... Root is clever, but his cleverness could not offset Marvin's weight.
>
> I do not wish the public to get the idea that I am trying to make Marvin Hart the champion.... It is not for me to say who shall be champion. It might be well, however, for the public to consider Hart, say as the champion pro tem. Put him on probation. This would stir up the now slumbering army of heavyweights and result in a number of hard-fought battles which would eventually establish the right of Hart or some other man to the championship honors beyond the question of a doubt.[346]

The question raised by the *San Francisco Bulletin* was, "Who is the Champion of the Ring, Anyhow?" Its daily writer contended that Hart had as much right to the title as anyone else did, as long as Jeffries was retired. So, at that point, it accepted him as the champion.[347]

A New York writer said that Hart was the world champion, and that no one was better, except for Jeffries. "Fitzsimmons hasn't shown any form... Fitz has about blown.... In the last two years he hasn't put up a first-class fight."[348]

Bat Masterson said Hart was the real champion and could whip any heavyweight.

> There is no other heavyweight in sight willing to try conclusions with the recently made champion, with the possible exception of the negro, Johnson...[who] would not be likely to score a victory in a battle scheduled to go to a finish.
>
> Fitzsimmons...stated emphatically that the only man he would fight was Jim Corbett, so that would seem to let him out of the running.[349]

---

346 *Louisville Courier-Journal*, July 5, 1905.
347 *San Francisco Bulletin*, July 6, 1905.
348 *Louisville Courier-Journal*, July 7, 1905, quoting "Tad" of the *New York Journal*.
349 *Louisville Courier-Journal*, July 9, 1905; *Reno Evening Gazette*, July 13, 1905.

Describing Marvin, Bat said, "Hart is an awkward appearing fighter when in action in the ring, but his awkwardness is more apparent than real, as any fighter who has faced him will acknowledge."

Speaking of who Hart should fight, Masterson said, "Gus Ruhlin will seek a match with Hart, and on the showing made by both men in their last encounter in Baltimore the Akron giant appears entitled to first consideration at the hands of the present champion. Ruhlin has not done any fighting, however, for about two years." Ruhlin had not entered the ring since his May 1904 12-round draw with Hart.[350]

Hart initially said that he would meet the winner of the Ruhlin v. McCormick bout.[351] However, Marvin was also reported to have issued a challenge to Mike Schreck.[352]

There was some discussion of a Fitzsimmons bout, but Bob went to Paris to fetch his wife, who was rumored to have left him. "Why the red-topped hurricane should start on a European trip just at a time when he could have fought Hart has puzzled the fight fans. At last the truth has come out. Fitz went after his wife."[353]

However, there was some speculation that Fitz wanted to appear interested in fighting when he really was not. In June, there had been some talk of matching the winner of Hart-Root with the winner of the then-scheduled Fitzsimmons-Schreck bout, which was then set to take place in Salt Lake City on July 4. However, eventually Fitzsimmons called off the Schreck fight, for alleged financial reasons regarding the posting of forfeit money. However, those who saw Bob in training said his reasons for calling off the match were mere pretext, that Bob knew he would lose and was done-for as a fighter, for in training, instead of getting stronger, he was getting weaker.[354]

The San Francisco Evening Post said the title would be clearer if Hart could knock out Johnson.

> The memory of the recent Hart-Johnson fight, when nearly every report was that Hart was rushing and was being cut to pieces with jabs and hooks...does not linger pleasantly. ... Nobody is especially anxious to see Johnson beat Hart. At the same time, the fact that Hart has drawn the color line will certainly not boost him. Johnson is one of the cleverest big men that ever stepped into a ring. Jeffries would probably beat him, as the big fellow apparently has most of his opponents bluffed so badly they are beaten before they enter the ring.

---

350 *Louisville Courier-Journal,* July 9, 1905.
351 *Louisville Courier-Journal,* July 5, 6, 1905.
352 *Louisville Times,* July 4, 1905.
353 *Louisville Courier-Journal,* July 10, 1905.
354 *Nevada State Journal,* June 16, 1905.

For the others, however, the chances are that Johnson will be the 'yellow peril' to be avoided for a long time. He showed this by the way he pranced around 'Miner' Jack Munroe, outclassing him and punching him at will.

Hart is the heavyweight champion as long as Jeffries is out of the ring. ... The best way for Hart to try to earn Jeffries' crown is to wipe out the smudge left on his record by Jack Johnson, for, though Hart did receive the decision it was anything but a clean one.[355]

In late June 1905, Johnson had easily "won" a 6-round no-decision bout against Jack Munroe, the fighter whom Jeffries had stopped in 2 rounds. In mid-July, Johnson won a bout against Sandy Ferguson when Sandy was disqualified in the 7th round as the result of foul low blows. Ferguson's stock plummeted. Johnson kept active enough to keep himself in the public eye.

The question was who Hart would fight next. Fitz had bad hands and was traveling to Paris. Gus Ruhlin was inactive. "To a person standing on the conservative line, it looks as though Hart has a pretty good grip on the title when compared with the none too promising bunch of 'heavies' at present claiming attention."[356]

A couple weeks after the Root fight, Hart said that he was the heavyweight champion of the world and was willing to meet anyone the public wanted, including Schreck, Fitzsimmons, Ruhlin, or even Jeffries.

Again discussing the championship battle, Hart was quoted as saying, "Root walked into a punch that landed between the kidneys and the short ribs.... Five minutes afterwards Root was still on queer street. Root was game and he gave me my greatest battle. He is a tougher proposition than Jack Johnson, the black."

Hart said that Jeffries had told him, "All you need is more cleverness. You have the punch, willingness and gameness." Hart did not know of anyone who had much of a chance to defeat him, and expected to be champion for a long time.[357]

The Police Gazette was still not convinced of Hart's claim to the crown. "Marvin Hart is the heavyweight champion only because he says he is. The sporting world at large does not share his opinion, and will not until he bests some better man than Jack Root." It felt that until he defeated someone like Ruhlin, Schreck, or Johnson again, he was not the champion.

Some were even speculating that Jack Johnson threw the Hart fight, or at least gave it away by not fighting his best. They felt that Johnson should still be considered as a viable challenger to the title.

---

355 *San Francisco Evening Post*, July 13, 1905.
356 *San Francisco Evening Post*, July 15, 1905.
357 *Reno Evening Gazette*, July 20, 1905.

> Although the fighting critics throughout the country are inclined to believe that Johnson considerately helped to string his own scalp on the Louisvillian's girdle by laying down, Johnson so easily and neatly trimmed Jack Munroe in the recent meeting, that he must be reckoned with as a decided factor.[358]

Referee George Siler reluctantly recognized Hart as champion, but said that he was the poorest champ since Sullivan.

> In looking the heavyweight pugilistic field over I can see no white man capable of trouncing Hart, so he is indeed fortunate that the crop of good, big fighters is scarce. Undoubtedly the best big man in the business at present is Jack Johnson, the colored heavyweight champion, and Hart shows excellent judgment in drawing the color line. It is the opinion of all fair-minded witnesses that Johnson beat Hart in their recent fight at San Francisco, and undoubtedly can repeat the trick, so it probably is better for the game that Hart drew the color line.

Mike Schreck was the only boxer to have knocked out George Gardner. He wanted a crack at the title.

Hugo Kelly, who had split two bouts and had two draws with Mike Schreck, and had split two bouts with Jack O'Brien, including a more recent 1905 W10 over O'Brien, fought Tommy Burns in late July 1905. Burns defeated Kelly, but robbed himself of the official victory by agreeing before the bout that if both were on their feet at the end of the 20th round that the bout would be declared a draw. Still, the performance served to boost Burns, who also held a 20-round decision over Dave Barry.[359]

The Police Gazette again said Hart's fight with Johnson was an "alleged fake fight" and that Hart could not lick Johnson "on the level," which was why Hart drew the color line - to avoid another meeting.[360]

In August, the *Police Gazette* reported, "Marvin Hart says positively that he will never meet Jack Johnson in the ring again." It said Hart's claim to the championship was "pretty groggy, and figuratively speaking is on the ropes." *The Police Gazette* had traditionally been staunchly opposed to the color line in boxing. It criticized Hart for his drawing the color line, even though every champion before him had essentially done the same.

> A black man, in my esteem, is entitled to just the same rights and prerogatives, as long as he is cleanly and decent, upright, capable and honest. Both Jeffries and Hart have fought niggers, as they style their colored rivals, before, and why not fight again? .... [W]hen he barred colored men he was thinking of no one on earth but Mr. Johnson....

---

358 *Police Gazette*, July 22, 1905.
359 *San Francisco Evening Post*, July 29, 1905.
360 *Police Gazette*, July 29, 1905.

> Mr. Hart knows, as well as he knows that he is alive, that Jack Johnson was entitled to that fight out in San Francisco, and he also knows, I'll bet my boots, that Mr. Johnson can lick him every day in the week, not even barring Sunday.
>
> I must say, however, in this connection, that I do not believe Mr. Jeffries barred Mr. Johnson for the same reason Mr. Hart has. Jim couldn't see any honor or dough in a win over Jack.... Again, I have always thought that Mr. Jeffries' virulent jealousy of Mr. Johnson's superior sartorial predilections had much to do with his denying him a chance.

The Police Gazette was calling for someone first to go through a series of hard fights to impress the public that he was entitled to the championship honor.

Gus Ruhlin was clamoring for a shot. He admitted being hurt and dropped in the 4th round of his first fight with Hart. He claimed that he cut Hart to ribbons in their second bout and that he dropped Hart six times, "and he was in such a bad way that the police jumped in to save him. He won't fight me, and he's wise not to."[361] The primary source accounts did not agree with Ruhlin's assessment.

Hart accurately said that he defeated Ruhlin in their 6 rounder, but the second fight was "about even." He said of their draw, "Ruhlin cut an artery over my eye and I suffered for a time from loss of blood, but toward the last I was myself and knocked Ruhlin down."[362]

In August, Ruhlin scored a KO18 over Hart manager Jack McCormick, but Ruhlin was really not an active fighter. He would not fight again for another 8 months.[363]

Ruhlin was not willing to meet Jack Johnson to legitimize himself as a top challenger. "Well, Gus says he never fought a colored man, and does not intend to begin now." Ruhlin though, praised Johnson.

> Outside of Jeffries, I think that this fellow Johnson can trim the world. Yes, Fitzsimmons and the whole bunch of them. I only saw him in one fight, but he's a marvel.... Why, he has a chance even with Jeff, in my mind. Jeff was a bit leery of him, too. I'm not saying that Jim was afraid of him, you know, but he didn't want any of it if he could get out of it. You know he drew the color line on Johnson, and he had met four coons before that time. I guess he knew a little about Johnson.[364]

---

361 *Louisville Courier-Journal*, July 11, 1905; *Police Gazette*, August 12, 1905.
362 *Police Gazette*, September 23, 1905.
363 *Police Gazette*, August 26, 1905.
364 *Louisville Courier-Journal*, July 11, 1905.

The Police Gazette reported that the smaller Jack O'Brien was not interested in fighting the husky Hart.[365]

The Police Gazette was getting Hart's age right, in September saying he was born in Jefferson County, Kentucky on September 16, 1876, and was 29 years old. It compared him with Tom Sharkey. "He believes in fighting all the time and in this way wearing an opponent down." It said that he was now a full fledged heavyweight and weighed 200 pounds.

It again addressed Hart's inconsistency in regard to the color line. "Like all Southerners he has inherited a prejudice against the colored race." It noted that he had refused to fight Joe Walcott after defeating Kid Carter, saying, "I am a Southerner and my folks would disown me if I fought you.... I could not go back to Kentucky again."

Yet, he had fought Johnson. It explained that Hart had initially refused to fight Johnson, but he was heavily in debt and was being taunted by Johnson and his friends of being afraid, plus he knew that defeating the top contender could possibly get him a title shot, so he took the fight with Johnson. Of their fight, it said,

> Hart, however, forced the fight all the time and the good judges who figured it out that he would make Johnson hold back, afraid of being hurt, had the right end.
>
> Johnson had repeatedly challenged Jeffries, but after Hart beat him that put an end to his claims for the championship. It proved also that Johnson never was in Jeffries' class.

By September 1905, the *Police Gazette* said it did not agree with the idea of a championship being handed down, but, "Hart has more claim upon it than anyone else just now." So, it was backing off of its previous position that Hart was not the champion.[366]

Jeffries, although not coming out of retirement, said,

> I am not bragging when I say that I could beat all four of them in one night. I mean Hart, Johnson, Ruhlin and McCormick. That Hart-Johnson mill was one of the saddest sketches ever perpetrated on an unsuspecting public... Not one of these men is better than a third-rate heavyweight.

Of course, it was easy to talk trash from the retirement post, unwilling to back up his words.

The Police Gazette both complimented and criticized Johnson. On one hand, it said, "Jack Johnson is the best heavyweight now before the public." However, it also said, "The fact that Johnson lost to Hart stamps him as a faker or as a boxer with a yellow streak in his make-up, and either defect

---

[365] *Police Gazette*, August 26, 1905.
[366] *Police Gazette*, September 16, 1905.

would kill his chances for first honors if pitted against such men as Jeffries or Fitzsimmons."

However, Fitz and Jeff appeared to be retired. "That leaves Johnson to fight such men as Hart and Ruhlin, either of whom he should defeat handily. But there is no reason why any such contests should be classed as championship fights, for they are only second rate fights at the best."[367] Basically, to these folks, if you were not the lauded Jeffries or Fitzsimmons, you were nobody.

Hart said he wanted to fight Fitzsimmons, amongst others. "I am ready to fight any white man in the world. I do not think any man now in the ring can defeat me. When I am beaten it will be recorded that it was a fight from first to last and that the victor was punished within an inch of his life."

Hart was also willing to fight Mike Schreck, whom he called a "rough and ready fighter and is full of grit." However Schreck had an odd September 1905 "win" over John Willie that may have been a loss. *The Police Gazette* reported that Schreck went down in the 7th round from a body shot and left to the jaw. In the 10th, Schreck went down claiming a foul, which was not allowed. In the 11th, Mike again went down. He was counted out and the referee awarded the fight to Willie. Yet, oddly enough, he then changed his decision and gave the fight to Schreck, but declared all bets off. Hart had bested Willie in their most recent contest.

Hart also expressed a willingness to box Jack O'Brien. "I have beaten Jack O'Brien and can do it again."[368]

In October 1905, it was reported that Hart had hired Tommy Ryan as his manager/trainer and fired long-time manager/trainer Jack McCormick. "Hart said he hated to do it, but he felt that Mac could not give him that scientific training necessary to the successful pugilist."[369]

---

367 *Police Gazette*, September 16, 1905.
368 *Police Gazette*, September 23, 1905.
369 *Police Gazette*, October 28, 1905.

CHAPTER 16

A Title Fight

Bob Fitzsimmons challenged Jack O'Brien to a 25-round battle "to determine who is best fitted to hold the heavyweight championship title."

Fitz claimed that Hart had ignored his challenges. It is unclear regarding who ignored whom, as Hart had expressed a willingness to box Fitz as well. Hart's manager Tommy Ryan claimed it was Fitz who was afraid of Hart. *The Police Gazette* opined, "That kind of talk sounds pretty funny to people who know how hard Fitz tried to get Hart to agree to a match, after the latter whipped Root." It noted that Hart had not done any boxing since claiming the title. Hart did not defend the title in 1905.[370] However, in Hart's defense, most of the talk after the Hart-Root fight had confirmed that Fitz was unavailable in Europe or had said that he would fight no one other than Corbett. Hart supporters might say that Fitzsimmons wanted a man who was more defensive minded and not as big, strong, and as rugged as Hart, and whom Fitz had previously boxed and almost knocked out.[371]

Since losing a 1905 10-round decision to Hugo Kelly, amongst his bouts that year, Jack O'Brien had a D20 with Jack "Twin" Sullivan and an October KO17 over then highly touted up and comer Al Kaufman. The 19-year-old 196-pound Kaufman had just turned pro, but had scored a KO1 over Jack "Twin" Sullivan, who in turn had a 1904 10-round decision win over Mike Schreck and the draw with O'Brien. *The Police Gazette* had given Kaufman a great deal of coverage despite his relative inexperience.[372]

Fitzsimmons and O'Brien were scheduled to box 20 rounds in San Francisco in December 1905. In training, O'Brien looked very fast with his feet. O'Brien said that he would use speed to peck away at Fitz's face, blind him if possible, and when he was helpless, try to knock him out. O'Brien insisted on the large 24-foot ring. It was obvious that he wanted a big ring so that he could utilize his fast footwork. Jack said the pace would be too much for Bob.

Fitz claimed to be in very good shape, and looked fit, but he also oscillated between saying it would likely be his last fight and that he might consider a fight with Hart if he won. The question was how much he had left at his age. O'Brien was 28 years old, while Fitz was at least 42, and had only boxed one 6-round bout, that with O'Brien, in the two years since

---

[370] *Police Gazette*, November 18, 1905, December 2, 1905.
[371] *Louisville Courier-Journal*, July 11, 1905.
[372] *Police Gazette*, October 14, 1905, October 28, 1905, November 4, 1905, November 11, 1905.

winning the world light heavyweight championship in 1903. Fitz was old and inactive. Even in late 1903, writers were saying Bob was past it and should consider retiring.

Although they claimed to be boxing for the world's heavyweight championship, the truth was that they were really contesting for light heavyweight honors, as neither would weigh over 175 pounds. Still, some might argue otherwise.

> The light-heavy championship is certainly involved… As to the heavyweight championship, Fitzsimmons and O'Brien have as much right as anybody to battle for it under existing circumstances, but other contests will be required before the question of superiority among heavyweights is settled definitely. Marvin Hart will demand recognition, of course, and as he has already figured in an event which was winked at as a world's championship, he is entitled to consideration.[373]

---

[373] *San Francisco Bulletin*, December 13, 1905.

On December 20, 1905 in San Francisco, before a crowd of 8,000 at Mechanics' Pavilion, Philadelphia Jack O'Brien fought Bob Fitzsimmons. When the boxers entered the ring, it was announced that Marvin Hart challenged the winner.

1 - The round was marked by O'Brien's marvelous footwork.

2 - O'Brien continued moving, although more blows were thrown.

3 - O'Brien opened with a left jab that made Bob wobble. Jack opened Bob's nose during the round.

Just at the close of the round, O'Brien suddenly stopped running and leapt into the center of the ring with a plunging straight left. It landed between the eyes, on the nose, and sent Fitzsimmons to the floor on his backside. Bob grinned and quickly rose as the bell rang.

4 - Fitz forced matters, but missed so badly that the impetus of his punches caused Bob to throw himself down to his knees. Jack used rights to the body to wear Bob down. Later in the round, O'Brien rushed and hustled Fitz to the ropes and Bob fell down. He was up quickly. It was not a true knockdown.

5 - Blood ran from Bob's nose and mouth, and his face was badly cut up. He kept trying wicked swings, but to no avail.

6 - O'Brien again used extreme speed to get out of danger. Some hissed his sprinting tactics.

7 - O'Brien further marked up Bob and opened up a cut over his eye.

8 - O'Brien ripped in a nasty left over the eye. When they both swung rights, Jack landed first with his short right to the jaw and dropped Fitz down onto his back. Bob scrambled to his feet at once, but he staggered a bit. A right to the jaw forced Bob to the ropes and a series of left jabs and rights almost put him out. Jack also struck him with several body blows. Bob was groggy and in a bad way.

9 - Fitzsimmons showed his gameness and recuperative powers, and O'Brien did all he could to avoid the vicious blows.

10 - 12 - These rounds were marked by Bob's futile efforts to land, and by the constant jabbing and uppercutting on the part of O'Brien, which served to gradually wear Fitzsimmons down.

13 - The round was more of the same, with O'Brien outboxing Fitzsimmons. Just before the round ended, Jack landed a wicked short left into Fitz's stomach.

After the bell, Bob went to his corner. While on his chair, Bob sank in a faint. When referee Graney saw Bob's condition, he immediately waived the contest off. Another version said after about 30 seconds in his corner, an exhausted Bob sank to his knees. His eyes were nearly closed, his nose spread, and his lips swollen. Bob began vomiting, and the blood ran from his mouth. Naughton claimed that Bob said, "Eddie, I'm all gone." Another paper said Bob tried to say something about being hit with a body shot, but then collapsed while seated, the blood flowing from his nose and mouth.[374]

Fitzsimmons had been dropped in the 3rd round with a straight left between the eyes and in the 8th by a right. The left hook to the body just before the end of the 13th round took the rest of the fight out of Fitz.[375]

O'Brien gave a speech, saying he took no credit for the victory. "I was too fast for the old man and set a pace I was at all times sure would win in the end." He just had to watch out for the one punch that might turn the tide of battle. "I am prepared to defend the title of heavyweight champion of the world, which I now claim belongs to me. Marvin Hart and all the pugs the public think are entitled to a meeting will be accommodated." O'Brien said he was now ready to fight any man in the world for the middleweight or heavyweight championship, provided he was white.

O'Brien received over $7,000, while Bob supposedly earned just over $2,000. The club earned over $6,000.

---

[374] *San Francisco Bulletin, Examiner, Call, Evening Post*, December 21, 1905.
[375] *Police Gazette*, December 30, 1905.

TWO "EXAMINER" FLASHLIGHTS, SHOWING FITZSIMMONS SPRAWLED ON THE FLOOR OF THE RING AS THE RESULT OF O'BRIEN'S KNOCKDOWN BLOWS

The Evening Post said Fitz fought hard, but was no match for O'Brien, who was too fast, too active with hands and feet, and too elusive and cautious. The game Fitz took a fearful beating. He had to fight both O'Brien and father time. His age was too much of a handicap.

The Examiner said Fitzsimmons was thoroughly beaten. Fitz was too slow for him. O'Brien was as nimble as a rubber ball, and he punished Bob throughout. The bulk of the damage was done with straight lefts as Jack danced about.

Referee Graney said that if Fitzsimmons still had the power in his legs that he had retained in his arms it would have been a different fight. O'Brien was too shifty. One writer said Bob was not his former self, but instead was a pitiful spectacle.

Fitz admitted that O'Brien was too young and lively for him, that he had Corbett's footwork, although Jack was not as big as Jim. He also complimented Jack's ability to duck and get out of tight places. He did not fault O'Brien for doing so much running away.

The next day, Fitzsimmons said he was done with the ring. He saw the openings, but he could not punch when he wanted to. His old-time speed was not there, and his feet dragged. He felt slow. "When I started to fight I found my brain and my muscles did not work in accord. I would see an opening, but before I could take advantage of it the chance was gone. I think men in all the professions find age dulls their faculties." Bob asked, "Could you picture O'Brien doing this to me when I was younger?"[376]

Although the bout had been at light-heavyweight, O'Brien began claiming the heavyweight championship. He believed that the championship reverted back to the previous title holder, Fitzsimmons,

---

376 *San Francisco Call, San Francisco Chronicle*, December 22, 1905.

when Jeff retired. "That makes me champion." Initially, the *Police Gazette* agreed that O'Brien had a clearer claim on the title. Jack claimed that he wanted to fight Hart for the undisputed title.[377]

However, despite his talk, when it was said that Alex Greggains would offer a February date to Hart and O'Brien, Jack declined, saying that he wanted to rest until March, and was more inclined to take on Tommy Ryan at middleweight first. "Hart? Certainly I'll fight him. When I'm done with Ryan, Hart will be accommodated immediately." Such reluctance to fight Hart, and the desire to fight at middleweight, took O'Brien out of the running for consideration or recognition as a heavyweight champion.[378]

The San Francisco Bulletin said O'Brien was not willing to fight Jack Johnson. He wanted Hart or Ryan because they would be the best money fights. "Beating Root gave Marvin something of a championship prominence, and while he laid claim to the title, he was not taken seriously by the sporting world." Most thought that O'Brien was the superior boxer. If it was a 20-round bout, O'Brien would be the favorite. However, in a finish fight, Hart's endurance and bulldog grit would stand him in good stead.[379]

---

377 *Police Gazette*, January 13, 1906.
378 *San Francisco Evening Post*, December 21, 1905.
379 *San Francisco Bulletin*, December 22, 1905.

CHAPTER 17

Next Up

In early January 1906, Hart and new trainer/manager Tommy Ryan were in Butte, Montana. On January 1, the two were the feature of the burlesque show at the Grand. Ryan and Hart boxed 4 rounds in an exhibition. Both appeared to be in splendid form.

Tommy Burns issued a challenge to fight for the championship. Hart representative Jack Curley said Hart would take the fight if the clubs were willing to sponsor the bout.

On January 2 at the Grand Opera house, Ryan and Hart boxed again.[380]

Jack O'Brien was negotiating a middleweight match with Ryan, and possibly even George Gardner, so he was not all that interested in a match with Hart after all.[381]

Tom Carey of the Pacific Athletic Club in Los Angeles had previously been negotiating a match between Ryan and Burns. However, Burns could no longer make the middleweight limit, and wanted to fight for the heavyweight championship. Down in Los Angeles, Burns was well thought of, and they wanted to see him in a big match that would attract national attention. So Burns and Hart were matched instead, the bout to take place on February 22 or 23.

On January 9, Hart, along with Ryan and Maurice Thompson, left for Pipestone Springs. Marvin was training for a bout set to take place a week later with Pat Callahan before the Butte Athletic Club. If Hart failed to stop Callahan he would forfeit $100.[382]

Middleweight Jack "Twin" Sullivan, who held a decision victory over Burns, joined Hart's camp as a sparring partner.[383]

Tommy Ryan spoke of the economics of boxing.

> It is not always the best fighters, and those who win the most fights, who are the best public cards. Neither is the unbeaten fighter of class necessarily any better as a drawing card than the fighter who has lost fights. ...
>
> Good cards can be divided only in two ways. The crowd hates one and comes to see him whipped, and the other is the popular idol whose every move is cheered and the crowd prays for him to win.[384]

---

[380] *Butte Miner,* January 2, 3, 1906.
[381] *Butte Miner,* January 7, 1906.
[382] *Butte Miner,* January 10, 1906.
[383] *Butte Miner,* January 12, 1906.

Ryan said, "Hart will be the pugilistic idol, and will be champion of the world for many years. He is big enough, game as a pebble, can hit a good punch, willing, so what more can you ask of a man. What's more, Hart can make lots of friends, as his ways make a hit."

Following the Callahan bout, Hart and Ryan would engage in a few short theatrical engagements and then journey to Los Angeles to put on the finishing touches of training for the Burns bout.[385]

Six and a half months after winning the title, on Monday January 15, 1906 at McDonald's gymnasium, the arena being used by the Butte Athletic Club in Butte, Montana, Marvin Hart fought an exhibition bout with an unknown miner named Pat Callahan. It was one of those deals where Hart was undertaking to knock out his adversary within 4 rounds or give him $100. Hence, although it was technically an exhibition, it was in fact a real fight. "Callahan stands on his record of outfighting every amateur he ever met."[386]

MARVIN HART, WHO MEETS PAT CALLAHAN AT M'DONALD'S TOMORROW NIGHT AND AGREES TO STOP HIM IN FOUR ROUNDS.

One source said Hart looked solid, weighing about 200 pounds. Marvin claimed to weigh 192. However, another source said that despite claims to the contrary, Hart appeared fat and not in the best condition, appearing to be about 220 pounds. One source listed Callahan at 165 while another said he was 170 pounds.

1 - Hart went at Callahan like a bull, beating his opponent black and blue with punches that would have felled a horse. However, Pat Callahan was a fearless Irishman who came to fight. It was a fight every minute. There was no clinching or stalling to avoid punishment. Callahan stood up and fought like a man with no quit in him. Marvin soon saw that he would have to earn the knockout, and fought like a whirlwind. He was in with no

Pat Callahan

---

384 *Butte Miner*, January 13, 1906.
385 *Butte Miner*, January 14, 1906.
386 *Butte Intermountain*, January 13, 1906.

walkover. Marvin landed the right and left to the nose. Callahan swung back wildly.

After some exchanges, the champion led with his right to the jaw and Callahan went down in a lump. However, he looked up smiling and slowly crawled to his feet at nine. He came up strong and they engaged in fast and furious exchanges that caused the spectators to hold their breath.

In the middle of the 1st round, Callahan covered up as he was coming toward the champion, as Hart was called, and then swung his right, catching Hart in the face with a wicked jolt that sent Marvin to a sitting position on the canvas. Like an explosion, the roar of the crowd shook the hall. Every man was on his feet, frantic with excitement. The surprised Hart stayed down less than five seconds.

Upon rising, he waded into the game Callahan like a raging bull. Pat kept at a distance, then covered his head and face and landed rights and lefts to Hart's body. Hart was doing his best to land a knockout blow. The round ended with Callahan weak but still smiling. His gameness set the crowd wild with excitement.

2 - Callahan was a bit more cautious, using his feet to good advantage and showing better defense. Then all of a sudden Hart landed his big right to the nose and Callahan tumbled over for an 8-count. Blood was plastered all over his countenance.

Callahan stood up to the champion and mixed it with him. Pat slashed in a right and the claret commenced to stream down Marvin's face.

However, a right to the jaw dropped Callahan again. He saved himself by clinching when he came up. Blood was splotched over the necks, arms and breasts of both.

Pat made no effort to evade Hart's terrific blows that were showered on his face and body. Hart hit Callahan hard enough several times at the start of the round to kill eight ordinary men, and although his fist seemed to sink into Callahan's body above the heart fully six inches, the game Callahan fought back.

After a few more blows, Hart cracked his right into the ribs and down he went again. Still, Pat gamely pulled himself up, staggering. Dazed and bloody all over from pounded lips and nose, Callahan had not gotten his bearings when Hart rushed in and jabbed him mercilessly and then knocked him to the floor for the final time with a sledge-hammer right after two minutes of the 2nd round had elapsed. He was out.[387]

Afterwards, Hart said, "Don't underestimate this chap Callahan. He is as game a man as ever lived, and he has an awful wallop in either hand. When he caught me on the nose I knew I had been hit, and Callahan will make a dangerous man for an opponent near his weight."

---

387 *Butte Miner, Anaconda Standard,* January 16, 1906.

It was the second time a champion got more than he bargained for from a Butte fighter. Folks remembered how Jack Munroe had hung with Jeffries. Afterwards, Callahan was not seriously hurt, but he was terribly battered by the beating he endured. Hart was described as "just a big bruiser, always hammering away."

Another local paper said Callahan was knocked out in the 2nd round, but "during that time he knocked the burly heavyweight champion down and gave him punch for punch that brought the blood streaming from the big fellow's nose. Hart looked to weigh more than 200 pounds, his opponent 30 pounds less." It was an exciting give and take battle. "After being knocked down three times in the second round, Callahan got dazedly to his feet and before he got his bearings Hart rushed in from behind and showered blows upon the miner until he went down and out."

Once again, Marvin Hart had been involved in an exciting battle. The man was pure fight, a true warrior. Still, even Butte was not impressed with Hart's skill.

> After last night's exhibition Hart will have to show the Butte fans before he can pose as a champion. They no longer doubt but that Jack Johnson and Jack Root both had him jabbed to death as was reported when he fought those men, and that it was only his ability to stand punishment that enabled him to defeat them.[388]

Jack Johnson wanted to fight Jack O'Brien, but even he drew the color line. Johnson "doesn't understand why O'Brien should draw the color line since he whipped Fitzsimmons seeing that he fought George Cole, Black Bill and many other colored aspirants within the past five years."[389] O'Brien's stance was inconsistent and selective. He had once drawn the color line against Joe Walcott. *The Police Gazette* had then said, "The Philadelphian bases his refusal on Walcott's color, but he probably has another reason."[390] O'Brien subsequently fought Walcott in a 1902 6-round no-decision bout. O'Brien said that he was going to first give Tommy Ryan an opportunity at his middleweight championship and then take on Hart. O'Brien was not eager for an immediate fight with Hart.[391]

O'Brien also had some marketing troubles. On January 26, 1906 in Ohio, when giving a 3-round sparring exhibition, in the 3rd round, Fred Cooley knocked down O'Brien with a right.[392] Cooley's career included a 1904 L6 George Gardner and KO1 Peter Maher, but a number of fighters had knocked him out. O'Brien and Cooley would eventually fight in a late 1906 bout and O'Brien would stop Cooley in the 3rd round.

---

388 *Butte Intermountain*, January 16, 1906.
389 *Police Gazette*, January 27, 1906.
390 *National Police Gazette*, October 19, 1901.
391 *Police Gazette*, February 3, 1906.
392 *Police Gazette*, February 10, 1906.

Hart had scheduled a defense of his crown against Tommy Burns to be held on February 23, 1906 in Los Angeles. Burns was a solid fighter, and though not the most deserving of a title shot at that time, he was willing, and the local club was willing to promote the fight and put up the money.

The Los Angelinos were impressed with Burns' performance against Hugo Kelly, whose record included 1903 W15 and D20 Schreck and D10 O'Brien; 1904 W6 Sullivan, W6 O'Brien, L20 and D10 Sullivan, ND6 O'Brien, and D10 Schreck; and 1905 W10 O'Brien, D10 Burns, and D20 Burns. Kelly had victories of some kind over Schreck, Sullivan, and O'Brien. Burns had recently defeated Kelly, though it was technically ruled a draw owing to the agreement for such a decision if there was no knockout.

Burns was a middleweight, coming off a loss, and his record was not overly impressive against top contenders: 1903 L10 Schreck; 1904 D6 Schreck (though Burns was better) and L6 O'Brien; and 1905 D20 Jack Sullivan, D10 and D20 Hugo Kelly (Burns better but agreed to draw if no knockout), and L20 Sullivan. Sullivan had recently won 20-round decisions over both Burns (October) and Schreck (November), but he was a middleweight, and easily made that weight limit, so he was not in the running for a heavyweight title shot.

In Burns' defense, all of the bouts where he struggled were at middleweight. Burns claimed to be weight drained and said that he would be more effective at a higher weight. Burns was considered to have defeated Kelly, and Kelly had a win over the vaunted O'Brien.

Despite the 1905 draw with Sullivan, Jack O'Brien had two earlier wins against Sullivan, including once by knockout. O'Brien also had wins over Schreck and a 6-round decision over Burns.

However, Jack O'Brien was playing a waiting game. He had not given the indication of any immediate willingness or interest in fighting Hart, which made sense given that he was dropped late in both of his 6 rounders with Marvin, and would be at a disadvantage in a bout of greater duration owing to Hart's superior weight, strength, and resiliency. Hart had called him out for a while even before he became champion, but O'Brien had not accepted a third match. Although after defeating Fitzsimmons, O'Brien said he wanted to meet Hart, it was reported that he was going to first meet Tommy Ryan in April for the middleweight title, so any such match would have to wait. Therefore, Burns was a serviceable interim match while awaiting more lucrative bouts.[393]

Unfortunately, for Marvin Hart, Tommy Burns proved to be a much better heavyweight than a middleweight. It seems that Tommy had been underestimated and overlooked by Hart. Hart's tenure as champion was to be short-lived, as he lost a 20-round decision to Burns, who clearly

---

[393] *Police Gazette*, February 3, 1906.

outboxed him. This ended Marvin Hart's short-lived reign as champion and began the 3-year reign of Tommy Burns, who defended the title several times, including a significant victory over O'Brien.

In subsequent years, Hart had mixed success, and would never again fight for the title. His style simply was not designed for a successful lengthy career, because all of those poundings had to take their toll. His record included: 1906 LND4 Mike Schreck; 1907 KO2 Harry Rogers, KO2 Peter Maher, LKOby21 Mike Schreck (Hart fought most of the bout with a broken wrist, until his seconds retired him); 1908 WDQ4 John Willie (Willie illegally punched on the break, dropping Hart), D12 Kid Hubert, WDQ5 Jack "Twin" Sullivan, LND6 John Willie (Hart dropped three times in the 2nd round, but came back to drop Willie in the 5th, though the 6th was even and Hart had lost the first 4 rounds); 1909 WDQ13 Tony Ross (Ross had Hart almost out and had dropped Hart to the floor, but Ross hit him while down), LKOby4 Mike Schreck; and 1910 LKOby3 Carl Morris.[394]

Marvin Hart had been a very entertaining fighter who was almost never in a dull fight. He could be hit and hurt, but he always came forward, always hit hard, and he could keep it up. He was a fan's delight. He fought often and took on any white fighter that would fight him. He crossed the color line only once, to fight the world's top contender in Jack Johnson. His victory over Johnson was controversial, but nevertheless it put him in the position to fight for the vacant championship, which he won. Hart refused to fight Johnson in a rematch and would not cross the color line again. Because Hart did not successfully defend the title as champion to further prove his mettle, sadly, he therefore has become one of history's forgotten champions. Some even questioned whether he was champion. A review of his career reveals that he was a fighter deserving of more recognition than history has given him.

---

[394] Boxrec.com.

Appendix: Marvin Hart's Record

BORN: September 16, 1876; in Fern Creek, Jefferson County, Kentucky.
DIED: September 17, 1931; Fern Creek, Kentucky, at age 55.

1900

Jan 15	William Schiller	Louisville, KY	KO 4
Feb 12	William Schiller	Louisville, KY	KO 6
?	Butch Fletcher	Louisville, KY	KO 1
?	Stormy Goss	Louisville, KY	KO 2
?	Paddy Minton	Louisville, KY	KO 1
Apr 2	Charles Meisner	Louisville, KY	KO 1
May 10	Tom Williams	Louisville, KY	KO 2

Tom Williams became Hart's trainer.

Jun 12	Lucas Siefker	Louisville, KY	KO 9

Siefker was knocked out at the conclusion of the 8th round, but saved by the bell. Siefker was unable to answer the bell for the 9th round.

Jun 26	Harry Rogers	Louisville, KY	KO 14
Aug 13	Kid Hubert	Louisville, KY	WDQ 7
Sep 18	Kid Hubert	Louisville, KY	KO 6

Kid Hubert became Hart's trainer, along with Tom Williams.

Dec 17	Peter Traynor	Louisville, KY	KO 17

1901

Hart sparred with Kid Hubert and Punch Campbell.

Jan 21	Al Weinig	Louisville, KY	KO 11
Feb 25	Australian Jimmy Ryan	Louisville, KY	KO 7

Hart was sparring Kid Hubert and Jim Watts.

Mar 29	Tommy West	Louisville, KY	KO 16

Hart sparred Steve Crosby.

May 24	Dan Creedon	Louisville, KY	KO 6

Hart traveled to San Francisco, but was unable to finalize any matches.

Hart became sick with malaria.

Nov 1	Jack Beauscholte	Louisville, KY	KO 10
Dec 17	Billy Hanrahan	Louisville, KY	LKOby1

1902

Jan 20	Billy Stift	Louisville, KY	KO 3
Apr 7	Dick O'Brien	Louisville, KY	KO 3

Hart sparred with George Grant, Pete Traynor and Joe Choynski.

May 3	Kid Carter	Louisville, KY	KO 9
Aug 18	Billy Stift	Chicago, IL	W 6

Hart sparred with Russell Hart, Tom Daly, Jimmy Simister, Jim Watts, and Kid Husbands.

Oct 16	Kid Carter	Philadelphia, PA	ND 6

Newspaper draw or slight edge for Hart.

Nov 10	Jack Root	Chicago, IL	L 6

Hart sparred with Jack/Jim McCormick, who became his trainer.

Nov 19	Philadelphia Jack O'Brien	Philadelphia, PA	ND 6

Two local newspapers said O'Brien outpointed Hart on number of blows landed, but two other newspapers felt that Hart had earned a draw because O'Brien was down and almost knocked out in the 6th round.

1903

Jan	Hart fractured his right wrist.		
Apr 2	Jack Bonner	Louisville, KY	WDQ 4
May 3	Philadelphia Jack O'Brien	Philadelphia, PA	ND 6

O'Brien outpointed Hart in the first 4 rounds, but Hart dropped O'Brien in the 5th and 6th rounds and nearly had him out.

Hart was sparring with Jack/Jim McCormick.

May 13	George Gardner	Louisville, KY	LTKOby12

Hart retired in his corner after the 12th round as a result of a badly broken right hand.

Nov 16	Joe Choynski	Philadelphia, PA	ND 6

The newspapers agreed that it had been a fierce 6-round draw.

Jack McCormick continued training Hart.

Dec 1	Kid Carter	Boston, MA	KO 15

1904

Jan 5	George Gardner	Boston, MA	D 15

Newsmen agreed that Hart clearly deserved the victory.

Jan 25	John Willie	Chicago, IL	D 6
Mar 16	Sandy Ferguson	Hot Springs, AR	W 20

Most thought the fight should have been scored a draw.

Apr 20	Gus Ruhlin	Philadelphia, PA	ND 6

The newspapers agreed that Hart had defeated Ruhlin.

May 20	Gus Ruhlin	Baltimore, MD	D 12

Hart traveled to San Francisco to try to get a fight there.

Dec	Hart was sparring Al Kaufman.		

1905

Mar	Hart sparred Sam Berger, Al Kaufman, Dave Barry, Jimmy Britt, Dave Sullivan, and Jim McCormick.		
Mar 28	Jack Johnson	San Francisco, CA	W 20

Hart age 28. Johnson age 26, just days short of 27.
This was a controversial decision. The crowd wholeheartedly supported the decision. Some newsmen thought Hart deserved it; others thought Johnson had outpointed him, while still others thought the fight was a draw. Hart was more active and aggressive, and the harder puncher, but Johnson was much the cleverer boxer and landed the greater number of clean blows.

May 8	John Willie	Philadelphia, PA	ND 6

Newspapers agreed that Hart had won.

Hart trained and sparred with Jack McCormick and Deafy Thompson in preparation for the Root fight.

Jul 3   Jack Root   Reno, NV   KO 12
Vacant World Heavyweight Championship. Hart age 28. Root age 29. Fight scheduled to the finish.

Oct   Hart fired McCormick and hired Tommy Ryan to train him.

1906

Jan   Hart and Tommy Ryan gave sparring exhibitions in Montana. Hart also sparred Maurice Thompson and Jack "Twin" Sullivan.

Jan 15   Pat Callahan   Butte, MT   EX KO 2
Hart contracted to knock out Callahan within 4 rounds or forfeit $100.

Feb 23   Tommy Burns   Los Angeles, CA   L 20
World Heavyweight Championship.

May 3   Mike Schreck   New York, NY   ND 4

1907

Mar 15   Harry Rogers   Hot Springs, AR   KO 2

Apr 1   Peter Maher   Hot Springs, AR   KO 2

May 30   Mike Schreck   Tonopah, NV   LTKOby21

1908

Mar 17   John Willie   Hot Springs, AR   WDQ 4

Oct 9   Kid Hubert   Lexington, KY   D 12

Oct 20   Jack "Twin" Sullivan   Boston, MA   WDQ 5

Nov 14   John Willie   Philadelphia, PA   ND 6

1909

Mar 12   Tony Ross   New Orleans, LA   WDQ 13

Jul 26   Mike Schreck   Terre Haute, IN   LKOby4

1910

Dec 20   Carl Morris   Sapulpa, OK   LKOby3

Acknowledgments

I want to thank all those who helped in some way with the research, photographs, editing, promotion, or general support of my endeavors:

Tracy Callis

Randy Essing

Tom Seemuth

Stephen Gordon

Katy Klinefelter

Tony Triem

Harry Shaffer

Zachary Daniels

Clay Moyle

Cheryl Huyck

Christine Klein

Ron Marshall

Dave Bergin

H.E. Grant

Michael Vogt

Christopher LaForce

Cyberboxingzone.com

Boxrec.com

Eastsideboxing.com

Pugilibri

Antekprizering.com

Pugilistica.com

University of Iowa Interlibrary Loan Services

University of Iowa Media Services

Library of Congress, Prints and Photographs Division

INDEX

Abrams, Zick/Zeke, 145, 148, 167, 168

Armstrong, Bob, 51, 68, 74, 115

Baker, Henry, 27

Barry, Dave, 92, 136, 147, 216, 221, 223, 240

Beauscholte, Jack, 31-33, 37, 62, 239

Berger, Sam, 88, 90, 92, 136, 147, 240

Bonner, Jack, 24, 27, 33, 38, 41, 62, 66-68, 240

Britt, Jimmy, 136, 147, 172, 240

Burns, John, 27, 30

Burns, Tommy, 136, 187, 188, 223, 233, 237, 241

Butler, Joe, 69, 81, 101

Byers, George, 21, 24, 33, 37, 39, 54, 66, 73, 115, 189

Callahan, Pat, 233, 234, 241

Callahan, Tim, 16, 17

Campbell, Punch, 21, 239

Carter, Kid, 30, 33, 41, 44, 48, 50, 53, 54, 62, 63, 67, 68, 73, 79, 81, 84, 101, 104, 112, 119, 140, 155, 225, 240

Childs, Frank, 21, 37, 47, 66, 84, 133, 144

Choynski, Joe, 21, 23, 27, 35, 37, 41, 42, 45, 47, 62, 68, 69, 84-87, 92, 101, 104, 135, 143, 186, 189, 239, 240

Chrisp, George, 62

Color line, 42, 61, 115, 140, 149, 155, 159, 160, 162, 168-170, 173-177, 179, 181, 214, 221, 225, 236

Corbett, Harry, 147, 193

Corbett, James J., 8, 27, 62, 80, 81, 83, 90, 146, 221, 248

Corbett, Young, 27

Corrigan, Patsy, 33

Coughlin, Con, 81

Craig, Frank, 24, 27, 38, 54, 62, 73

Creedon, Dan, 19, 21, 24, 27-31, 37, 38, 54, 66, 84, 189, 239

Crosby, Steve, 28, 239

Crowhurst, Ernest, 127, 132

Crowhurst, Frank, 143

Daly, James, 50, 240

Delaney, Bill, 92, 97, 98, 179, 197

Dooley, Mick, 84

Eagan, Joe, 218

Edgren, Robert, 98

Egan, Joe, 199, 204

Ferguson, Sandy, 39, 89, 115-119, 135, 167, 169, 177, 188, 189, 222, 240

Film, 4

Finnegan, Jack, 21, 66, 119

Fitzsimmons, Bob, 4, 5, 27, 45, 66, 79, 81-84, 87-101, 104, 106, 110, 113, 115, 119, 125-132, 181, 185-188, 191, 196,

243

197, 206, 212, 219-222, 224, 226-231, 236, 237, 248

Fletcher, Butch, 6, 239

Flynn, Jim, 177, 187, 189

Gallagher, Jim, 138

Gans, Joe, 28, 61

Gardner, George, 28, 33, 34, 41, 42, 54, 55, 68, 73-83, 85, 88-101, 104-110, 112, 125, 133, 135, 155, 167, 182, 186-190, 194, 197, 214, 223, 233, 236, 240

George, Dawson, 98

Goddard, Joe, 84

Goss, Stormy, 239

Graney, Eddie, 91, 97, 178, 230, 231

Grant, George, 42, 239

Green, George (a.k.a. Young Corbett), 27-28

Greggains, Alex, 89, 92, 98, 135, 141, 145, 146, 148, 149, 151, 154, 155, 166, 167, 169, 170-178, 181, 182, 232

Grim, Joe, 68, 81, 101

Haines, John Klondike, 42, 115

Hall, Jim, 16, 84

Hamm, James, 131, 132

Handler, Jimmy, 28, 31, 33, 34, 39, 50, 62, 73, 112

Hanrahan, Bill, 24, 30, 33-38, 40, 41, 67, 73, 75, 84, 85, 239

Hart, Russell, 45, 240

Harvey, Charley, 51

Hassler, George, 14, 15, 38

Haywards, Jim, 136, 151

Horton law, 13

Hubert, Kid, 11-17, 19, 21, 24, 238, 239, 241

Hurst, Tim, 28, 29, 36, 76

Husbands, Kid, 14, 51, 240

Jackson, Young Peter, 21, 62, 112

Jeffords, Jim, 19, 62

Jeffries, Jack, 31, 37

Jeffries, James J., 4, 5, 8, 21, 33, 45, 51, 63, 76, 81, 90, 119, 132-134, 140, 179-181, 184, 186, 191, 194, 195, 198, 206, 214, 216, 248

Johnson, Jack, 23, 28, 37, 41, 42, 55, 69, 71, 74, 84, 92, 99, 115, 133-141, 143-182, 184, 186-188, 190, 191, 193, 197, 201, 206, 214, 216-219, 221-226, 232, 236, 238, 240

Jordan, Billy, 92, 151

Kaufman, Al, 134, 136, 138, 140, 142, 151, 227, 240

Kelly, Spider, 88, 148

Kelly, Hugo, 187, 188, 223, 227, 237

Kennedy, Joe, 88, 92

Kenny, Yank, 62, 66, 115

Kilrain, Jake, 123

LaBlanche, George, 39

Law, 13, 29, 30, 37, 46, 54, 61, 62, 67, 81, 114, 126, 132, 175, 204, 224

Lorraine, Hank, 239

Madden, Billy, 123, 177

Maher, Peter, 62, 63, 68, 74, 81, 84, 88, 89, 101, 119, 125, 236, 238, 241

Martin, Denver Ed, 68, 115, 133, 136, 137, 138, 140, 143, 144, 146, 151, 177

Masterson, Bat, 189, 220, 221

McAuliffe, Joe, 84

McCormick, Jack/Jim, 37, 62, 67, 75, 81, 85, 101, 112, 123, 135, 136, 137, 138, 140-142, 151, 189, 191-194, 196, 198, 205, 209, 216-218, 220, 221, 224-226, 240, 241

McCoy, Charles, 8, 24, 27, 28, 37, 38, 39, 44, 45, 50, 51, 61, 62, 66, 68, 80, 84, 102, 122, 134, 140, 189

McGrath, Tim, 88, 115, 168

McVey, Jim, 101, 149, 177

McVey, Sam, 101, 133, 144, 148, 169

Mechanics' Pavilion, 92, 229

Meisner, Charles, 6, 7, 239

Minton, Paddy, 6, 239

Mitchell, Charles, 158

Morris, Arthur, 238, 241

Munroe, Jack, 68, 105, 115, 125, 132, 136, 150, 180, 222, 223, 236

National Athletic Club, 120

Naughton, W.W., 140, 149, 150, 159, 167, 168, 180, 196, 199, 203, 212, 214, 218, 230

Nelson, Battling, 158, 172, 205, 213, 217

O'Brien, Dick, 19, 27, 37-40, 66, 115, 239

O'Brien, Philadelphia Jack, 24, 41, 62, 67, 68, 81, 84, 92, 101, 125, 126, 132, 143, 148, 154, 182, 186-188, 223, 225-227, 229, 236, 237, 240

O'Donnell, Steve, 84

O'Rourke, Tom, 33

Peppers, Harry, 46, 66

Plumb, Dido, 16, 21, 62

Pollock, Abe, 113, 114

Rocap, William, 85

Rogers, Harry, 9, 10, 18, 238, 239, 241

Root, Jack, 4, 21, 24-26, 28, 30, 31, 37, 39, 41, 46, 48, 54-63, 68, 74, 75, 80, 85, 88, 99, 101, 104, 113, 155, 182, 187, 189-223, 227, 232, 236, 240, 241

Ruhlin, Gus, 8, 10, 33, 68, 84, 87, 101, 115, 119-125, 133, 136, 186, 188, 221-226, 240

Ryan, Australian Jimmy, 7, 21, 22, 24, 25, 54, 239

Ryan, Tommy, 8, 21, 22, 23, 24, 26, 31, 37, 38, 41, 46, 50, 54, 66, 83, 112, 125, 188, 189, 226, 227, 232, 233, 234, 236, 237, 241

San Francisco Athletic Club, 141, 145

Schiller, William, 6, 7, 8, 11, 239

Schreck, Mike, 74, 186, 187, 188, 194, 195, 199, 216, 219, 221-223, 226, 227, 237, 238, 241

Seitz, John, 11

Sharkey, Tom, 5, 10, 35, 68, 84, 105, 119, 122, 139, 225

Siefker, Lucas, 8, 9, 239

Siler, George, 38, 39, 48, 49, 67, 68, 110, 111, 114, 201, 223

Smith, Australian Billy, 66

Smith, Jem, 27

Stift, Billy, 9, 19, 25, 27, 31, 37-40, 46-49, 54, 62, 68, 74, 88, 112, 135, 143, 187, 189, 190, 239, 240

Sullivan, Dave, 16, 29, 34, 138, 240

Sullivan, Jack, 187, 227, 233, 237, 238, 241

Sullivan, John L., 16, 84, 248

Thompson, Deafy, 191, 192, 198, 205, 241

Thompson, Maurice, 191, 233, 241

Traynor, Peter, 14, 16-18, 42, 239

Updike, Hal/Albert, 206, 208

Updike, Lee, 205

Walcott, Joe, 21, 24, 25, 28, 33-35, 38, 41, 42, 46, 55, 62, 66, 69, 73, 74, 81, 84, 99, 101, 104, 115, 118, 188, 189, 225, 236

Watts, Jim, 8, 11, 19, 21, 22, 24, 25, 37, 51, 68, 239, 240

Weinig, Al, 19, 20, 21, 37, 39, 41, 48, 50, 68, 74, 84, 88, 112, 239

West, Tom, 21-25, 27, 28, 33, 37, 48, 54, 62, 66, 239

White, Jabez, 158, 170

Williams, Tom, 8, 9, 11, 14, 17, 21, 239

Willie, John, 46, 101, 112-114, 115, 156, 182-184, 187, 189, 226, 238, 240, 241

Wilson, Billy, 148

Yosemite Athletic Club, 135

Other Books By Adam J. Pollack

John L. Sullivan: The Career of the First Gloved Heavyweight Champion

See mcfarlandpub.com or amazon.com

In the Ring With James J. Corbett

See lulu.com (paperback or hardcover) or amazon.com (paperback)

In the Ring With Bob Fitzsimmons

See winbykopublications.com or amazon.com

In the Ring With James J. Jeffries

See winbykopublications.com or amazon.com